MY OWN ASHES

A Hero's Journey with Mental Illness and Addiction

KIRK STRAWBRIDGE

OBOL HOUSE
PUBLISHING COMPANY

An imprint of Huntsville Independent Press

2112 Morningside Drive NW, Huntsville, AL, 35810

Obol House can bring authors to your live event. For more information or to book an event, contact Obol House Publishing Company at +1 (256) 678-0411 or visit our website at: www.ObolHouse.com

Cover design by Chris Treccani - 3 Dog Creative
Interior design by Chris Treccani - 3 Dog Creative

The text for this book was set in Adobe Garamond Pro.

Manufactured in the United States of America
First Obol House paperback edition December 2026

1 2 3 4 5 6 7 8 9 10

The Library of Congress has cataloged the hardcover edition as follows:

Names: Kirk Strawbridge, author.

Title: My Own Ashes

LCCN (TBD)

Identifiers: ISBN 979-8-9943699-6-8 (PBK)

979-8-9943699-7-5 (HCV)

979-8-9943699-5-1 (eBook)

My Own Ashes

FOREWORD
Jill W., Substance Abuse Expert

When I first met Kirk, I saw more than just a man working through addiction—I saw someone fighting silently against layers of unrecognized pain, confusion, and the deep loneliness that often accompanies mental illness. His story, told with raw honesty and unflinching vulnerability in *My Own Ashes,* is one that will stay with you long after the final page.

As a counselor specializing in substance use and mental health, I've walked alongside many who, like Kirk, found themselves at the intersection of trauma, undiagnosed mental illness, and addiction. But Kirk is not just another case or statistic—he is a gifted storyteller, a former history teacher, and a human being who lost everything and still found the courage to examine his life, his patterns, and ultimately, his truth.

My Own Ashes is not a recovery manual, and it's not a redemption arc neatly tied in a bow. It is something more valuable: a clear, deeply personal look into the mind of someone who never quite fit into the mold society demanded of him. It offers insight into the confusing, isolating experience of living with undiagnosed mental health issues, and the destructive ways many try to cope when no one—sometimes not even themselves—can name what's going wrong.

This book is important because it tells the truth. And in a world full of filters and façades, truth is revolutionary. For those living with similar struggles, *My Own Ashes* might feel like the first time someone has put into words what you've always known but couldn't say. For those who love someone who struggles, it may offer a perspective that breaks through the walls of misunderstanding and frustration.

Personally, I relate deeply to many of the challenges shared in this book. As someone who has faced depression, anxiety, OCD, and likely undiagnosed ADHD—and as a mother raising children with similar challenges—I know how difficult it can be to navigate a world that isn't built for neurodivergent minds. I also know how critical it is for stories like this to be heard.

Kirk's voice matters. His pain matters. And now, his story can help others feel less alone and more understood.

You're holding something rare. I invite you to read it with an open heart and an open mind.

CONTENTS

INTRODUCTION

This leap of faith has been delayed far too long. The leap is what I refer to as whatever this project will become, but I am hoping it will be a book that receives some attention. I cannot imagine failing at this point. Why? Because when I get my heart set on something, it takes a great deal of effort to remove it from my mind. As you will see, this has worked for and against me during my life. Failure, before my fall, was unacceptable. I took the results as proof of my fitness or unfitness to live free as a real person. That is still a challenge, but times and attitudes have changed.

So, what about this book business? A book or any piece of art can endure forever as a testament to all a person was on this earth. Wow, that is setting myself up for the f-word (failure). I set grandiose expectations and compare my actions against the highest standards. I do have faith, though, that what I have been through and what I have learned is important to write down. In addition, I believe that others can identify with aspects of my story and gain valuable insights into their own lives. More than money, I seek people who genuinely care about what I have to say. That is worth more than any material thing.

Faith is a necessity to fulfill one's potential. However, I am not talking about religion unless that is the kind of belief that your particular soul requires. I am beginning without any safety net below me. There are parts of my story that are painful for me to speak about. Others have little issue with sharing their most trying times and emotionally driven decisions and outcomes in written form. Well, it might seem that way, but in truth, it is not as easy as it appears. I do not know what will come of any of this, or if anyone will care about this journey I have been unknowingly apart of. Despite anything, I had to write this book for reasons you will come to understand. That is why faith has to hold a place in my life. You will also find, in the following pages, that faith is one of the hardest things for me to grasp.

I want my story to matter. There is the fear that I will work, love, and do all that I can, only for no record of my life to exist. This is equivalent to not counting as a person who lived on this Earth. And, this reminds me so much of those troubling years as a young person, because the thought of not mattering was always there. More on that a little later. So, not only must I get published, but some significant number of people need to recognize my story as something worthy of scrutiny and praise. They must READ it, to put all this in the simplest terms. I hear the voice that says "slow down," and I always pay attention to every person's point of view. Now I recall what I said about faith, so I must keep some on the ready at all times during this writing project.

The act of writing has aided me in figuring out some of the things that inspired the book. It has been like therapy. For most of my life there was no serious attempt to find treatment for mental illness, and later on, addiction. Many people grow up like me as far as mental health not mattering very much. This is the perception that I wish was not true, and please take my case as an example. Despite all my brooding on why I did not fit in, professional medical help was necessary to firmly secure some answers. In fact, it has taken a whole body and mind approach, including big-picture ideas, therapy, and medicine to arrive at a better place where I can seek contentment at the end of the rainbow. Now I am stronger than ever before.

You will learn that education was and still is crucial to living a life of reasonable expectations and fulfillment. I believe in all forms of education, including common sense. I went to graduate school for a long time, received advanced degrees, and was a teacher prior to Depression and addiction tearing me away from what I love. I tend to see fancy questions of existence and what we should do with it as fundamental to every person out there. Well, maybe it is just me, because I need meaning and purpose in my life in order to feel like I am not wasting time.

Yet I am someone from a small southern town without connections to any elite person or status. My family has been great even if we do not always agree. I sought education because there were no other obvious paths to take. It turned out research and writing suited me well, so I continued on in History for as long as I could. There is a duality to most people I reckon, and the same is true with me. The country boy side never felt completely at home around professors and professional conferences where they were in attendance. Old scars are hard to rise above, and mine include low-self esteem and other disorders you will learn about in these pages.

Most books of the academic kind (and this is not one) begin with a sound question that is answered throughout the chapters. So, if I have to nail down my question that launched this project it would be: How did unceasing sadness and loneliness in my youth contribute to the mishaps and terrible events that stalled my progress as an adult? It is not that I desire to give readers a play-by-play of my childhood. However, I found it necessary to detail my young self in order to make sense of where I am now. Hopefully, I can consistently offer other people the thoughts of a person with mental illness, how he handled life, and how he found the hope to reach his potential and become the person of his dreams.

I demur to say that a transformation happened over the course of the events I will discuss, but that might be accurate. I hesitate to use this word because of my feeling that I became more like myself rather than a new person. My point of view is that we remain ourselves on the inside even when we no longer resemble that person on the outside. Through it all, I needed to respect who I was and live that way. Sometimes I use arrogance as something to aspire to, but I mean this word as representing pride in one's self no matter what hazards threaten to disrupt us. For me arrogance is necessary to some degree in order to live as a whole person committed to a purpose. Oh, and you will see dear reader that I lacked personal pride for most of the story I am about to tell.

I often turn to Romanticism as a means to explain who I am and have envisioned myself to be at my most confident. I enjoy the poets and authors of this movement that we usually place in the early nineteenth-century. In my mind, I am a modernized Romantic which may be too contradictory to make any sense. Despite this possibility, art itself is important and is part of that idealized self I imagined as a child. I like to create things. I have a sensitive side that I see in the great works of art that fill my mind with only positive affirmations of what life can be. But with romanticism and art comes sadness that this old world has never aligned with how I feel. Most of what we see appears as cold, and people act like calculating con-artists who want nothing more than to take and take without giving. This contradiction has been tough to counteract for most of my life, but I think writing these pages has helped me to reach a more optimistic view of everything.

Along with romantic poems, movies will be consulted here. This is part of my teaching D.N.A. In class, it is helpful to allude to any media that young people might know and find interesting. Sadly, as the years passed by my references have become increasingly old and unknown to the average college student. Nevertheless, I find great art can often speak in a way that is superior to my words and my unique way of thinking. In sum, I use movies to make declarations about my life, my thoughts, and my mental health journey. Consider this book a mental health coming of age story. We love stories that are either directly or metaphorically about the stages of life and the challenges we face maturing toward some more enlightened future.

Speaking of enlightenment, I feel that I have gained it. How? This book will tell that story, and once again, the process of writing aided me in reaching a place of greater truth. We must treat mental health with more respect. If I had to pick one category of analysis to interrogate and unveil a person's true nature, it would be mental health. For me, mental health is spiritual, scientific, and artsy all at the same time. Instead of ignoring it like occurred in my youth, we should be teaching mental health in every school. What is more important than the filter through which we interpret every single thing that happens?

I desire that the work done on this project will help any people who suffer from mental illness of any kind. This is one of my favorite sayings: Be part of the solution and not the problem. I found a better way to exist by first recognizing mental illness, dealing with it unsuccessfully and then through safer means, and now I see myself as part of the solution. Some people like to say: pay it forward. Maybe that fits, I am not sure. We are never as alone as we think, and there are lots of people around who can almost read your thoughts. By that I refer to folks who have a deeply felt understanding of your trials and the bad and good things that resulted. I tend not to give commandments like many in the self-help world, but this book can be classified as a story that promotes people helping themselves. Self-knowledge is the best way to combat any kind of mental issues.

Let's quickly break down the book by chapter and subject. "The Golden Child" recounts many experiences and thoughts early on in my life. This is necessary to formulate some sense of who the man became. "We are What We are Not" and "My Life as a Hole," detail young adulthood and the disorders and faulty thinking that plagued most of my life. "Darkness in the Mourning" sets the table for both profound truths I have learned and that point at which mental illness led to addiction. "Dreams" is indeed about dreams of all kinds and surveys the darkest days before the dawn. The conclusion is all about lessons learned and wisdom accrued. I should add that I do not separate what some folks call "high-brow" topics from what is disparaged as "low-brow." I place, side by side, my education, research, and years of deep thinking about big questions with practical knowledge and the everyday concerns of a country boy. There is no reason why people cannot learn about the great thinkers. For me, I emphasize the works of Ernest Becker, Carl Jung, and Friedrich Nietzsche in this book.

I want to be an intellectual, I want to be an artist, I want to be a known writer, I want to be a cynical modernist—I want to be me. Some clichés are right on the money, and one of these is that teaching that we must be ourselves. I think that most desire this but are overburdened by life's calling to work, work, and work some more. Well, work is necessary in some sense but should not preoccupy all your time and cannot define all that you are. If you are doing what you love, then that is a different story. I have faith that we all can find what we want to do somehow. The thing is that it rarely arrives to us easily or in the package that we expect. Every story matters. I tell my story now realizing that change had to take place to move to the next step of my personal evolution. You see, my nature is to obsessively focus on the past. I am always looking backward, in fact, but I found a way to escape those pains that keep me from moving forward.

In the story to come I like to ask lots of questions, as I have the heart of a teacher, after all. Some will be answered while some are meant only as a means to advance a subject further or make a concept more intelligible. I have few memories of science classes. They all together form a blur that I am glad to forget. However, the cycle of a butterfly is interesting to me. There are four stages that must happen to allow an egg to become that colorful creature we enjoy seeing now and then. At each phase of its life, the butterfly looks different. In fact, the larva does not resemble the finished product at all. It might be true that we cannot call the caterpillar a butterfly—that they are distinct and different things. Then, there is another view one can take. What we see from stage 1 onward is always the butterfly. The essence of it is still there despite the changes that take place. To me, we cannot have it both ways. Either the butterfly is not as such until the last of the process, or it is a butterfly all along. This question tests our understanding of how the world works and reveals something about our inner perspective. I like that. What is your answer, dear reader? I think I favor the idea that the butterfly exists at every point on its timeline. This does not agree with science I am sure, but I have never let facts get in the way of how I feel.

CHAPTER 1:

The Golden-Haired Child

I was so much older then, I am younger than that now.[1]

I want to be a hero, and I am prepared to write myself that way. Whatever the outcome of my writing efforts, I hope to explore how a mentally ill, highly inhibited man transformed his life and became a hero. Doing so makes sense to me, in part, because of my extensive education in history. There will be some history here, I expect, because my story is a small part of a greater one that all people experience every day. So I must have faith, but also be arrogant. Yes, I think I have decided that this is part of the recipe in the book, as well. I must turn away from the old voices that instruct me to run and hide from every chance to shine. In the past, those guys never let me enjoy anything, and always reminded me that I was an impostor. Therefore, your author must make great effort to think of himself as important enough to write about and make grand declarations using his life as the foundation. In writing about me, I hope readers glean much more than merely that information about the people and places that are part of this random life.

So much has been revealed to me through dreams, reading, and introspection, that I feel different now than I did before the terrible times. However, I need to unearth my younger self to understand why he did or mostly did not do this and that, to feel confident about the big statements about life I have under construction. My story is often missing many pages or has been told incorrectly, and so I can only explain to you how I felt in a general sense. There is a lot of pain here that I will probably try to make lighter and easier to ingest. If you are thinking that is not a good thing to do, you are right. But I trivialize my story compared to others. I will keep an eye out for that, but it is likely to happen.

The good news is that I am an over-thinker. This might yield some conclusions worth reading that, in turn, make my life worth remembering. My perspective is as broad as the widest shot from an old John Ford, John Wayne Western movie. Details are frightening things, I find. They can be scary, and I mostly have avoided details in my life. Math is full of details, which is one more reason I tend to run from it whenever I have the chance. It is not too arrogant to consider what each of our lives means to eternity, and how spiritual forces have manifested in the small details of our days. My mental approach has aided me in education to a great degree and harmed my personal life about the same. Somewhere in my overthinking, I live with mental illness as a cause, effect, or probably both at the same time. I plan to tell my hero story from the mental health perspective, which is essentially the intellectual, thinking side of our being.

Sometimes I wonder if I am a new person or not, and if deciding that either way makes any difference. Stubbornness is another quality of mine you are bound to discover, and some of us humans can find ourselves holding on to something, like a part of our soul, for way too long. Similar to that idea, a person can doggedly work from the wrong script way past the point at which they need to scrap it and start over. I am getting closer to talking about one of my favorite subjects: identity. I plan to do a lot of that, but not quite yet. To get to the point, I think I have been fighting the wrong war all my life. My priorities were only those propagated by the laziest and most indifferent people we meet in life. My story has been distorted, and I am now ready to refocus on the good things in life, and one of those is writing.

I often feel that I am running out of time, but that may be more of the bad voices speaking. This is the feeling I have, because so much of what I realize now requires a lot of work and a late start. If my life were a movie, the hero would have been fooled and would have to regroup and refocus late in the second act. Regardless of any of that, time is something else I want to discuss here in these pages. I have always been obsessed with time. This is primarily the case due to mental illness and a general nervousness about failing to do things right (perfectionism). I have tried to defeat time. As anyone can guess, those battles never turn out in my favor. Time is also significant to me now that my dad left the living realm in 2021.

I have much sadness to share with you, but I also intend to move forward with some wit and a few lighter moments. Surely, I do not want to be depressed and never wish to worsen or cause the depression of another. Some people say I have a dry sense of humor, and the problem with that is that words on a page are not the best way to express it. That doesn't matter, though. I am trying to tell a story about a hero who does not have the typical, all-is-right-with-the-world ending. However, I am certain that I want my story to be one about overcoming and learning to be more true to myself. All of this is conjecture, though, because the thing itself is not a thing yet. Writing always has lots of surprises.

Most often, I need to wade in the deep end a little while before I start to swim. Or to put it another way, it takes a while for inspiration to come to me. After all, until the thing begins to breathe and become something rather than nothing, how can I know what the something is? We shall see. I believe I have experienced highs and lows, the penthouse and the outhouse, you might say, which could make this project something unique that people may want to read. I have not traveled around the world, and my life has been unusual because of things that *did not happen.* From my perspective, the hero's journey has taken twists and turns impossible to predict. Dear reader, I hope you will find something in this that benefits you and your life.

I possess a competent understanding of history, which enables me to broaden the scope of my work to incorporate the ideas and concerns we all share. I have always been interested in the meeting of older notions and habits (which could be called tradition, if you prefer) with new, head-turning, life-altering innovations. In other words, when the old and new meet, they often have conflict, and humans must sort out what we think about it all and how to live in an environment that somewhat makes sense. Does it not all impact mental health? Yes. Dear reader, you might conclude that my interpretation of mental health is broader than expected. Therefore, there will likely be some discussion of history, along with thoughts on modern life. Everything circles back around to mental health, what works, what went wrong, and what it all means to recovery.

I have recently come to understand something: I often see myself as watching some other character participate in life rather than being the actual person, myself, participating. In other words, if life were a movie, it feels like I am watching a character acting in it rather than genuinely being part of it. What does this mean? Not sure. It could indicate that I can detach from situations and analyze them, putting myself in the place of each of the "characters." I believe I possess empathy, and this is one of my strengths. It could also follow that I disassociate from my body and whatever is happening at a given time. This realization may also be reflected in the pages that follow, which have yet to be created. It is crucial to explain some harrowing things, where I spent years learning how to separate my authentic self from what was happening right in front of me. In other words, some things are so bad that it's hard to believe they are happening.

Fooling myself carried me forward for many years until those unfed demons hijacked my life and almost made it a tragedy. To be clear, I am speaking of demons like addictions and mental struggles, rather than hell-born demons. I have made progress just by sitting here and writing without feeling overwhelmed by regret. Eventually, we need to approach life with a permanent, conscious zeal, knowing that time should never be wasted on anything that consumes it. Not everything we pick up in life is something special, but I want to make something special out of every thing. Most people I know do not understand. The same goes for you when you craft your own story. At the very least, I think this is a story of misunderstandings, crisis, mental health, philosophy, and a striving to reach an enlightened place that is sustainable and lasting. Indeed, I think it is important, because it is the only story I have. It must turn out heroic. How can I manage my life otherwise? How can the hero stand himself unless his anguish, regrets, and disasters lead to a fulfilling conclusion?

All that you have read thus far is a little sample of how my mental illness colors my thinking. It has taken a stream-of-consciousness approach. Thoughts never stop, and sometimes gently merge with—and other times crash into—other thoughts. It takes a lot of effort to make sense of them and communicate effectively, but it can be a fun and creative process. Usually, the hardest part is just getting started. It is almost like having to choose randomly, picking from an innumerable number of possible points of departure on a wheel that loops continuously. This can be somewhat daunting, because every beginning sets a specific course that is not the same as leaving from another chosen exit. I am thinking about airports and specific flights as a way to help myself explain. For sure, I want to communicate with you, dear reader, in a manner superior to my conversations with others so far in life. A life's goal is to be able to express myself completely and to thoroughly understand others in such a way that I never have before. Throughout my life, it is rare that I genuinely believe I understand something.

I do not remember many specific things from my early childhood. It is very foggy until puberty, and even then, memories exist only sporadically in patchwork form. Mental pictures can be sorted and cataloged only a bit, one from another, of events that would seem insignificant to most people. Don't worry, this isn't me starting at zero and recounting all the boring details of my life as if most of it is something you should already know. The task I am undertaking will not follow a strictly chronological narrative. Hopefully, it would not be a narrative at all.

My former therapist, whom I had promised to keep seeing even after I left Bynes, once told me that my emotional and mental patterns checked every box typically seen in survivors of sexual abuse. I don't recall this happening. Other counselors have said my distress, disorders, and overall sensibility seem to stem from an unknown trauma of some kind. There is more to the story that may just be lost forever. Recovering related incidents and mental snapshots is not likely.

During this year of discovery, I remember seeing an old picture of this hero as a golden-haired kid of about four or so. This has been stored in my mental imagery and occasionally is recalled with a smile. And, this idea of a golden-haired, blonde boy has featured in my mind as something symbolic of losing, then finding whatever materials that compose my best self. The picture resonated immediately as one representing purity, naiveté, unsullied hope, and youthful simplicity. The image could have been one of many other children with similar features, as one's appearance does not stand out as much at this age. It struck me that this could be a portrait of the hero as a young man in a story, without any of the traps that come with the slings and arrows of actually living. I have no idea what occasion sparked the taking of the photo. That's a good thing, as I can imagine anything I want to accompany it.

It has been easy during the low points of the hero's journey to forget that such images exist. Not once did that blonde boy cross my mind during the dark times. Now, I can work to reclaim him as myself and not merely a photograph. I must say that young man was handsome and had what looked like a genuine grin. He had the true "yellow" blonde hair that only existed in the 1980s. I wish I could visit the past, know what he was thinking and feeling, and be aware of only the things that contributed to his pleasant appearance. There were no hints of that world-weary scowl that later became his trademark. There was no contemplation in the young boy's eyes, unless it was of the sort that attended only to immediate and probable possibilities. Every potential was there, except for worry, as everything was in place and the future was protected. Yet, the future was only assumed to be another pleasant series of moments where no one—or nothing—would be missing.

I do know that images like these originated from the first house, located near the middle of the small town, where everything began. I recall that there were bunk beds. There was a yard, a barn, a fence, a German-Shepherd, a living room, and a back porch. Most of all, there was a swing on that porch where certain people came often. There was a Christmas when I infiltrated a closet and discovered toys meant to be wrapped and then unwrapped at a later date. Also, behind the little house was a short but steep hill that led to the road, mostly flat, and a narrow bridge beyond. The hero remembers his father there, on one of the rare snowy days in Alabama, carefully sledding him down the hill.

These memories are scattered and disordered, and not much of the real events and places can be identified with assurance. That boy passed his birthdays and his time in the big house in the country. This became home. It seemed large, but it was a modest home with an upstairs and a downstairs. One had to explain whether they were going up the upstairs, down the upstairs, up the downstairs, or down the downstairs, specifically. There, and at his grandmother's house, is where the boy stayed most of the time. Almost every hour of every day was spent at these places. He did not like to talk or commiserate with people who should have been familiar, such as cousins and acquaintances, or with strangers. I have been told that he did not like to leave these places or separate from his beloved mother. He was loved, and according to some sources, could entertain by being funny and doing impressions. The only one that can be proven was the "mawking" of a televangelist. Finally, the man became convinced that episodes in the spotlight were not unusual for the boy. People have said these things to me but was not convinced for most of my life.

There were five who lived together: two parents, two boys, and one girl. The blond-headed boy was the youngest of the family and always seemed much younger than anybody at any kind of gathering. The get-togethers were something to be avoided, he always thought. Mama and Daddy were hard-working and honest to a fault. There is no question that the hero was and is a "Momma's Boy." Lately, instead of feeling shame for this designation, he thinks it is something to be proud of. Oh, one of the many things that should have occurred to him much earlier in life. What is real and what is imagined remain so indistinct as to be mysteries to this day. Here, life seemed to be happening without him ever cognizant that he was part of it. It seemed he was never part of it, really—only an occasional guest-star. He has come to a firm conclusion. Something occurred very early in his timeline that had a profoundly negative impact on him, an experience he cannot recall. For this reason, he can only fail at identifying the culprit or cause, but the evidence persuades him to believe.

I have always wanted to know the connection between the golden child with a short career, trauma, mental illness, and the man who is now present. Pondering all of this has occupied a significant portion of my life. I have ruminated so much, but I do not think that is the same as the meditation learned as part of my mental health ordeals. The boy was lost in a world of imagination. His reality was almost entirely inward and invisible to the rest of humanity. I can remember many stories and numerous sheets of paper filled with sketches and doodles. I composed little drawings of objects in the room or people on television. All of his creations were held as secrets, reckoning no one else cared about them. This began a trend with the boy, which continued with the young man, of not sharing his innermost self with anyone. Drawing was one thing for which the boy was known, and it gave him a minor sense of pride. The man does not know how to construct a proper hero story based on incomplete evidence and numerous unanswered questions. Only the work of putting down some stuff on paper, he believes, will uncover or rediscover how the boy became the man with so much undesirable baggage.

Some may know, but for those who do not, I should briefly discuss the template of what is commonly called "the hero's journey." It is a trope frequently used in stories dating back to at least the ancient Greeks and continuing in all media to the present. The parameters and basics of the story are so common and frequent that our subconscious mind detects them without our consciousness explicitly realizing what is happening. Here is a short overview. An unlikely hero is chosen to embark on a mission that will bring him (yes, it can be a her too) out of his comfort zone and away from all he knows. The provincial young hero usually hails from no place of importance. At first, he rejects the offer, saying something to the effect: "Why me? I am insignificant and not worthy of the task." After his journey begins, the hero faces numerous hazards along the way that represent his most deeply held fears. In the end, the hero is victorious and returns home a changed person, having acquired a special object or knowledge to share with the community. This is an abridged outline of the hero's journey. Of course, many details vary. But, I bet you can think of something you have seen or read that features this basic plot.

Star Wars is my go-to starting point for discussions about the classic hero narrative. Just know when I say *Star Wars*, it probably refers to the first three films, possibly to the second trilogy, and never to the last ones (by our chronology, not the movie). In my opinion, most fans are unaware of why they love these movies so much. *Star Wars* is not science fiction. No. It should always be classed as epic adventure/fantasy storytelling. Luke Skywalker is the hero who begins as no one living in nowhere. Obi-Wan Kenobi is more or less a wizard who prompts Luke to join him on a quest across the galaxy. Luke accepts and returns as a new hero: a Jedi. I believe that humans love this story form because it mirrors the process of growing up, facing obstacles, and emerging as an adult. In recent years, it is disheartening that a mega-rich corporation, driven by limitless financial ambition, would fail to comprehend and appreciate the essence of *Star Wars*. Such an organization might even impugn and ruin Luke Skywalker—one of the last, classical heroes.

Probably I should stop down this road, as it leads to bitterness and not excavation of the intended topic. At any rate, my hero's journey is ongoing, and will hopefully continue to progress as I write this thing. It is necessary to include some biographical information. I guess the subject of this emerging hero's journey is the same as the process of writing it: how one discovers their self, among the many minefields of life, in a way that can sustain positive mental health for eternity. That is what I am thinking now, anyway, but that could change depending on the topics that are stressed. I want to accomplish a few goals that hopefully are not too far out of my reach. It feels that way now, but every journey begins with a step, they say.

Everyone understands that childhood scars follow a person into adulthood. I want to know how the influence of a strange young life, and one scarcely remembered, formed a man with a formidable mental illness. I want readers to feel the story and be moved by it, and those I love to understand. If anything here applies to you, dear reader, I hope it helps. Additionally, I plan to contribute significantly to the ongoing discussion about what life truly is or should be. Those ideas are floating around, anyway, but who knows if I can adequately articulate them and put them on paper. There is another thing: I am trying to edit life in some way that transforms my hero's journey into a story of significance and greatness. Like many childhood things, I want to say, "That doesn't count, I want a redo." The great artist Paul Simon has a song that expresses the core of what I mean. I love songs that can capture something that feels impossible to say in any other way. Here are some words from "Rewrite" that help you understand:

> ...Yeah, I'm working on the rewrite, all right, Gonna change the ending
>
> Throw away the title, toss it in the trash. I'll eliminate the pages
>
> Where the father has a breakdown, and he has to leave the family
>
> But he meant no harm. Gonna substitute a car chase, and a race
>
> Across the rooftops, where the father saves the children, and he holds
>
> Them in his arms...[2]

When answering any question about three wishes or if you could go back in time and relive any part of your life, I maintain that I would like another opportunity at childhood. Since October 2021, I have been consumed with thinking about time and how to control it. Well, that began before this date, but for different reasons. This is when my father passed away. When life took a horrible turn, I imagined myself in a different place and situation from unmanageable fear. When I see a Google article about time machines or anything related, I read it. So, yes, I want to go back in time, and like the song, start the rewrite. You know what, though? It is unlikely to happen. It seems I have to settle for a metaphorical rewrite... or maybe not? I would like to think that I can weave the unfortunate and terrible aspects of the hero's journey into something satisfying, life-affirming, and healthy. That is a huge task, and it is precisely what I am doing right now.

Hopefully, I can impart some wisdom based on a life of sadness and unrealized potential. That mission offers some motivation for trying to write my story. As a youngster, I can confidently say I did not attend many things apart from family gatherings. It would not be an overstatement to say that I hated leaving home and was nervous about doing so. Also, I was not a "joiner." There was no Little League, Pee-Wee football, Boy Scouts, 4-H, or anything at all. The world of my imagination was almost the only one I inhabited. At various times, looking back, I think I could have had agoraphobia. Here is a revelation that has never been spoken or written: I was terrified of most life situations well into my teenage years. As a result, the golden boy's social skills were underdeveloped. Even among cousins, aunts, and uncles, I felt an unwelcome stranger. A mild stutter did not help the maturation process. My mom was the only person I could trust or spend time with for very long.

I was not enthusiastic about doing any activity outside of those that relied on the creative process to "make things up." Maybe it was that I only trusted to engage in those things the mind can gather up from thin air. Rules were pitfalls to run from. Part of my personality and perhaps the mental illness is obsessive doubt that I can understand spoken or written directions. Unlike many young males, I had no desire to take things apart or put them together. I did not take shop class and was terrified by the thought of it, due to a loathsome unwillingness to complete any type of project (like that staple, the birdhouse). The idea of performing tasks with my hands, especially in front of others, made me sick with terror. In Biology class, I was unable to successfully disassemble dead critters, locate their organs, or recall their locations on the tests. I felt stupid. I never knew about having severe anxiety until much later. So, I carried the assumption of incompetence in all things that mattered to adults, and in turn, remained afraid of most aspects of day-to-day living. I did not function, and I was well aware of this fact.

I thought I was dumb and that the condition was incurable. Many are surprised by this declaration, given my later academic success, yet it was true. This constant self-assessment held me back socially as well as in other areas I plan to relate in this writing. Avoidance is a key word that explains many aspects of my life. The once-golden child sought out strategies to hide and avoid basic activities that most boys are expected to perform. I think humans are performers most of the time, and this sensibility is central to how I process life. You may be thinking that the explanation is rather vague, right? It was due to the reality that there was nothing the child believed he could complete correctly in the material world.

No instructions could be followed to perform the most basic work. He would always mess things up. In my mind, I surveyed the likelihood that someone would scream at me for being so obviously inept. The thought was devastating. Every little thing would prove my uselessness as a normal person. So he did not do these things, such as opening or closing a window, throwing or catching something, putting something together, putting gasoline in a vehicle, holding a real conversation, moving heavy things, knowing what people meant when they said things, working with any kind of machinery, and we could go on forever. Few places or subjects consoled him, and grim anxiety filled his young life. He was never entirely free from potential hazards. Despite the boy's efforts, he was eventually forced out of his comfort zone and into a world where he did not feel at home.

The desire to escape participation in so many small acts and greater responsibilities of life had destructive consequences. Feeling dumb, acting like it, and then the feeling that everyone knew about his obvious shortcomings, formed a vicious circle that trapped the boy in a state of sedentary thinking and living. He effectively banned himself from most everything part of acculturation and bonding with others. He was sworn, by a secret oath, not to get involved in outward life. This was Alabama— the Deep South—in a typically conservative little town. Males were supposed to conquer things, build, play sports, compete, win, work with their hands, be fearless, fight, be handy around motors, etc. Thus, our young hero did not feel heroic at all. This must be stated with some force: he did not feel masculine. I had vague but accurate notions of proper manhood (or boyhood) and not once felt confident that I met the criteria. Further, I hated this fact and was horrified that others probably regularly reviewed and laughed at my unfitness. Did everyone know, he wondered? Perhaps not everyone… he might be able to fool some of the people. Alas, he was not confident about this possibility or anything else that was not part of his inner world of colors and characters.

Chief among all other manly arts, as a teenage male, was playing football for your high school. Even among other southern states, football in Alabama is especially important. There is no other sport that even compares to the passion and ever-present obsession folks have for this game. It is expected that all healthy, well-adjusted males will play for whatever town they represent. The talk of your future football career begins in infancy, often with cutesy remarks to moms about raising a future linebacker or running back.

Organized football starts at around five and ends for most at about 18. During this period, males have the opportunity to establish unimpeachable toughman credentials that will last a lifetime. So, pressures to play are set early on and only grow louder for any teenager without an obvious physical or mental malformation. Before being qualified for varsity football, every youngster is scouted and assessed for his future potential and position. So, playing big boy football begins in the minds of the townsfolk before it commences in reality. It is expected that all healthy, well-adjusted males will play for whatever town they represent. I could not and did not. Although I enjoyed football and didn't mind the collisions that characterized it, I knew I couldn't be on the team. This betrayal was equivalent to turning one's back on a town and a peculiar, martial way of interpreting the world. It was a mystery to all why I did not play. After all, I was a decently sized kid with at least average coordination at that age.

My father was an excellent athlete and a successful football player. He was only familiar with a life that involved intense physical activity. Beginning very early, my dad worked and hobbied hard almost every day of his life. He was an expert bird hunter, dog trainer, and marksman. At any point in his life, for as long as he could, Daddy could be found playing sports, doing toilsome physical labor, or hunting. As an athlete, he was good enough to get a scholarship to a minor college program. He was the quarterback of the high school football team. As far as I can gather, my dad excelled at every sport he tried. He had a great sense of direction before GPS and navigated without any external aids, relying solely on his senses. His work was never sitting, talking, selling, directing, or computing; instead, it was always physical and laborious. He was not a large person but, as you might assume, was very strong from a lifetime of lifting, throwing, pushing, pulling, moving, hammering, swinging, cutting, trimming, shooting, etc. In short, there was no doubt that my father met and exceeded the manly standard during every phase of his life.

The difference between my blue-collar, sports-loving father and me is painfully obvious, now just as it was back then. My dad and I had trouble finding things in common. However, we both enjoyed watching sports and certain Western movies. I have given a lot of thought to how to express myself regarding this time in my life. I cannot do so to my satisfaction. So, I can only state that I was perpetually afraid of doing the wrong things, was wholly certain that I would do those things, and therefore feared partaking in what to others caused no forethought whatsoever. Building bird-houses and such have directions, and those are similar to rules, and rules cause pressure, and his mind retreats. I guess the boy needed no limitations to have no fear, as is customary in creative arts. Anxiety has a way of making one more nervous and sweaty, the more one tries to put on a calm face. Trying but faltering in the battles to conquer anxiety, the boy only became even more conscientious and sad about his shortcomings. No day was safe, and only the night brought some reprieve from the boy's forlorn thoughts.

I did not realize until recently that a desire to control time and a discomfort associated with male authority figures link back to these teenage years. Entertainment was a refuge, and it was a much happier alternative to real life. Oh yeah, and there were no directions to follow. On television, stand-up comedy, Saturday Night Live, and David Letterman all seemed interesting, creative, funny, and somewhat calming to the youth.

The appeal of comedy was there early on, and this interest was his alone. It felt like these shows were just for me and not for anyone else in the world. And, everything worth watching happened during the late-night hours when no one else was awake. Under the night skies, my mind could be freer to think, analyze, and create. I did not always get the jokes, but the hero knew something unique and subversive was going on here. No people in a hundred-mile radius appreciated all of this great stuff, other than him.

The former golden child, now awkward youth, could not share his interests with his father or any other "real" person. His father did not watch goofy comedies. Instead, Daddy was passionate about hunting and was very good at it. Hunting, in my dad's point of view, meant walking miles and miles each day and being very handy with a gun. This was not the sitting around until an unlucky animal roamed into your vicinity kind of "hunting." Not at all. Daddy trained dogs, but people also needed training in the art of this real sport. I am trying to say that my father's habits begat a culture of toughness that exceeded the capabilities of this young, terrified boy. What about that manly hunting banter, using coarse language and unknowable, symbolic half-words that have inside-joke meanings? Oh my, the boy fell way short of the standard. I knew with certainty that any attempts at trying to fulfill the role of the gun-toting sportsman would end in embarrassment. Like with almost everything, he did not want to try. His one-and-only hunting excursion was not substantial enough to warrant talking about here. I confided in my heart that I had disappointed him, and his shame lingered, never completely leaving his soul.

As a teenager and then well into adulthood, our young hero could not feel comfortable around men who had any kind of leadership role. Sometimes, he hated them. Experiences with male authorities usually occurred in high school. Teachers, principals, and coaches were kept at arm's length as much as possible. The boy would not play football for two primary reasons, one of which has to do with the ultra-masculine culture that accompanies the most macho American game. I knew the sport well enough, enjoyed watching it, but could not participate. The typical football coach and the competitive environment he forged would probably fit under the category of one of pop culture's favorite catch phrases: "toxic masculinity." I could not be yelled at by strangers, and I knew that was bound to happen.

That is the first reason that is connected to the second. I could never follow instructions or perform any football act correctly. I believed this one hundred percent. This would be a disaster for the whole community to hear of or see themselves. After all, the men of the town watched and dissected practice just as closely as the games on Friday night. Just thinking of the coaches and their unfettered bluster made me almost physically sick. I had to take a sad course of action, but the nature of things back then left no other reasonable alternative. Playing would cause him to panic during school hours every day, and he would be unable to perform academically. Heck, he would be a total wreck and probably be committed to wherever people with mental health issues are sent.

To understand myself and have anyone gain something from my story, I must talk about the ubiquitous violence so accepted as part of growing up. One could simply not play sports for the team, not sign up for shop class, refuse to hunt animals, keep some distance from unbearable people most of the time, and feign any number of reasons for not engaging in various manly arts. This could all be undertaken half-successfully, but at a psychological cost of not living up to expectations. There was a more direct threat to my physical body, however, that was more nightmare-inducing than any scenario heretofore described. The possibility of a fight happening was never far away in the time and place of my upbringing. Dear reader, do not overlook or underestimate the impact on a young man or woman's mental health when continuously exposed to bodily harm. Fighting was an omnipresent specter that haunted me, and it did not matter what non-fighting situation one was engrossed in at the time. This was true of every school day from Kindergarten until the last day of the last grade. For this and many other reasons, I felt nauseous every morning before school.

A fight was a noteworthy event to be recorded, remembered, and sometimes encouraged. Official school policy frowned on fighting, and some adults spoke out against it on Sunday mornings and at dinner tables. Yet, everyone knew that fighting was kind of cool as long as you were in the right, and, most of all, won. Dads were proud of their boys who fought well, which in the currency of growing up as a male was about equal to scoring a winning touchdown. There was no covering up, forgetting, or changing the results of a fight. Everyone would know the details and outcome, invariably. Winning or losing a fight was a judgment on a boy or man's character; an instant verdict that brought glory or shame. Certainly, physical conflict was a way to prove or lose one's manhood. And yes, females fought sometimes. There was not much at stake in catfights, regardless of the brutality or cause. Simply put, the community did not care.

You can probably guess how someone with my assumptions and fears would try to avoid fighting. It was impossible to do so. After all, any obvious shirking of the responsibility to fight would itself be a cause for dishonor. Backing down marked a young male as a target for endless physical and verbal battering. One might have to fight more often because they didn't fight on an earlier occasion. In other words, the culture of my youth demanded that every male greet violence with acceptance and a little bit of jocular glee for the opportunity. I was always frightened of getting involved in a tense confrontation with another boy. I did not feel like I knew the required information to be a successful fighter, and much like with hunting or football, I believed myself to be less than manly. Violence was as ugly to me then as it is now. Yet, I must be more honest here, with you, the reader, than I ever have been on this subject. No common-sense rationales were suggested as alternatives to brawling. No person in range of my hearing ever said: "There are no winners in a fight."

No situation or setting was too benign to be completely safe from punches, tackles, biting, gouging, and other forms of aggression. A shoulder brushed against a shoulder, a look in the eye, a rumor of a rumor, an improper greeting, a rough sports incident, a female, name-calling, boredom… these are just a few excuses for brutality among endless others. If someone slighted you, then it was customary to begin preparatory posturing for a throwing of hands. Perhaps it would happen, and perhaps not, but our hero always knew that perceptions were everything. Once the "bowing up" started, there was no turning back. And so many boys were sloppily indiscriminate with their teasing, touching, slapping, cussing, grabbing, etc., that it was easy to be roped into a tussle. In my mind, everyone else was probably stronger than the now brunette youth. He did not need to be reminded of the lack of building, lifting, pushing, hammering, towing, throwing, welding, wrestling, and such in his background. He knew a physical contest would eventually come and expose his lack of manly credentials. What happens to all the anger? Sometimes, enough is enough, right? Yes, he had plenty of that but rarely let it surface. What happens is that anger becomes mistaken for other emotions but remains anger in disguise, and then pours out somewhere in adulthood.

As for the topic of fighting, I had a close, negative comparison between myself and my father and older brother. My brother was big, strong, and never minded a fight. He was very good at it. My brother was well-known in town as someone not to mess with. As a result, some kids assumed I was skilled in the art of combat, which only made matters worse for me. There was at least one almost-fight that happened because of this false assumption. Daddy was a very physical person, and I never doubted he had been in fights before and could be again if necessary. Once, while taking me to school, a large, notoriously violent kid was beating up another guy in the parking lot. Without hesitation, my dad picked up the big kid and restrained him with ease. "Wow," I thought to myself. So, I had two people very close to me whom I did not compare favorably to at all.

Although I regretted my precarious lack of manliness, the youth enjoyed mocking what he saw as the expressions of pretentious masculinity all around him every day. This is true of the man, as well, except for the everyday part. It is partly a Southern phenomenon, but it is unquestionably not confined to the Southern states. Dear reader, you may or may not know the type. Many of these young males were fraternity boys in the future (you can tell), but that was not a requirement for the fake masculinity outlined in this paragraph. One must have work boots, so that was a given. The haircut back then was a little shaggy, combed into a swooping, half-moon shape down to the eyebrows. Haircuts could not be long enough for a young man to be confused with a hippie. Each of these guys had a little or a lot of money to afford the proper costume. And this one seals the deal: one must drive an enormous truck, preferably with persistent mud stains on the bottom. There was something about the young man that prevented him from playing make-believe in this way. I would have been embarrassed to do so, therefore I was not walking in step with most of my peers.

As I hope to make clearer as we proceed, I opposed and privately mocked the false bravado and silly charade presented as real life. He is completely clueless about why that was put in him and from what source. Also, he could not think about this distaste for so many ordinary conventions of life, in a systematic and studied way, in those days. In other words, I realized that a lot of things were artificial and meaningless, but I couldn't pinpoint the reasons why. I did not want to do them, and I wondered why others did, but I couldn't explain that to a single person. Thankfully, I knew wearing work boots alone did not qualify someone as a working man.

As for those awful senior photos that are taken, he never could relate or even grudgingly pretend he believed in all of that. He hated pictures of himself. There was no interest he could plausibly put a name on thus far in life. By the way, kids may still engage in these unpleasant activities, regardless of what I say. It may make a person well-adjusted, as I have no idea.

Before we proceed, I would like to pause to clarify my general situation as a teenager in high school. Dear reader, do not assume that our hero was an outcast or extremely unpopular. This was not the case. I was not directly bullied, as it was just that I could easily sense a culture of violence always eagerly in wait for the slightest spark. I was handsome (some say) and came from a lower-middle-class, seemingly normal, family. My grades were usually somewhere between mediocre and good. Instead of being an obvious target for scorn and ridicule, I was not anything. I never stood out as uniquely cool, nor was I counted among any typical school clique—athletes, rebels, druggies, the best and brightest, etc. I stepped out of actively living the high school/teenage experience. The struggling youth attended school but was not part of it in any way. So, his body was there, but he never felt like a participant in the happenings there. He did not belong and must have appeared like an extra in a teenage movie with the occasional speaking part. Any evidence to the contrary, when the hero truly engaged with someone, was treated as an aberration that must have been a mistake.

Recently, I learned about a concept from sociology that helps me understand many of my difficulties with other human beings. To be clear, this sociological construct was not known to my teenage self. Now it makes perfect sense. Randal Collins has written about how every exchange with another person, whether in person or not, has either a positive or negative emotional payoff. So, if emotional energy is like currency, every interaction is a payment to or deduction from each individual. This means everything, from an everyday hello between two friends to a gathering of hundreds of people. When emotional energy is gained, that ritual is reenacted endlessly because it is mutually beneficial. Interaction Ritual Theory confirms many things I already believed to be true. When it came to socializing, I had a sense that what I observed from afar was a type of performance. And he always watched everything and listened even more. From the bashful boy's point of view, every human somehow knew what to say and do, to this person but not that one, when each was called for. This activity was mysterious and the source of consternation. Sadly, he felt the downside of interaction rituals. He greeted most social exchanges as a job, and it was work he did not know how to perform. So, more and more, the interaction rituals informed the youth that he should avoid interaction rituals, if you know what I mean.

For a social ritual to occur, Collins argues that it must naturally exclude some people. When these events take place, there must be a tacit understanding that a defined number of others are not participants. For instance, when two or more people have a running joke or an inside joke among them, each member of the group refers back to it repeatedly. It brings those involved positive energy, and this is not for other people who are not "in" on the joke, you see. Reader, also consider how two people exchange a greeting or handshake only with each other. Yet, the same applies to any gathering, such as a concert, where people who are not there are not part of the fun.

As far as I perceive the theory, every social interaction is like a little club shared only by those people involved. As I viewed life back then, this explanation of ritual interactions is right on the money. Indeed, it felt like being excluded, day-to-day, from all the goings-on of people, whether in high school or not, but especially there. It is one thing to see it all now and wonder how foolish I could have been to dissect life in such a way. Yet, it all stung and caused great anguish, no matter how we view it long after the fact. Imagine one hundred acts every day, likely more, which signaled to someone their non-membership in every conceivable social relationship. That is very tough to handle.

In the tale of woe that is unfolding here, I have yet to mention the greatest heartache and regret of my youth: the frustration of relating to and being with females. I will discuss dreams later on, but I should mention that I still have unhappy dreams about girls from the past. There is something in my unconscious about women that remains broken and un-repaired that my mind cannot leave alone. My missed chances, stupid decisions, and chronic inaction all add up to a miserable record with the opposite sex. Like practically all boys of that age, women were on my mind all the time. As you can probably guess by now, dear reader, get ready for an honest but sad summary of my lack of a love life.

Nothing was more mortifying to consider, and no outcome more dreaded, than trying and always losing the romance game. Talking to any girl was a herculean task. Anxiety killed any realistic chance for a positive encounter. Then, some notion, maybe depression or another form of mental illness, convinced the boy that nothing ordinary could work for him. The female problem consumed my mind and tormented me in a manner more painful than any other obstacle. It sounds almost funny, perhaps, but it has been seriously traumatic for me. There was no way to have confidence when my frame of mind (should I say mental illness?)

repeatedly reminded me that I was stupid and fated to fail at everything. There was Jane, for example, who I now think liked me. She was pretty and smart. I didn't know how to approach her, so the words never materialized. She wanted nothing to do with me, I thought. Why would any female show an interest in me, given my many shortcomings and lack of manliness? This was frustrating beyond belief.

To be more accurate, my lack of success in the romance department was a terrible burden that contributed to a wrenching depression. To help explain, I should note that I was the youngest in my family on both sides. My cousins were getting into serious relationships and getting married while I was still in high school. Also, most of the other boys at school, even the unattractive, ignorant, or plain awful ones, were able to have relationships with the girls. So, everyone I knew seemed very capable of having success with love or lust, while I remained a solitary young man. Part of the problem was that I had nothing to say to them. I lacked the words, and at times wrote things down to have a script to reference. This only worked over the phone, obviously. It was a mission impossible to avoid the landmines and overcome all those factors working against me. So, while I desired a relationship, I also could not fathom having anything to say to the girl in one with me.

My heart was broken by the only female ever to show me an obvious, without-a-doubt attraction or flirtation of some kind. Before this, I had only had a girlfriend for about a week, once. Invariably, girls stopped talking to me after it was obvious I could not communicate in words or any other way. Karen was a pretty, blonde, type-A personality. Karen initiated contact, and it seemed there was instant chemistry and mutual interest. She laughed at my jokes, which were all I had in my arsenal. Nonetheless, when roughly two weeks had passed I was the only one in love, still smitten by the first real opportunity for a relationship. As it turned out, I had failed the test, and it was over before it began. She remained the apple of my eye for a few years. Why? It was that feeling I received, right when the non-relationship started, that was new, long-awaited, and glorious. I would do anything to recapture that excitement of the whole body and spirit. It felt wonderful that a pretty female paid attention to me. In the final analysis, it was not the individual but that brand-new inner joy that was irresistible. To be honest, I carried a torch for her until I met the next would-be love of my life about ten years later.

I did not take advantage of the good opportunities that could have come my way, and instead half-heartedly chased the unattainable and unrealistic. The hero's life would have been much different, he feels, had he been able to make any successful movement toward closing the deal on a high school relationship. A real and healthy one is what I mean. Most likely, he would have gotten married around 21, and life would have surely played out in a much different manner. He would have had a few kids, like most of his peers, and probably would have pursued a practical career. No one knows for sure if the hero would have been happy or miserable with this outcome. Yes, there was Jane at least, and maybe another, who was compatible and probably genuinely liked the almost tall and handsome young fellow. Two things worked against me. Until this day, the hero cannot discern between casual banter, flirtations, and strong signals of romantic interest. So, I was inevitably completely unaware of the existence of a female admirer, regardless of her most blatant signs of courting. Also, he possessed an all-consuming self-loathing and hatred of his own body. This inability to gauge if someone shows interest in me did not end in youth. There is no telling how many positive relationships, and really friendships of every kind, slipped through my fingers.

All of his deficiencies made the no-longer golden-haired boy certain of his total inability to be a productive member of the community. This, he did not doubt. As his twenties passed by, so did any realistic belief that a woman could like him, and certainly love was too much to ask. A romantic relationship became like a fantasy. Women were as mysterious as birdhouses, but they caused an intolerable loneliness that hurt him immeasurably.

When it came to relationships, he supplicated daily to meet his future bride. After all, the boy knew marriage as the desired and only conclusion to a successful relationship. So, while putting an unrealistic and disturbing amount of pressure on himself, the hero surely sabotaged any opportunity that came along. Another way to put it is that I was so awkwardly intense that I was probably repulsive to the opposite sex. I can remember feeling so dejected for weeks or months when a date (a rare thing) went wrong, which it always did. Dates were few and ill-conceived, as I could not make contact myself with any woman whom I liked. To be as clear as I can, I was not living in reality at all. It will not make sense to take a healthy approach to analyzing this time in my life.

The hero felt as if there was an inaccessible void between him and everything he wanted. Or, you could think of it as a giant glass door, or window, separating him and relationships of all kinds, acceptance, strong friendships, and happiness. He could stand behind the window and see the other side, but could never pass from one side to the other. There was no opening to start moving forward. All that was real life was as indecipherable as advanced math. There were no directions that explained how to turn toward a more promising path. However, he could see people being happy, getting married, having fun, hanging out, being carefree, and generally understanding how to live from day to day without anxiety. That is how it felt. The hero was outside his skin, watching himself struggle and fail to become part of the theater of life. He was not part of it. The sad hero felt literally like everyone possessed knowledge that he did not. It was as if everyone but him had read the instruction manual for life, including how to do every minor and major thing. The boy felt left out of practically all worthwhile pursuits that were part of an incomprehensible world.

I became suicidal around the age of fifteen. Reflecting on this at age 43, I am embarrassed to admit that. I am very closely guarded most of the time and do not like confessing this even to myself. Also, it is a very stupid thing to consider doing. Plus, I now understand how painful life can be for the unfortunate, and so many humans have to come of age in tragic circumstances far worse than mine. It is an honest admission, however. Although I did not attempt to complete the act, I was reckless at the time and did not care about myself. A major but one-car accident took place, a car slammed into a heavy garbage container at high speeds, and the boy received a concussion. The thought of going to school each day seemed overwhelmingly futile. Nothing would change. No outlet was available for me to reach out beyond my mind and my room, so it seemed. I did not feel like I had any real friends, the kind that one could confide in outside the school halls. Many times, I cried, feeling so unable to connect with the people all around me. Other kids knew it all, and I knew nothing. I did not know who or what decided to prohibit me from entering the world of love, fun, and sociability, but I was confident the ruling was permanent.

I would like to mention today's events and how they relate to my battles with life. I went for a long walk through the downtown residential area of the town where I live. The main part of the trek took me through a nice, middle-class neighborhood of older homes. The houses were well-worn, modest but manicured, densely packed, yet with plenty of lawn space requiring some yard upkeep. There was nothing special about it, but that is what I noticed. The smell of newly cut grass was apparent, as was the sound of lawn mowers. It is Spring, and so it was pleasant and not yet oppressively hot in the Deep South. I imagined the kind of people who lived there to be older couples. It felt relatively safe, and there was a semi-regular flow of slow-moving cars without it being too arduous to walk down the side of the road.

The sights and sounds of my walk stirred memories of feelings and places that had remained dormant for many years. Primarily, the day reminded me of my grandmother's home and the surrounding neighborhood. I had only one grandparent growing up and spent a great deal of time at her house. She was a great cook and always had scrap paper for me to use for drawing. As the youngest grandchild, my time spent at her red-brick home lasted longer than that of my older cousins and siblings who had busy lives involved with this and that. She had a sizable yard, which seemed enormous at the time, with the most beautiful azaleas of all colors, a perfect oak tree for climbing, and a big dirt pile for creating interactive stories with my G.I. Joe figures. The neighborhood is just as memorable to me now. It was a very short street with a big, steep hill that acted as a barrier one was forbidden to go beyond. The closest neighbor was an older lady I visited frequently, and her name, to me at least, was Aunt Bea. Today's quaint scenes, along with the smell of grass, took me back to this time and place. It was unexpected. Nothing happened on the walk, but I realized it had been so long since I strolled through this kind of environment. Instead of being anxious and worried about dangers, everything was safe and a little familiar. I would say I felt the illusion that I could be one of the people who lived here, just walking to my house or a neighbor's.

Suddenly, I realized what I had been missing since the reign of the golden-haired child: belonging. It is little moments like these that can remind one of a thought or emotion long buried in the back of the mind. Sensory experiences, particularly the smells in this case, can almost transport one back in time, The little episode evoked memories of having close neighbors whom you knew for a long time, as was the case at my grandmother's. In those days, one could walk up and down the street knowing who lived in this or that house. You knew that person enough to say hello every once in a while. I feel I am almost being nostalgic here, which is something I hate. I hope not. Although it is simply true that I have not been in a position to walk around a "normal," all-American street like this, rather than one that seemed foreign, unsafe, and transient. It is not the warm, Norman Rockwell-esque feeling that I want to convey to you here. Many others have discussed this to a tiresome degree.

Instead, I hope to emphasize the most important and relevant idea that entered my consciousness today: roots. Like a tree, all people have some kind of roots, of course. By using that word, I do not mean beginnings as in origins, though. I am talking about the increasingly rare thing of how some people have ties that bind them to something sturdy and even permanent. Most often, this refers to something physical, such as a house, street, or homestead. That kind of life has not been one I have known for a very long time. I should mention that my family's residence was in the country, where people were spread out far enough that we hardly ever interacted with them. In addition, my parents taught me that many of those individuals were somewhat untrustworthy and unsavory. I am fumbling with my words trying to express a source of authenticity one can turn to and feel connected to at any time.

Feeling rootless has been a part of my lifestyle and a major contributor to the chaotic and tumultuous nature of my life over the past year and a half. I do not have children and have never owned a home. Having kids of my own was once in the plan, but that project did not get off the ground before it imploded. The young adult lived mostly in apartment complexes in his twenties. I have learned that, increasingly, modern American apartment dwellers will not even look each other in the eye, much less exchange anything pleasant. Like many in recent years, I realize that I suffer from the lack of a fixed, immutable home base in both physical and symbolic senses. Now, I cannot feel this place (apartment) where I live as anything approaching permanent. My lack of sleep is partially due to restless thoughts that remind me I have no relationship or bond with where I lay my head at night. In the past, the hero never gave much credence to the notion that fears of this kind were important. Mostly, he just wanted to avoid the burden of house payments. Now I can see this was an error. At the same time, this downcast emotion is probably both a result and a cause of his lifelong sense of not belonging.

Recent news of the impending sale of my childhood Home is adding to my baleful worries about the future. This has never occurred to me as a possibility in my life. Like many things, it came without warning, though I should have foreseen it was only a matter of time. There have been yard sales, rumors of yard sales, and some noise about eBay. Now, I feel homeless. Where I live is not home and can never be home. There is only one, and it will soon be gone and sold to new owners. I am sure they will decorate and reconfigure the hearth and habitat of my life into something unrecognizable. Some relics will remain, sure, but of little consequence. In all candor, this feels like a tragedy. I dislike it when things avoided refuse to go away. And, it may be to the benefit of the one I love who lives there, admittedly. I am sure you can see how the confluence of recent events offers no bright, sunny forecasts for my life. I am reminded in this moment of every billboard, commercial, film, bumper sticker, and daily planner that tells us that a person is nothing without a home.

Not having a plot of land, something with walls and a ceiling, and children is like not being counted among the other adults and is even un-American. After all, not everyone gets to leave the kiddie pool and swim in the real one. The "American Dream" can encompass many things, but most often it contains the hope of a middle-class home with a white picket fence and the rest. This was how real people carried out their lives in the many examples of what "good people" do. I am trying to say that these symbols I lack are like being less of a person. Those founding fathers, such as Thomas Jefferson, James Madison, Benjamin Franklin, Alexander Hamilton, and others, more or less agreed with my last sentence. In the revolutionary era of the late 1700s, the men we call founders generally believed that land ownership should be a prerequisite for voting. Furthermore, a permanent place called home was the difference between a decent, honorable American and a not-so-trusted vagabond. Certainly, this sentiment is not as prevalent today, but the South is still more traditional than the rest of the country, I must remind you.

Well, I should be as clear as possible as to what I mean: even today, land, a home, kids, and a marriage are all barometers for ranking males on the manliness scale. Movies, at least the ones I have watched, clearly convey that the good guys we cheer for have something to protect, such as a wife, kids, or home. I do not know what I would talk about if I were to venture to my father's former hangout spot, filled with old, retired men. If your grandkids are not up to something, or if your roof or air conditioner doesn't need some repair, and if you cannot relive old sports glories, then I definitely wouldn't fit in. Perhaps my tendency to be overly critical of myself and others causes me to overemphasize my point in this paragraph. But I think I am at least half right about the importance of roots. Additionally, therapy has taught me that my feelings are real, regardless of whether they may not seem logical to someone else.

His hometown can provide neither roots nor a sense of belonging for several reasons. He never felt accepted or even liked in the town where he attended school. Unlike many young males, he did not take ownership of where he came from in any meaningful way which provided a sense of self. Technically, it was not even his hometown, as he grew up outside the city limits close to the Mississippi line. Sure, there were people there he cared for, but the naysayers and the bewildered greatly outnumbered them. His primary obstacle in that town, however, was the high school. Although the young man was socially barren, he was a decent student. The youth performed well on any test or project that allowed him to utilize creativity and imagination. Yet, I was never encouraged or helped by anyone during his high school career. The teachers hated him. The boy possessed some rare abilities that were never highlighted, directed, or utilized in a useful way, and often went unnoticed. Nepotism and Cronyism ran rampant at that place. For most of my life, I did not think about having roots in any conscious way. Recently, it has become clear to him that this is one of his life's deficiencies. I must gain some ground here to inch closer to contentment.

The picture I wanted to understand better and relate to an audience is coming into focus. I hope that you can see an overall characterization of the hero during his youth. Additionally, you can perhaps imagine the challenges that awaited him in adulthood based on his unfortunate difficulties/misunderstandings as a younger person. It is not all a sad story, and I hope to be able to share that with you as well. The once-golden-haired child, who looked happy in the picture, faded from his reality and memory. Only now does the man realize that this was as if a death had occurred. The worst of his harmful thoughts began around the age of twelve. Young adulthood, or the teenage years, or however you say it, felt like being thrown out into the wilderness without any survival skills. More than that, he did not recognize familiar places or faces as being anything or anyone he could now relate to. Everyone knew the secrets of the brand-new world, but he did not. He was in a losing game. This state of affairs lasted, to different degrees, long past his teenage years. I want to connect what seems like a late start in the race of life to the hero's mental illness and addictions. I must understand the part of my life that was so mysterious in its unreasonableness.

Hopefully, I can somewhat skillfully delineate what mental health means to me in the following pages. I think it means almost everything. Dear reader, have you ever sensed there is more to a word, a feeling, a person, a place, or a thing than the dictionary definition of that thing? I am betting yes. Mental health is a conundrum of a term, in my humble opinion. Without sound mental health, we can accomplish precious little.

In contrast, a torn muscle, broken leg, problematic back or shoulder, loss of a limb, or other tangible injury, does not prevent people from consummating and executing countless tasks and life goals. We take every runny nose, congestion, sore spot, ache, and pain seriously and strive to remedy these issues with medication and doctor visits. It is socially polite, if not required, to ask, "Are you alright?" after a person turns loose a coughing fit. Though one is less likely to lend a hand when it comes to others' behavior that can be classed as belonging to that indefinite world of mental issues. It is easy to say we should pay more attention to people suffering from apparent mental illnesses. That is certainly needed, but it's not quite what I'm referring to. I think it is a good idea to acknowledge sadness and social stagnation, as well as everything that we cannot immediately identify by its medical name. In other words, there is much more to mental health, and thus mental distress, than can be verified by armchair doctors or even real ones.

There was no mental prepping for the highs and lows that came my way, and the same can be said for every person I knew as a youngster. Therefore, it is neither beneficial nor correct to discuss how some people failed to prepare the hero for life. I am sure the failures exist, but there is too much at work here, and probably it is expansive enough to attribute the causes to that word: "society." That is another way of expressing: I do not know. Perhaps I will learn more as I progress in my story. One theme might be how I can view so much of my history as what could have been. Add to that, the powerful but too-late determinations that most of what I desired was there for the taking. With this in mind, I hope you can appreciate how devastating mental illness is as to blind someone to the very things their heart sought out. Regardless of my current perspective, the boy and the man were not equipped to overcome the many issues they faced in this existence. So, that's just life, I guess.

Outlasting the most hazardous storms of mental anguish was made possible by reading, writing, listening, and learning. The hero is near his best self when engrossed in the intellectual side of life. With that in mind, I enjoy classic stories and myths, and one comes to mind now that seems particularly fitting. There have been many different tales about the search for the Holy Grail—the cup Jesus used during the Last Supper. These seemed to have been originally authored during the Middle Ages and remain part of the popular consciousness to this day. Any fans of the Indiana Jones movies know this to be true. Many scholars and non-scholars interpret the quest for this most sacred of objects as having a hidden meaning. The search is not for a physical object at all; instead, the stories present a metaphor for an individual passing through different stages of life while gaining the necessary skills along the way. Or, the lost Holy Grail can substitute for any person's major life purpose of finding…fill in the blank. The term itself is often used to describe something precious and rare in a given category, such as the Holy Grail of stamp collecting or something of a similar nature. In most Holy Grail stories, though, the seeker usually cannot find and/or keep the prize for which he is obsessed.

I prefer to view Grail lore as describing the onset of adolescence and the subsequent search for an identity and a sense of wholeness. These years tend to create a shock to the system, where many realities of life are expected to be learned. Puberty and, thus, sexuality are one of those. Indeed, adolescence is a time when many young males and females begin to formulate notions of the world that encompass complexity and danger. In other words, the safety and certainty of being a child is replaced by a world of desire, fear, greed, and complex motives. This is a simplistic way to describe the grail myths I know, but there is a mountain of readings on this topic, should you be interested.

I am not sure that the hero of this story successfully navigated his way into adulthood with the proper knowledge or coping mechanisms. I am sure he did not. His grail experience did not go as expected. In other words, his path did not fall in line with the successful completion of the hero's journey. This, like most notable findings, I did not discover until late 2021. The tools were there to see it all along, but I could not slow my mind long enough. And that could only begin after the storm blew through my life, tossing me toward unprecedented and alien environments. I hope there are no expiration dates on rewrites.

CHAPTER 2:

We are What We are Not

"The truly creative mind in any field is no more than this: A human creature born abnormally, inhumanly sensitive. To him...a touch is a blow, a sound is a noise, a misfortune is a tragedy, a joy is an ecstasy, a friend is a lover, a lover is a god, and failure is death. Add to this cruelly delicate organism the overpowering necessity to create, create, create, and create—so that without the creating of music or poetry or books or buildings or something of meaning, his very breath is cut off from him. He must create, must pour out creation. By some strange unknown, inward urgency he is not really alive unless he is creating."[3]

My favorite movie is *The Godfather*. To be more specific and accurate, my favorite movies are *The Godfather I* and *The Godfather II*. Yes, these are two different films, but I consider them two epic installments of one very lengthy epic movie. Besides, it is impossible to choose between the two, as one features Marlon Brando and the other Robert De Niro. I have several favorites, but no other movie exudes genius so thoroughly and offers so much sage commentary on life as *The Godfather*.

I would like to provide a brief overview for those who have not seen it. Yes, plenty have not. It is an Italian Mafia movie that centers on the lives of two generations of the Corleone family. Although there is violence, the main portion of the drama revolves around the family's struggle to remain preeminent and powerful while navigating enemies, including law enforcement and rival Mafia factions. It is much more than the typical gangster flick. The youngest son, Michael, becomes the hero of sorts after being thrust into the leadership role of the family. Throughout the film, Michael makes plans to preserve the family's life and fortune while seeking revenge on the mobsters who nearly assassinated his father. Michael was never meant to be a Mafioso, but he had to rush to his father's aid to protect him and the empire the Godfather built. In what I think is the key scene of the film, Michael asks his mother if a man can lose his family by being strong and trying to protect it. His mother does not understand what Michael is saying and replies that family is a permanent state of affairs. Michael responded with, "Times are changing."

The Godfather is a tragedy about family and choices made, and how those decisions can subvert the very thing in life one holds dear. Michael was a war hero who was never intended to take over control of a crime syndicate. Once his father, Vito, is badly hurt, and his brother, Sonny, is murdered, it is left to Michael to summon the strength and cunning to do whatever it takes to protect his loved ones. However, by assuming command amid a family crisis and engaging in murders himself, Michael's obsessive desire to defend the Corleones isolated him from his closest family. Michael orders the death of his brother for being disloyal, and his wife leaves him. Michael sits atop the most powerful Mafia family but has become a distant, cold figure estranged from those he loves. Thus, the essence of tragedy here is that by trying and doing everything to save his family, Michael unwittingly authorizes the deeds that destroy it. This is cinematic brilliance at its finest, teaching a very hard life lesson.

While pondering *the Godfather's* tragedy, I have considered parallels to decisions and events in my life that did not turn out as planned. There are various bits of wisdom in popular culture that relate to becoming too single-minded and overly zealous in securing what one wants in life. Most of them say something like this: "If you want or love something, you must learn to let it go." This is not exactly what I am talking about, but it is in the same ballpark. The great psychologist Viktor Frankl was much closer to what I mean. He offered an example of an insomniac who is desperately trying to get some sleep, and is hyper-aware and concentrated on making his desire come true. Therefore, a person like this goes to bed with all their brainpower aimed at achieving restful sleep. Yet, the fear of not sleeping itself creates anxiety that, in turn, defeats his purpose and takes him even further away from getting rest. Therefore, by consciously pushing hard toward an outcome, one can inadvertently undermine one's wishes. I know from experience that this is undoubtedly true, especially when it comes to sleep. I have an ongoing battle trying to get enough sleep, and this has always been the case.

Defying my wishes has been a recurring problem throughout my life. Once again, I did not realize any of this until recently, over the last year or so. I was taught to work hard to achieve whatever end goal. So, it has often been the case that I thought trying and praying stridently for something would make that something become reality. There is nothing wrong with the spirit of this philosophy, but living has taught me that all-out effort does not guarantee anything. Too often, my INFJ preoccupation with some wonderful thing in my mind, to the exclusion of all else, has hindered my hopes and dreams. Also, I am a perfectionist and have, for too long, been a victim of the old "all or nothing" mindset. Either my plan is working perfectly or is a disaster, she either loves or hates me, I am brilliant or stupid, etc. Like Obi-Wan Kenobi preached to Anakin, only a Sith (evil guy) speaks in absolutes.

Combined, these factors can erode one's mental health and contribute to difficult times. For instance, my long battle with sleep deprivation has not been aided by "working harder," and that has instead caused it to worsen. The anxiety of not sleeping starts to creep into my conscious mind as bedtime approaches. By the time it arrives, I have worked myself into a frenzy of thought after thought, each careening into one another when I am supposed to feel relaxed. Once racing thoughts arrive, peacefully falling asleep becomes a rare occurrence. Not sleeping turns into a fear of not sleeping that affects my whole day. So, sleep worries make all the waking hours more anxiety-ridden. Fortunately, I do take prescribed medication that helps.

I believe self-sabotage is the ultimate form of humans acting against their conscience to achieve success. After being introduced to the concept in rehab, I was sure that self-sabotage did not apply to me. Why would I intentionally want to do anything to derail my most cherished desires? Yet, it was true, and I had to face reality. Moreover, now I confess that my case is severe. Most people likely assume, like I did, that there was no way they could practice this kind of self-harm. There are many reasons someone indulges in self-sabotage, and they all have to do with our human survival instinct. Yes, being less successful can trigger, somewhere deep in the unconscious, a feeling of protection. Some worry that success will bring more responsibility, as in a job promotion. In relationships, people betray themselves due to the trepidation of letting someone get too close to them. I, like many, have never considered myself deserving of praise and therefore feel uncomfortable sitting in my achievements. Some in the modern world feel more secure away from the bright light of doing something very well. You see, we do not think to ourselves, "Okay, enough of this, it is time for self-sabotage." Our tactical undermining of ourselves occurs somewhere, not in our conscious minds, with us unable to recognize our self-destructive actions. Philosopher Frederick Nietzsche had much to say on almost every subject, including the following:

> But the worst enemy you can meet will always be yourself; you lie in wait for yourself in caverns and forests. Lonely one, you are going your way alone! And your way goes past yourself, and past your seven devils! You will be a heretic to yourself and witch and soothsayer and fool and doubter and unholy one and villain. You must be ready to burn yourself in your flame: how could you become new, if you had not first become ashes?[4]

A scene from *Star Wars* can add to the point I am making. Most of you are aware that the film's themes and action coalesce around a specific father-son conflict between Luke and Darth Vader. Training to be a

Jedi under the tutelage of Yoda, Luke enters this mysterious cave of dark forces. To summarize, Luke encounters the arch villain Darth Vader, kind of, but not really. In terms of the film, the confrontation may be in Luke's mind, or it could be just a vision, but not a real, flesh-and-blood fight. Anyway, Luke strikes him down, and Vader's helmet falls to the ground. In the mask/helmet, Luke sees a reflection of his face staring back at him. Luke encounters his fate should he succumb to the dark side's powers. So, Luke's true enemy is himself, because within the hero lives the material to transform into the galaxy's most heinous villain. Despite the laser gunfights, aerial battles in space, alien landscapes, and all the rest, the movie is really about the things that count here on earth: growing up, becoming an adult, and facing yourself and your father's legacy.

Along with self-sabotage, there is a phenomenon known as "impostor syndrome," which is part of my interconnected tapestry of dysfunctions. Many people burdened with this condition do not truly believe that they deserve good things to happen to them. Sure, we claim we want and deserve all that the heart fancies, but somewhere a voice of sabotage lurks within. And yes, it is our voice, so both the yearning for good things and the belief we should not receive them are part of the same being. It is not odd at all and is an aspect of being the complicated thing called human. Too many times than I can estimate, I have heard, "you are a wannabe, not as good as people say. Those people are wrong." It is only a matter of time. This applies to almost any work or relationship situation.

Now I must add "avoidance disorder" to the terrible stew of ailments and distortions we have been cooking. My condition was severe and perhaps still is. For reasons not entirely clear, the hero put others on a pedestal, believing most people to be smarter, more cultured, wiser in the ways of the world, and cooler. Interactions with almost all other people convinced him that he lacked intelligence and social skills. We cannot say he was one thing all the time, of course. However, he had predictable tendencies that we can summarize, and the young hero was remarkably gullible and easily deceived. He viewed any individual who acted confidently and even arrogantly as assuredly having a stranglehold on life. Now he can better judge how people can appear well-adjusted but feel terrified and inferior on the inside. Avoidance is the first and last resort for him and has been his most consistent ally when faced with anxiety and sadness.

Although it may be difficult for others to understand (perhaps not, I am not sure), the young man believed the literal, surface representation of every person and thing to be true. That is sadly the way it was, long past the point of becoming an adult. He now feels that the hero was extremely naive and can still be easily swindled. Taking every utterance and action as sincere, he easily felt less-than and as someone who should not attempt things. By things, I mean practically anything. So he avoided every situation he could where he knew his shortcomings would be exposed, especially in a competitive activity. He still did not know where one could find the book of life instructions that others surely had read. The boy avoided life itself. He just refused to enter the race.

It would have been beneficial for the young me to listen to those negative voices and discover their true source. There is a concept called "Internal Family Systems" that can be very helpful for those who are serious about their mental health. Professional psychologists and therapists tend to agree with taking all our "people" seriously. IFS treats the good and bad advice inside us as people with whom we can converse. If you want to call it voices or that old devil vs. angel on your shoulders, or something else, it does not matter. I am referring to the various perspectives each person has in their mind that influence their decision-making process. We are composed of many complexities and change continuously over the lifespan; therefore, humans are bound to have various opinions and inner conflicts. No matter how illogical, the beliefs are real and there, probably, for a good reason. Often, the mind will tell us to do something counter-productive out of some desire for familiarity and/or self-preservation. So, your brain can react to danger in a way that feels safe and is an instinct, even though the behavior is increasingly ruinous to body and mind.

I approach each voice of advice as representing a person who is either trying to help or manipulate me. That way, I think I can start to overcome the bad urges with the guidance of the more logical, inner therapist. This is a classic case of easier said than done. Detrimental actions are difficult to conquer because they have become consoling. Thus, we gravitate towards them before we are capable of having more reasoned thoughts. How many of our acts and decisions do not make good sense? In other words, some of us become reliant on self-sabotage because it is a well-practiced response we do not have to think about to act on. This is not unlike the instinct to put our hands out to brace ourselves when we fall. I feel that my brain wants to protect me from disappointment and pain, and urges me to do what comes very easily. Hurting myself, before someone or something does, has been a constant ever since my memories began. It is my old companion. I can exit a situation and, in a way, control it by putting it in my rearview mirror. To achieve this, it may require an initial loss to regain some sense of comfort.

The instigators of my self-destruction are the twin misfortunes of a crippling lack of self-esteem and little to no ability to trust others. For instance, I assume most people will abandon me once they see through my persona to the pretender within. This is a guarantee, I reckon, due to my incompetence in so many areas of life, including the complete lack of birdhouse skills. For years, from adolescence into my twenties, I could only see my faults and had this obtrusive mental block. My brain treated the compliments and the good works as trespassers to be immediately removed. This is me striving to get close to the truth so you understand, but almost without fail I threw away any proof that Kirk was a good person. People have an amazing capacity for fooling themselves, taking this to heart, and disregarding that. Self-esteem is the foundation of positive mental health. It is the bedrock.

If my self-worth were a volume button, it was turned all the way down to zero. This is not a melodramatic moment, because it is regretfully accurate. To continue my little metaphor, I had no idea that the dial could be reversed in the other direction. This significantly impacted my quality of life in numerous ways. For one, I relied on retreating by fading further and further away from a social scene once I felt unwanted or ignored. This occurred frequently and easily, and likely served as a defense mechanism.

Yeah, seems probable. This was the modus operandi for him for a long time and, sometimes, even to this day. From the age of 12 to roughly 14, he did not speak at all unless necessary. Not in public, that is, and that mainly refers to high school. Considering his life up to the present, this era has been like being lost in the wilderness without hope. This is when the hero begins to view the world outside his body as if things were happening to someone else in a movie.

Yet, the real trouble was that nothing was happening to him. It was as if he did not exist, and no one could recognize the sadness he surely must have been conveying, right? Maybe the school counselor was uninterested or unable to provide some support, but I know counseling was never more than a passing rumor. There was nothing for him or with him. The youth was aware that this was the time of bodily changes, so he was not that oblivious. Very importantly, this is close to the age when males start to play football for the "real" school team. Readers may know what I mean all over the country and the world, but those in the South understand football madness better than anyone else. Everything important enough to matter was now about football and not imagination or jokes. The players belonged to a private club, but they also bestowed membership on the prettiest or most eager girls. Never again did anyone in school talk about something the hero liked or understood. He well remembers that sense of complete detachment.

Probably more than anything else during those harrowing days, the man recalls having a chronic lack of anything to say. There are introverts and loners, and he is both. Then there is something worse: habitually searching for but failing to find any words that make sense for the situation. At least, that is what it felt like. Rarely did the young man believe he could speak on any subject that would register with others his age. This became a total preoccupation, a thorn in his side, and a heel of Achilles, especially when it came to members of the opposite sex. It was the stuff of nightmares. He could not converse about cars, assembling things, hunting and killing, guns, or playing football. Then there is another mountain to climb on top of all that: what in the world do girls want to talk about, anyway? I have real remorse, now, considering all those opportunities squandered in the silence. Nothing ever came out of his mouth without sounding awkward to his ear. Fear of not having something to say was a self-fulfilling prophecy that helped to fuel the anxiety factor. And, his anxiety was already near-intolerable. He did not know what panic attacks were, but some he had came as a result of social anxiety.

I lost potential romances and every other kind of personal connection in large part due to my issues with participating in any meaningful exchange with another human being. I remember searching the cobwebbed parts of my brain, desperate as to what normal people would enjoy talking about. Inside my mind, there was plenty. Truthfully, I did not care about the success of the football team, but never would I utter such a heresy. The hero was indifferent to practically every topic others tended to hold in high esteem. And, he lacked that useful talent of faking interest. I wondered to myself: what was so wrong with me, given that every other person appeared to have endless things to say to one another? I only thought in terms of what others might want to hear and dared not be honest with myself. Once again, I wished that I had access to the textbook that everyone else had read. Surely, there was a chapter in it about exchanging words.

From time to time, humor supplied some hope of escaping the doldrums of social incompetence. For years, I at least attempted to turn all conversational opportunities into performances to showcase my comedic abilities. After all, every single look or word between people is a ritual. And for each occasion, there is a verdict rendered along with winners and losers. I was good at making people laugh. Girls like to laugh—I realized that. I remember, more than once, entertaining the whole class at lunchtime with an older boy who must have known about comedy. It must be that watching Saturday Night Live and David Letterman as often as possible bled into my psyche enough to pick up some rhythms and timing. Most of all, I could always create stories, characters, and situations. Absurdity agreed with me, as life itself was mostly a repetitively cruel, unintelligible joke. Yet, it was fatiguing to me, and probably to others, to turn everything into comedy. Instinctively, I understood that not every-thing was funny and did not want to appear foolish. Looking back, I am guessing this is one reason why people drifted in and out of my social circle at will. It gets tiresome.

By now, you should understand that I have had terrible problems with forming and sustaining relationships and feeling any sense of belonging anywhere. Still, there is a bit more to the picture. There existed no real-life alternative role models for a strange kid to emulate. I think most of you understand small towns and their limitations, and mine was especially pessimistic for reasons never clarified. On top of that, my teenage years occurred before the widespread adoption of both the Internet and cell phones. It was the last generation where this was true. So, access to other versions of and opinions on life did not exist for me. By different, of course, I mean compared to the standards of personhood and manhood that lived in a small southern town, and whatever you are now presum-ing is most likely an accurate assessment. Not fitting the standard meant being a nothing; a strange oddity who was simply left out of the pageant of life. You may wonder if I felt more at odds with myself than I appeared to others. This is possible, yet the feelings were just as real, regardless.

I believed I had been left out of the main currents of culture and sociability. A term called "Othering" helps explain my young life and the struggles of many people around the world. Most likely, every person has both Othered someone else and been on the receiving end of it. Othering is not a term commonly used in everyday vernacular, but it is well-known to academics and others curious enough about the Humanities. It is rather simple. As human beings, we identify with something, no matter how anti-social the individual may be. Even the most isolated person is cat-egorized by one or more of many factors, such as occupation, ethnicity, nationality, race, family heritage, and hobbies. Othering is the process by which we shape our sense of self by defining it against the alternative attri-butes of another group that possesses unfamiliar, unacceptable, or inferior characteristics. So, to be a member of group X, it means there is at least a group Y that, by its exclusion, establishes the attributes to be part of X.

If you are an X, it is somewhat easy to decide that the Y people are less sophisticated, smart, strong, racially pure, deserving of leadership, and the list of possibilities goes on and on.

Othering is not a particularly difficult subject to consider when you think about how people tend to take simple differences in culture or race and magnify them into an identity. Discussions of Othering in any setting often inspire folks, first, to consider the racial/ethnic implications. Therefore, I am not black, so I am white; I am not white, so I am black; I am not Middle Eastern, so I am European, etc. In America, many southerners set themselves apart because we are not Yankees, who many believe live and act differently. Ask southerners, and they will respond that northern people talk too fast and curse too often. Country folks have habits and proclivities that differ from those of city folk, as many have expressed countless times. The urban crowd is sophisticated and worldly, and will tell you so, because they are not like dull country bumpkins. The possibilities are as endless as there are ways of creating a persona distinguishable from another one. So, it might be accurate to say that who we think we are is based on who we believe we are not.

Othering is not always evil, but most of the time it leads to conflict and hard feelings. Nations have gone about the process of Othering, especially in the modern, industrialized world. A good example is how Great Britain and France have historically viewed one another with hostility, engaging in name-calling and war over centuries. Competing for colonial holdings and world supremacy, the two greatest European powers portrayed their enemy as the antithesis of everything good in the world. I am referring to the 17th to 19th centuries, approximately. England thought of their hated rival as lazy, incompetent, wasteful, and overly-sensuous (effeminate), and saw themselves as hard working, thrifty, masculine, and innovative. To the French, however, the British were perceived as lacking refinement and culture; they were essentially viewed as thick-headed, greedy, and unscrupulous. The U.S.S.R. and the United States Othered each other for much of the twentieth century during the Cold War. Thus, in both examples, a national character formed largely due to shallow perceptions and stereotypes. Here, as in many cases, Othering aids in instilling national pride but can also produce hatred and exclusion of non-members.

In the tragic, extreme examples in History, Othering sanctions humans to commit the most egregious and monstrous acts upon (supposedly) fundamentally different, enemy subhumans. Othering can sharpen perceived differences between groups that might be quite inconsequential. World War II and the Holocaust surely exhibited the worst of Othering. With endless examples, native peoples around the world have been Othered during the process of contact with and colonization by conqueror nations. It would not be a surprise to find opinions from the contemporaries of Christopher Columbus reputing Native Americans to be savage, heathen, and uncivilized compared to civilized, Christian Europeans. Many times, the Other is portrayed as something of a "boogie man" to fear. Othering is not limited to any particular place or people on earth, as it can manifest in many ways both large and small. So, while Othering applies to regions, nations, and races, we can see how it pertains to everyday relationships.

Belonging is the opposite of Othering, and heroes like me battle the dragons and other monsters of life to attain it. I never did during my younger days. Psychology implores us to take seriously the human need for fellowship and belonging. Well, I think common sense tells us this, too. And this is not a thing that can be short-lived, as it must be sustained to achieve satisfaction with one's membership. Identity can certainly change over time, and one can be a part of multiple groups simultaneously. As someone who had terrible anxiety around others, it is likely not shocking that belonging did not come my way. Closely related to belonging was my ongoing frustration with having an intimate partnership based on core values and passions. I am not speaking of a romantic relationship, though it could be found there. I describe what and who someone is when every artifice is removed. This has been a lonely endeavor, and I am unsure if it has ever been successful. In the places where I lived, went to school, and everything else, people normalized hunting and killing as the standard for males. Well, that is not the full spectrum, but it is a good start. I did not qualify and realized that I never could.

Othering, as I interpret it, cannot be understood without some recognition of the "zero-sum mentality." Many people interpret any gain by one to automatically entail a loss by another. It is an idea that is easily grasped when considering sports and other contests between individuals or teams. Team A wins, so Team B must lose. The zero sum is likely present wherever Othering has taken hold. In terms of civil rights equality, I do not need to remind anyone how we often calculate that one person's rise up the ladder must mean a loss of status or rights for another person. Simply by living and observing others, we can recognize the pervasiveness of the zero-sum mentality in the modern world. People want to win arguments and force others to lose them. Person A wants to win favor at school, work, or among friends and family, and becomes an opponent of Person B, who wants the same thing. Person A succeeds, and Person B detects they are now less than as a consequence. Most components of life need not be construed in this manner, though.

The zero-sum mentality was everywhere in those days, so naturally it infected my mind. Some competitions require a "loser," yes, but life is no game, and we should move toward more uplifting philosophies in most respects. As a young male, the unending culture of violence transferred its logic from the zero-sum game. The weaker in physical strength and character had to be rooted out and exposed for display. Those who dissented in some way, actual or imagined, deserved always to lose, and the stronger performed that job. By strong, I only refer to the males or females who aligned with whatever was thought proper to be and do. By not fitting the mold, I assumed I was on the losing side. The alternative is to envision oneself as a different, unique, or eccentric entity with valuable contributions to share. Oh, Othering and losing is by no means merely something that is erased by maturing into adulthood. Some adults are more like children than children. Many times, I have cringed at the thought of being less loved, approved of, or appreciated because of the fitness of another to be loved, approved of, or appreciated. I am thinking of authority figures and/ or people I love or want to love.

Othering likely begins very early in a human being's life. Of course, a toddler is not aware of the concept at all, but they can perceive the attitudes of adults on some level. Is Othering natural or unnatural? Is it an innate part of us from birth, or is it more of a thing that is learned? Most agree that we tend to Other people not within our kinship circle, and this might provide the blueprint for all of humanity's narrow-mindedness. Religious differences, such as people who do not go to your church, or not all, or are Christian instead of Muslim, Buddhist instead of Christian, Catholic and not Protestant, agnostic instead of…whatever, are among the first to be marked as different in an individual's young life. Kids develop notions of class distinctions based on who wears the most expensive clothes versus those with the lesser-than brands and styles. Certainly, Othering based on race and ethnicity begins early, as well. This is one of the most unfortunate aspects of modern civilizations—we tend to use physical differences to promote an "us vs. them" mentality. Unfortunately, people learn and teach that my way of worshiping God or gods, my skin tone and features, my language, etc., are the norm, and yours constitute the Other.

Even when considered on the micro-level in my life, Othering can have hurtful consequences. Kids can be mean, and they eventually figure out how to ostracize their peers who do not belong for whatever rea-son. In my school, there were the athletes, rebels/drug users, the smart kids/never do wrong-ers, and the poor/strange/maladjusted, from broken homes types. I was always the man alone on his island. Perhaps I Othered myself. In any case, I felt like an oddball and outcast from every possible group culture, including each costumed community of cliques. As an out-come of it all, I severely doubted my manly credentials, thought no one could love me, feared that I was not mentally unwell but just born wrong, and wore the disgust for my inner being around every day, constantly, like a scarlet letter. I believed I was weird to abstain from the hunting and fishing, muddy, football-crazy, hyper-macho ethic and lifestyle.

Perhaps I will never learn the ultimate origins of why I did not and could not go along to get along. Was mental illness the source? Only now can I look back and realize how my young adulthood would have been much easier if I had mustered the will to play the necessary games. Then, I have to remind myself that it was simply not on the table as an option. A voice inside quietly murmurs that perhaps someone will come across this writing with a similar story and provide the answers. It does not matter, as I am still unable to go back in time. What bothers my mind from time to time is missing out on what is referred to as "puppy love." Just to be clear, I refer to the euphoria of being young and in love, and I came close enough to feel what might have been. With females, friendships, and all things social, the zero-sum and all-or-nothing-ism fomented a virulent form of pessimism that blanketed my life with distress. My instruction in mental health teaches that one is never too late for most of life's precious gifts, but some things only live once and then vanish from view forever.

The hero felt like an almost-but-non-member of many high school communities. He had cool acquaintances from his childhood who were no longer friends, ever since the start of varsity football. His not-quite friendships rarely translated into doing things outside of school. To be seen, have fun, and chill with others at night, one had to circle "the block" downtown. It was sadly essential to do this to appear cool and let others know your status and availability to engage in risqué activities. Not surprisingly, I was unable to integrate myself into the "happening" scene.

For one thing, he lived by rather strict rules that discouraged him from spending too much time floating around downtown. Frequent home check-ins were mandatory. Additionally, I was unfamiliar with what I was supposing to be doing except for going in circles. He knew that some pathway must have existed that led to the parties, being around the cool girls, and feeling closer to acceptance, but he did not know where to start. Almost this and almost that, he was not quite anything.

Some manner of rebellion could have helped him during his teenage years, but that phase of growing up simply did not emerge until midlife. I have always felt a deep desire to stand out from the crowd. The status quo was boring and fake, and I realized this from an early age. During the 1980s and 1990s, we all received the same corporate brainwashing to conform, to just do it, to have it your way, and so on. Times have changed, but do we still live mostly in "a material world?" I cannot say for sure. And yes, it is very healthy and not contradictory to desire both belonging and singularity simultaneously. Rebellion is helpful within some common-sense limits, and it is degrading and unhealthy to always accept all of life's ridiculousness without some level of discontent. We should all agree that everyone needs a sense of rebellion. Yet, I did not explore it for reasons that you probably already know: I did not know how. There was no place or thing familiar to me that promised danger. My household was very strict. Once again, I wondered: How do people obtain this kind of information? Where?

My family upbringing and the values of my parents made youthful indiscretions and assertions of individuality practically nonexistent. I remember going over to a classmate's house for the first time, and seeing his dad had beer in the refrigerator. I was shocked and asked myself: "Oh, so this is allowed?" My parents had no vices and insisted that their children had none too. So in days long gone, I did not comprehend what beer was and how it was different from liquor, and I knew nothing about drinking except that bad people did it at bad places. Of course, I had heard about various drugs, liquors, and wines, but these had no relationship to my life. Certainly, I overheard whispers of stories about kids sneaking away to indulge in sinful behavior, somewhere, but all of that might as well have been on some other planet. For me, drugs never entered the picture, and I understood them about as well as quantum physics. Forget tattoos. There was a dingy Grunge culture, and it mostly inspired certain dress and dispositions, along with sullen, bratty non-conformity. I think every kid should try following an independent path, questioning those in power, and discovering their specialness. Life has taught me that burying something important will cause greater harm somewhere down the line. The denial of self can have a deadly domino effect.

With defiance hard to even fathom and organized sports out of the question, there was little left to make the hero feel masculine. If one did not pursue sports, then he needed to test boundaries, break rules, and run with the fast crowd. I guess we could say this was the alternate route to acceptable boyhood. Self-awareness was my curse, and I feared being Othered, sticking out like a sore thumb, and not acting out my part to make that saying, "boys will be boys," true. Young males have been, still are, and likely always will be given the green light to pursue what they seek in the world. Manly men are bold and live by some version of the "seize the day" mantra. The "best" of the best are future mayors, school board members, football coaches, and community leaders who get what they want and expect. It is only looking backward after the storms of youth have passed that someone can be nonchalant about the devastating pain of mental illness, rejection, and Otherness.

Males of really any age are supposed to make things happen if that means in sports, in love and courtship, in leadership, and acceptable, "manly" forms of self-expression. There is an expectation that boys will occasionally act obnoxiously and cause minor disturbances. They get punished, but that is to be expected. There have probably been millions of mothers or fathers who, when talking about their male child, roll their eyes with a laugh and a wink at the mention of his latest misdeeds. Just to make sure I am clear, males are supposed to engage in shenanigans, fight, flirt, play hard, drive fast, and every so often stay out past the curfew. Wow, that was not me. It never left my conscious mind that I was incapable of filling the roles handed down by tradition. Ultimately, if a youthful male was Othered, he then became more feminine by the rules of that closed-minded, closed-off world. Yep, it is true. What traits compose the Othered profile, in terms of whatever is not masculine and thus feminine? It would be a mix of a soft-spoken countenance, a willingness to compromise, color coordination, waiting one's turn, a mild temperament, disinterest in weapons and sports, a lack of aggression, and more. Okay, so some of those might be silly.

American culture holds aggressive male behavior in high regard—or at least it did in the 1980s and 1990s. I somewhat recall dressing up and pretending to be a cowboy at about 5 or 6, and no other character represents America better. There are different versions of the cowboy figure, but the most visible has been the man who secures or protects something through the use of violence. He has no problem with it and considers it his self-defined duty to dispense justice. Instead of cowboy, one might as well use the term "Old West hero." We love this type of man in movies, even those set in modern cities, the future, or wherever. Country music has long promoted this kind of male exemplar as preferred over the urbane, city-dwelling, over-educated, feminized Other. The idealized American go-getter could well be Clint Eastwood (this has been true, is it changing?) and his rugged, make-my-own-rules, not entirely the good guy, sometimes rule-breaking, style of living. You may doubt what I am saying, but this is more or less accurate when you think about it. In my opinion, not much has changed, but perhaps the cowboy's costume has evolved.

Although I could not articulate it back then, easy violence was welcomed as a legitimate means to deal with conflicts. For me, physical aggression can be implied just as forcefully as it can and is dealt out literally, person-to-person. Revenge fantasies are simulated all the time in movies and video games these days. As a teenager, I could somehow sense when words were real threats, when handshakes were adversarial, when body language was foreboding, and when looks could be deadly. And they were, as far as destroying someone's self-worth and safety. No matter what anyone prefers to say out loud, we recognize that physical force is a reliable and sometimes preferred tool for mediating between people. At least for my generation, boys did not need to be told this. But I was not enamored with violence as a young man and avoided it. As an adult, I have felt violence close up, the real kind, and found its practitioners (who promote it) dangerously unintelligent.

As in the case of films, music of any era mirrors the societal norms and preferences of people. Country music especially likes for the cowboy type to win over the polished, slick-talking, fast-moving, secular, doesn't mow his grass, male, who has never operated or touched a tractor. Modern Country radio is describing one form of the archetypal American man every day and hour. The music itself is a vapid substitute for organic folk music, portraying common people and the culture they create and inhabit. I think that Country tries and fails to provide male heroes and a value system that is widespread and usable for a broad demographic. In other words, the music presents imagery that overcompensates for several modern concerns, such as the one where men feel less masculine if they are not working in the spirit of birdhouse building.

I think music is but one example of how we, as a culture, deal with the unsettling belief that we have lost something. In my youth, kids were also overcompensating, and some continue to do the same thing as grown-ups. Yeah, I think I will concede that during those days long ago, toxic masculinity always simmered and sometimes leaked out with results ridiculous to tragic. Truthfully, the toxicity I witnessed never stopped and might be just as alive today as back then. This is another piece of the puzzle that helps understand the overwhelming sadness that should not have been there. No one pulled me aside to let me in on the secret that it was all a bunch of bunk. So, Country music did not invent the toxins; it is just a current reflection of that mentality that keeps turning out boy-savages.

Toxic, fake masculinity is the enemy of good sense, wisdom, and most of the things that cause folks to be happier than sad. Earlier, I said that writing this should inform me better about what this is, and now I can verify that as very accurate. There is a certain antagonistic atmosphere that makes me uncomfortable. It is like being besieged. It has something to do with over-maleness, intimidation, censorship, peer pressure, competitive one-upmanship, and zero-sum reasoning. If you are not willing to play the game and say the right things, you become Othered and shunned. Many, if not most, males thankfully grow out of this stuff. Where do you find it? In sports, hanging out, and engaging in traditional male pastimes such as firing weapons; these are a few places that come to mind but surely not all of them. Let us call it the playground mentality. Where this philosophy holds the key to power and belonging, being or acting intelligent is a major liability. Close–minded banter, feats of meanness and cruelty, stories where the cowboy archetype prevails, and recollections about disregarding the rules are a sampling of the subjects that dominate the day. I resisted the playground mentality most of the time, but I occasionally fell into its trap.

His lack of manliness left behind a mental wreckage that still haunts the man. Deep down, he suspected that there was more to being a man than what my culture popularized. However, this mild speculation never came to light. He thought almost entirely in terms of what others wanted and expected, and no one helped him climb out of this un-winnable paradigm. If there was encouragement, it went completely unnoticed. There was not much that he allowed to leak out of his tightly controlled thoughts, anyway. He was the most steadfast pessimist you could ever have the misfortune to meet. Though not afraid of physicality itself, the wannabe hero assumed he could not fight as well as others. After all, boys brag a whole lot, and he did not know it was possible to lie so enthusiastically. He could not see past any facade.

He was the easiest target for dirty tricksters who ever walked the earth. The young man lacked all the skills and foreknowledge applicable to the playground. He was a timid soul and was extremely aware of his difference from others. Often, he questioned how the offspring of the quarterback and head cheerleader was such a malfunctioning disaster. If you didn't play football, you better have a compelling reason for it, such as getting into serious trouble. Short of that, one should be employed with bird-house-building as part of the duties. Instead of fulfilling my role, I just felt useless.

Education offered a small amount of self-respect. He became very good in school over the years, but at 18, he was only beginning to become his future self: a super-student. Any subject or project that rewarded free thought, such as reading, writing, creativity, or analytic thinking, was his kind of fun. He wrote bad poetry for years, but it was not as bad as that of his peers. The world of ideas appealed to him more than anything else. Possibilities were exciting. Essays were easy and opportunities more than burdens, while English and History became the young man's favorite subjects. They are first cousins — if subjects were people. However, I hated Math and could not pay attention to it for more than thirty seconds. Likewise, finding a fixed solution among a field of numbers seemed somewhat like instructions for building a birdhouse. It was never going to happen.

Anyway, your author became the best History student in his school and then in the county. Yes, he was the History star of the county academic competition, even though his teacher hated him. Nevertheless, I almost felt like a real hero for the first time. It did give Kirk pride and, for some reason, a little optimism that Karen would fall in love with him. That did not happen. Still, little did he know his winning performance foreshadowed a brighter future for him in the academic world than in any other role of his young life.

The young man was considered the "smart one" of the family, even though his high school grades were only average. He hated his school and had little belief in himself, so he was not the most motivated student in the world. It did not matter much, as practically no one from his school received a scholarship to a major university. He had no career plan or any idea about the future except that he was going to college. High school graduation came and went, leaving him feeling rather lonely and empty. Next, he followed a few classmates to a local community college and then to the University of Alabama. He was not surprised, but disheartened, to find that college people also had access to the secret, how-to manual of living that was still tucked away somewhere unknown.

The young man assumed college was supposed to be fun and carefree, because the television had told him so, over and over. He did not regularly converse with any person who had been to college. Zack Morris from *Saved by the Bell: The College Years* was more of a mentor than any actual human being. He noticed how others he knew delighted in a greater degree of freedom and a larger pool of potential girlfriends and boyfriends. College would not be easy at all. It was a different environment and atmosphere, with new people who all knew something that he did not. Soon, the college kids, too, would see through his mask to that hidden, pretender-person. Fitting in would never be on the menu. Nothing had changed from high school, and if anything, the hero's love forecast promised no happy respite. These kids were likely smarter, had more financial resources, and came from more affluent educational backgrounds. "Uh-oh, it is like the Wild West now, lacking even basic rules and with endless chances for my stupidity to show," he thought. How the man wishes to go back there and be all he could have been. Meeting the demands of academic rigor was never the problem, but his unrelenting social impairment held him back from rising to his potential.

I have a clear memory of my going-away-to-college party, but for unfortunate reasons. This was, I think, about two days before I was to leave Home for the first time and live at a college apartment. My mom invited my grandmother and a few aunts and uncles. Everyone was excited for me and asked questions about my plans and such. I recall distinctly being afraid that I would vomit, pass out, or cry in some combination. It was miserable, even though I appreciated the party. Here was another trap all too common: I was appalled by my inability to enjoy this, so my sadness seemed illegitimate. Suddenly, for the first time, it became real that I would be moving into a place without my family close by. It felt like a lightning bolt to the brain, flashing images of the future, and they were all scenes of hardships faced all alone. That thought repeated in an unending rotation in my head. So, I smiled through the pictures, but I felt assured that this was the day when my weaknesses would be exposed to all. That scared me, as well. It seemed not to matter that my voice of reason reminded me that I should be happy, like most college kids. I would not be alone, the voice interjected. No, any logic had left me replaced only with unreasonable, stifling fear.

It was bad, really bad. He experienced the loneliest feeling of his life soon after the party's conclusion. After everyone had left, his mental distress cratered to its lowest depths. He could no longer avoid what, in his head, seemed a grim reality very near. He believed the coming storm would make him so anxious to become physically sick, that no one would care about him, and he would miss classes and then fail college altogether. That night, he had what probably could be called a panic attack or nervous breakdown. Yet, he did not know to call it that, nor could he summon any effective remedy for it. Crying fits that he could not contain coincided with rapid heart rate, difficulty breathing, excessive sweating, nausea, and an unsettled feeling over the whole length of the body. His thinking was flawed but consistent with his usual perfectionism, all-or-nothing thinking, catastrophizing, and other well-worn patterns. Already, before his journey even started, the scared boy had rationalized out the most likely outcome. It would bring shame to him and ruin his "the smart one" reputation. He had to succeed no matter what.

The first few weeks of the university ordeal felt like nothing else I had experienced before. There was no scenario where survival was likely, and I easily believed it could end in some calamitous, total-body disintegration. Tuscaloosa is always hot, and in August, it felt like being inside an oven. Paved roads and concrete everywhere had a kind of roasting effect on him wherever he went. There were books in his hand, and inconvenient sweat incessantly poured out of him. And it was always lots of walking. There was an introduction to the problematic nightmare of college parking on top of everything. So, he did not know the tricks and the secret spots, thus he hiked long distances.

Every class was a challenge to keep from falling out of his chair. This is true without embellishment, dear reader. He daily anticipated not making it and passing out in class. The man now writing finds no suitable words to paint a reader an accurate description of that dreadful experience. After those days, I never required any proof that one's mental state controls the body. The pain never quit. It was as if my entire physical and spiritual being was in rebellion all at once, demanding to shut down, or else. My vision was blurry, and I was unnaturally exhausted each day. After sitting through the day's classes, he returned to that apartment, shut the door to his room, and plunked down on the bed until forced to trek out again in the heat. He was too weak to do anything else, including speaking to his roommates. He made it one day at a time.

This routine went on for weeks, then months, with the apparent realization that I needed major and immediate help. Previously in life, it had entered my head that something was not right and that it had to do with mental illness. Still, these weeks were the first time I remember believing some kind of intervention was needed from a psychiatrist...or, well, who knows? Again, I was at a loss as to where to turn. Never can I recall any discussion with anyone about the field of mental health or how to find any relief. The specifics were uncertain, but it seemed unlikely that I could continue in college, barely hanging on, unless some steps were taken to address the issue. My grip on reality was tenuous. There was no hope at all that I would last, here, all alone, without eventually having a significant collapse.

Feeling distraught, I summoned the only thing I thought I knew about mentally sick people and where they go. I asked my parents to take me to the "nut house." I begged. I had heard that term before and had falsely considered treatment to be like what was portrayed in movies and television. I could only assume that I had lost or was losing my mind. There was no sense of the totality of mental health services, different levels of care, counseling, inpatient vs. outpatient, etc., and little knowledge about medication. I would amend that and say zero. Certainly, I was a "the sky is falling" type of person anyway who always assumed the worst. I did not receive any manner of mental health treatment then or for a very long time. I felt Othered as a problem instead of helped as a person.

You could say that a stigma existed, for sure, but I am adding something more: the mentally ill constituted an Othered population. What might be charming eccentricities to one person are often labeled anti-social or crazy by another. Growing up, it was not rare to hear people of any age describe various others as insane and deserving of a bed at a mental hospital. Crazy was not considered a treatable issue, but instead was viewed as either a character flaw or a lifestyle choice. By issues, I mean those that cannot be explained away by circumstances or rationalized as normal. It is Othering at work when people stop being sick and in need of care, and instead are treated as a problem to be hidden away and forgotten. The rules of conduct were more traditional and less malleable in a small southern town than in New York City, Chicago, or any major city. So, to try to make it a little plainer, it did not take much more than not belonging to be classed as crazy, mentally unfit, or anything like that, according to the consensus of an Alabama country town. What might be termed a mental health diagnosis in today's world then amounted to accusations and character assassinations.

Tradition does not necessarily benefit people, and it may not even make sense. Academia taught me to examine traditions for validity, relevance, and fairness. Unfortunately, I learned that people struggling with mental illness just refuse to act normally. I gathered that the dominant culture prescribed that a troublesome guy with "mental problems" would benefit from a thorough ass-whipping. Thankfully, treatment of people with various illnesses, such as anxiety, Depression, PTSD, obsessive-compulsive disorder, substance abuse disorder, and Schizophrenia (many others) has come a long way. In some of the darkest days of humanity, people with real diseases and disorders were thought to be demon-possessed. People were treated with all sorts of magic and nonsense. Those who need extensive mental health care, though, can still be deemed weak and morally deficient.

Despite the recent celebrity campaigns on behalf of mental health awareness, there is still shaming and Othering taking place. There is a disconnect between the public's understanding of what "mental" means and the reality that I and many others live. So many people interpret that word as something separated from and independent of one's physical body. People bizarrely talk of the mind as an amorphous entity less real and material than the arms, legs, chest, eyes, fingers, etc. Everyone has heard someone utter statements like this: "Oh, do not worry, it is just all in your mind." The idea expressed here is the lazy assumption that a mental problem is different from having a broken leg or other physical injury. Any issue classified as mental is perceived as a temporary hiccup or even self-inflicted malady to be overcome just by trying harder. Of course, no sane person would tell someone with a broken leg to get rid of their medication or crutches, wheel chair, whatever, and start walking like nothing is wrong. Mental illness is a physical illness. You might be surprised to learn how many people still cannot properly grasp the nature of mental illness.

My undergraduate career began in 1998, and the sensitivity to and respect for people with mental illnesses has grown since. Without qualification, I was dragging myself around day by day with the belief that no one would grant that some disease lived within me. It led to self-loathing because apparently, I did not deserve even a visit to a mental health specialist. Nearing a breaking point, I wanted to finally lay my hands on that elusive instruction manual and just feel better. I did not know what crazy was, but it had to be something like what I felt. Or that is what one inner voice told me. By age 20, I had at least survived those terrible first weeks of the University without missing even one class. Things did get better, but I was hiding and not confronting the illness. My energy reserve was funneled entirely toward school with no social connections. By that, I mean I was still forging ahead, desperately, to what I presumed would be a one-and-only chance at college education. There would never be the Hollywood, good-time, college life, but my grip on remaining a viable college student was stronger. This is important: I began to gaslight myself by forming a false narrative in my head based on all the misinformation and despair.

The college years tested his coping ability, but they proved the young man could be laser-focused on some tasks while abandoning everything else important to a well-rounded life. A familiar state of affairs typified the hero's life as an undergraduate. He attended class, was on the roster, completed the work, and showed increasingly good grades, but he was never really a participant in the college scene. He was a spectator. As in high school, the young man never once felt part of anything outside himself and his inner contemplation of the subject matter. He did not belong at the on-campus party headquarters apartments where he resided. Again, others seemed to understand immediately and instinctively how to operate in this context. Maybe that was not the case, but he supposed it was true.

Everyone except him was in on the fun, confident, and greeted hanging out very naturally. They went to parties and met new friends. He recalls the one party he attended during his time at the University. People from his hometown and these new folks intermingled effortlessly, as if they had all known one another for years. The young man was unaware of what was happening or how to participate in it. It was like stepping into a different dimension. With nothing to say, he was a silent witness and then an eager deserter of this horrid thing. He was sure parties were not for him and never went to another one. Oh, and he still had no idea how to rebel.

The serious student focused solely on attending class and completing the required work. In this regard, our hero most often completed projects well ahead of the due date. He rarely spoke even to his friends/acquaintances/roommates. He could hear them socializing at night, which offered more proof of his isolation. "They must think I am the most anti-social weirdo in the world," he thought privately. Still, he had nothing to say to his peers. Based on intuition and his life experiences, he believed that every new face cared little about the big questions and almost anything else pertinent to his interests. Colleges are full of alternative thinking clubs and meetings, but he dared not venture to places where strangers dwelled.

Though in such a situation, his schoolwork greatly benefited. He was pleased to see he could write fairly well and was propositioned by other students to "help" them write essays. I learned more about the "big questions" of life that count. These are the topics of origins and meaning: why we are here, what we are supposed to do, who we are, and where we come from. He got good feedback from his professors, especially those who taught History. The hero discovered a curiosity about the Humanities in college that easily surpassed high school lesson plans. These professors were something else, he thought. How do they know so much? More than knowledge, his professors began to unlock a world of independent thinking, and it was these contemplations of humanity and existence itself that fueled those superpowers. The seeds of an intellectual life sprouted here, a kind of lifestyle that might allow him to avoid building birdhouses altogether.

He had a penchant for creativity along with a knack for analytical thinking that was well-rehearsed and well-suited to the Humanities. All his life, he had honed an ability to make stories out of the materials in his head. Professors were very intimidating, but a very young one seemed less so and was willing to discuss intelligent topics with me. Probably, he bothered his favorite professor in his office, too much. As this world opened, he stepped into it slowly, but steadily, from these days forward to the present.

Plus, there was validation possible here that the young man had not found elsewhere. His grades improved each semester, and more than one professor noted his talent in their feedback. He never considered that he could receive laurels of any kind from this world that so perplexed him. So, he discovered that he enjoyed higher learning, but he was unsure where it would lead him.

Those big questions remained front and center for the rest of his life. Sometimes they provided him with intellectual stimulation, and other times they caused him great sadness. I do not think it would have been possible to begin this project and get this far if I had not finally found some satisfactory answers to the questions. I should emphasize that some aspects are incomplete, not total. Without some belief I have learned some wise lessons, and without some grasp on what life is and should be, how could I be so pompous to write this? After life descended into a horror show in my early forties, I initially did not have writing on my mind. As for the meaning of life, it is both ordinary and esoteric at the same time; important to everyone, while an enormous proposition usually reserved for intellectuals. I am moving forward with writing based on a faith hopefully not misplaced. Sometimes it is a struggle, and the old insecurities take over for a while. Regardless, I've been thinking a great deal about the big questions and how I will address them in this project. First, I had to recover (in a permanent fashion) from the worst but most edifying years of my life that cost almost everything but taught me much.

I graduated from the University of Alabama with honors, but I had not learned much about the rules of living and how to forge a relationship. There was a paradox with the young man. He was fascinated by the books/ideas that delved into what it means to be human, yet he could not decode the nuts and bolts, the everyday exigencies of living on a day-to-day level. The more he tried to reach out beyond the world of his mind, which was growing fertile and worthy of cultivation, the more he was disappointed. Much later in life, he came to realize that trying harder does not guarantee success. I needed a second education with emotional intelligence and self-esteem as part of the curriculum.

He was lonely. In fact, lonely is a word that could be applied to almost every period of his existence on this planet. At 22, he had never heard of the hero's journey and was unaware that he was part of one. It sure did not feel that way. Big questions and studies could feed the inquisitive side of the young man, but the desire to be with another person simply remained wholly unmet. More than this, it felt like he would never be able to break through the wall that kept him and any love interest miles apart. He could not imagine how things could ever change, as women did not seem to like anything about him. Nothing he tried succeeded, and once more, his attempts were so embarrassingly inept as to inspire no more confidence than during his high school days. Only now does he see how life's avoidance and unrealized hopes had left a giant hole in his heart. For what seemed the longest time, he searched for a means that could perhaps fill the emptiness at least for a little while.

CHAPTER 3:

My Life as a Hole

There was a time when meadow, grove, and stream,
The earth, and every common sight,
To me did seem
Appareled in celestial light,
The glory and the freshness of a dream.
It is not now as it hath been of yore;-
Turn wheresoever I may,
By night or day.
The things which I have seen I now can see no more.
The Rainbow comes and goes,
And lovely is the Rose,
The Moon doth with delight
Look round her when the heavens are bare,
Waters on a starry night
Are beautiful and fair;
The sunshine is a glorious birth;
But yet I know, wherever I go,
That there hath past away a glory from the earth.[5]

The Romantic poet William Wordsworth penned the above excerpt from "Intimations on Immortality" long ago. He took great inspiration from the natural world. In a way, that also meant that childhood was "natural" and, for this reason, something to be celebrated. I am taking liberties, but I am assured my interpretation is not wrong. Artists like Wordsworth revered nature and wrote about it as containing some true essence of God. Being out in nature was akin to what modern folks would call a spiritual experience. At least, the poet's insights applied to the unspoiled, unaltered, natural environment. Similarly, Wordsworth and other poets of his persuasion wrote about childhood as a time of purity and wonder, contrasting it with adulthood, when human beings are sidetracked and worn down by responsibilities. As young people, we are the most natural, as I see it. He famously wrote that "the Child is the Father of the Man," in that our young lives are so instrumental in shaping the person we become.

I must say, he is one of my favorite poets. I have noticed a recurring theme in the work of Romantic authors, which is the close relationship between happiness and sadness. If I am wrong on this idea, then so be it. Wordsworth rejoices in the rainbow and other symbols of nature, but then pivots toward negativity, noting that "a glory from the earth" has "passed away." This is a lot like how depression feels, for your humble author. Being apprised of the world's potential for resplendent wonders underscores the reality that great things are exceptions to the rule and always come to an end. Depression is recognizing the things that are good and beautiful, that are transcendent, and then feeling downcast, regardless. That good stuff does not inspire me or comfort me, and it is incredibly depressing to confess to myself that the rainbows of my life do not and will not bring me good cheer. In turn, the happiest things hurt the most. For even the best of creation can easily become tainted, and likely will given enough time.

It is time that the poet could not defeat. As a child, rainbows were magical; as an adult, they are just a phenomenon one can learn about in a science book. We experience the world as children and do not demand to understand it. That comes with time as we grow up. Time allows us to gain insights and education, and the natural world is a little less interesting. Dear reader, this is not the truth for everyone; it is just one way to see the world that I can identify with. The most interesting part of the poem featured here is how Wordsworth acknowledges that he cannot recapture the spirit of childhood. It is gone. In my recovery, I would do well not to overlook that recover is right there in the word. So my never-ending project is finding links between specialness that vanished at an indefinable time, and probably from childhood, and positivity in adulthood that can contain my mental illness and sustain my recovery.

This may not be the first time, but it is the first time I can recall with certainty hearing an official diagnosis of mental illness. I was almost married and about 27, and had been in turmoil for weeks. Symptoms were vague enough to be attributed to so many different ailments as to not cause that much alarm at the doctor's office. There were headaches, slightly blurred vision, light nausea, and excessive sweating. Worse than that, his heart was beating like a marching drum, and this caused him great alarm. Also, he could not control the rapid-fire thoughts, including the voices insisting that he could die. My mind had been racing non-stop, and each thought predicted doomsday scenarios. At my most ill, every subject in my mind links to another, and then that pathway forks into two, and then that one the same, again, without end. This was not the first time nor was it the most severe. I knew something was physically wrong, but I didn't realize that worries and fears can manifest as an array of bodily symptoms. I was still under the delusion that mental illness was distinct from "real" physical issues.

At the clinic, I took this short questionnaire to gauge my level of depression. Many of you know what I am talking about. It is very hard for someone to put their mental anguish on a numbered scale, but of course, doctors try their best to know how sick you are. I don't even remember my main source of worry back then. I answered the questions honestly, such as: the one that asks how often you feel sad, have you had thoughts of hurting yourself, do you have problems sleeping, have you felt hopeless more than…whatever times a week, etc. All my answers confirmed having depression to a severe degree. The nurses, I remember clearly, looked at me with pity as if I had set a record for sadness within the walls of that place. That sizable and busy clinic seemed shocked all around. To me, it was no surprise—I had known no other reality in my life. So, then and in the future, when someone inquires how long I have been depressed, I can only chuckle and reply, "always." Anyway, the doctor confirmed I had Depression and Anxiety Disorders. There was more to the picture, other disorders and unknown, not-sure-what-to-call-it dysfunctions. This was not the first or last time I felt like I was dying.

From my perspective, it is better to feel terrible and put a name on it than to experience protracted symptoms with no idea of the source. There is a sigh of relief when medical personnel verify what you have always known. Without some kind of diagnosis, you appear to yourself as a defective human being and just plain crazy. One can imagine himself as something like a broken toy that, for undiscovered reasons, escaped the factory and then made it to the shelf. It made me ask, "How come I couldn't feel happiness?" and there was no answer except: "Guess I am just a bad person." I had witnessed how human beings get excited over good news and feel, apparently, a pure excitement not diluted by worry or expectations. It was never this way with me. In this episode, I cannot recall what medications were prescribed. I do think it was a temporary fix, and no steps were taken for long-term care. Well, there was no fix whatsoever. Countless times, I have thought myself on the brink of melting down, breathing too hard, or not enough, and this was just another one. There were no follow-ups, strategies for holistic treatment, appointments with specialists, or medicines beyond a few weeks. Through it all, I was not convinced anything would ever get better.

Years before engaging in the steps to attain better mental health, and before self-medication, my only antidotes for sadness and anxiety were humble and simple things. In graduate school, my routine and determination to excel meant I had a one-track mind dedicated solely to studies. My habits were born out of the need to avoid feeling overwhelmed and out of control. My work never ended, as there was always the next project on the horizon. Therefore, it was necessary to work every day for a preset length of time to ease my mind and rest. And the night was welcomed back in those days. Once enough work was done, my brain informed my body that it deserved to ease into bed and begin the steps toward sleep. These steps included nightly prayers to be rigorously repeated. Only with enough accomplished would my mind even entertain the idea that the day could end. This was a good feeling. It was not a sense of victory over the day, just a belief that I at least had broken even. But until I reached that level, there could be no safe or warm feelings. So, a vigorous work schedule was a must every day, regardless of any other matters that needed my attention.

For the majority of my life, I lacked self-care and failed to take stock of what I truly wanted in the big picture. One outcome was that I never set aside time to work on self-discovery. If I had reflected more on my life, perhaps I would have reassessed the causes of my sadness and corrected the story I was telling myself. Even then, I needed a rewrite or possibly a new beginning. Interestingly, my choice of shirts to wear this morning reminded me of something I want to discuss in this section. From a closet with an ample supply of shirts, I chose a bright-ish blue one with a red-flower pattern. As some people obsess over shoes and have too many, I do something roughly equivalent with shirts. Recently, I have become increasingly fixated on purchasing more shirts with floral designs. So, every day I can put on a different collared, buttoned, nice-looking, flowered shirt. It is a small thing, right? This is an unremarkable snippet of daily life, you would think.

Well, it is not as small a matter as one would logically assume. I do this because I can and desire for my costumes to express beauty, and for that beauty to buttress my mood. Yes, I say costume, because everyone wears one with some degree of conscious recognition. Your dress is an integral part of your presentation to the world. I wear those shirts to express something I want to say and be. I decide that my clothing choices will not convey anger, express some clichéd proverb, or display any logo I do not feel like endorsing. Oh, and all my clothes are blue. This is because I like the color and see no reason to deviate from it. I wear what I want, because I am becoming who I want to be. I am not ashamed of that person and even want others to understand him. When I choose one shirt over another, I am expressing my unapologetic, personalized pride in myself.

It is not a midlife crisis. I would never use a word like 'crisis' to describe what has been going on recently. If it were, I guess it would be the blandest one of all time. Additionally, I have plans to get a tattoo, and my hair is long and hippie-like. These things mean more than they appear, as I am just now acting on repressed impulses ignored for too long. Though all this could be reasonably reduced to superficial posturing, the costume each of us wears can have a more heartfelt meaning. Or not, it just depends on the person. If one is trying to be something false, aping some celebrity or trend, then fashion choices could be empty and silly. Or, an outward appearance can correspond to a feeling within and be a healthy expression of the self, and the word self represents the truest and whole person you know you are and/or strive to become regardless of how others judge you. The costume can be a distinct indicator of standing out from conformity. Clothes do not make the man, but they can be an external tribute to what makes the man.

Here, I will credit the styles of the young folks; those in their twenties and thirties. I was a young kid during the 1980s and an inhibited teenager during the 1990s. The movies were good, and some of the fashions too, but materialism was running wild and uncontrolled. These were those years of greed and conspicuous consumption, unsurpassed by, well, anything. It was the height of name-brandism, or the pressure to dress oneself in the "in" attire. In this part of the world, young people wanted to avoid being branded as Walmart shoppers. It seems society has moved past the fixation on name-brandism to an extent. There is a much higher esteem for second-hand clothing and thrift stores today. Oh boy, in the previous century, insults would come your way for dressing with an obvious disregard for the nouveau. The old and tattered, with actual or pretended holes and blemishes, would be a problem back then. So, at least in one way, my lifelong search for authenticity aligns with contemporary popular culture.

I have secretly judged myself as inauthentic at every stage of life. I do not know what to call it other than extreme pessimism or depression. My contributions to the world were insignificant compared to those of others.I could not fathom being good enough to earn a place of respect among other young people, who were everything the young man was not. He did not participate in activities appropriate for his age and thus was left out. Silently, I did not blame others who eventually stopped inviting me to social engagements. For instance, the youth could not attend the pool party because he disliked how he looked shirtless. Plus, the rules were too confusing to him. There was playful frolicking among the boys and girls, and it was too much to process. He did not go camping, or riding around in the mud, or fishing. These all likely called for skills from that instruction manual. He was dumb, so it was better to avoid, avoid, and avoid. The hurt inside was contradictory: he did not wish to be invited to stuff he dared not attend, yet he desired to be the kind of real person who would be asked to go.

Little displays of personal preferences I have been making lately were not possible back during the confused years of my life. This is probably not a surprise to anyone. It might be a challenge for you to understand how a person could be so deflated as to be uncomfortable with the most benign forms of self-assertion. Or, maybe it is clear and makes sense. During the years that should have been rebellious, the hero struggled mightily to carve out an outward appearance that reflected his inner sensibility. It seems obvious now that this is very unhealthy and likely to cause disaster at some point. The man now also wishes my drawing and all types of self-expression had not withered and died. Art was so crucial to his story, but the man in his late twenties still couldn't believe it. He had no faith. This is further evidence that struggling to live out a role at one time in life can endanger the self at another part of life.

I lived as an incomplete entity constantly under construction, and believed myself to be less than the real people with full and satisfied lives. As a teenager and then long after, a pool of discontent and self-ex-pression, and therefore identity, remained untapped. It was a hole that contributed to pre-existing mental illness and later addiction. The hero should have felt the call to a journey of discovery, but never knew the door to adventure even existed. I use the words "not possible" purposely, because I did not possess the tools to be a healthy young man. He refused the call to adventure again and again. Whole people were not terrified to leave the house, mingle with whomever, build bird houses, and play football. They always seemed to be doing the appropriate thing while armed to meet any contingency.

Real people were not hard to spot. Look in any direction, and they could be seen sharing their thoughts with others and perfectly fitting their given roles. This took place at a rather constant rate, with real people conversing with one another, talking, laughing, and planning to do the same things later at another location. Those who matured at a rate consistent with their age sought out mates and moved freely and unharmed among family and friend groupings, both separately and together. They earned their place in the human ecosystem by doing what was right and being what was right. They had the correct answers to all life's tests, and we know every minute of existence promises some measure of competition, meeting a standard, or letting someone down. Real people met every occasion with glee or cool disinterest. They did not "freak out" or feign sickness to avoid an interaction. Every motion caused a reaction, and every reaction a judgment, and the laws of the jungle were not forgiving. I did well with academics but deemed myself a failure due to the unavoidable trials of life.

It has been fascinating to observe how other humans expertly navigate social settings and apply the same skills to their general living. I always wished for one-on-one scenarios with no distractions, so I can hear and be heard fully. I honestly have no clue how many people become lost in the sea of faces with so much body language and words flying here and everywhere. He worked hard at maintaining calm and functionality in these situations. Inevitably, I sought out some refuge and/or just sped out the back door. When talking with one person, someone else inevitably interrupts, but no Hollywood director stops the show to say, "Alright, that was ruined, let's restart from the top." No. The confusion continues non-stop, and people seem not to mind being bombarded on all sides by looks, questions, and intimate details. There are smiles all around, although no communication is taking place, and I cannot possibly gather enough information from any source to think or feel anything about anything.

Every tedious act and decision made him tired all the time. At no time was the hero free of judging eyes, either those of others or my own, until I reached the safety of the bed. Every social setting was a cross-examination, and every movement and glance invited public scorn. Walking into a room meant that all faces turned to look at him and likely dismissed him as not a full person. At any store or on the street, the public could sense that an impostor was on the scene, I silently thought. Yes, I tried to act in ways that were appropriate and normal. One must be friendly, but not overly so, with a smidge of self-importance. I have a long-standing practice of stoicism that others interpret as aloof or "laid back." But it was all a performance directed at being as close to acceptable and cool as possible.

It is accurate that the hero was an angry young man, but one would not have known that fact. He did not recognize this either, so he did not believe his internal turmoil was part of human maturation. Anger is not the most apt word. Inside, he felt much like Holden Caulfield, but had never heard of *Catcher in the Rye* until many, many years after his season of youth. Come to think of it, I had no access to any countercultural, anti-establishment, or dissident viewpoints. Every inclination, worry, and desire of his must not be normal, because the other boys were perfectly adjusted and content all the time. They perfectly played their roles. I looked up to the cool crowd and hated them at the same time. Therefore, I wondered why I was not the person I should be, assured that his private reflections and forlorn spirit were both violations of the rules.

It was a very conservative world. To this day, I am not sure how normal or not this was, but I suppose that doesn't matter now. He would have some interest in James Dean and the movie *Rebel Without A Cause*. He always gravitated toward classic films, believing that something great must be hidden within them to earn their honorific. In this case, however, he did not feel an affinity with James Dean and found the film a little ridiculous. That kind of 1950s cool that so many males find appealing, mostly seemed untouchable and unrelatable. Ah, I would have to know more about cars and motors, he perceived. Returning to the main idea, the worlds of hipness and rebellion mostly did not penetrate his bubble. He was mindful that he had still not read from life's rulebook and also lacked the gift to know what was acceptable to do. Thoughts of stepping beyond any realms of safety were nauseating and sure to result in humiliation. I am aware, presently, that worrying about how to act in a rebellious way is missing the point of rebellion.

There seem to be some people who, at birth or soon after, have an innate, gut feeling that something is fundamentally wrong with this world. I like those people. They are sensitive and often unstable. Maybe I was one and should have stood up to be counted. The people I have in mind tend to be the kind of social critics who are also artists and intellectuals. Perhaps these individuals create for money, or maybe they do not, but one can still be categorized among the artistic and curious either way. These dreamers and idealists cannot walk through life without occasionally shouting out their truth. Their eyes are opened to the myriad ways that we waste our lives worrying about the insignificant. Someone who thinks about the big questions must at some time confront the reality that: 1. things as they are did not have to be this way, and 2. circumstances as they are do not have to continue indefinitely. These are essential concepts to begin tackling the big questions, and sadly, it seems most humans on earth never reach that threshold. The world teaches us daily to settle for mediocrity and then be thankful for it.

I have overstated the word rebellion too often. It was not rebellion I was pining for so much as originality, sincerity, and authenticity. This last word means the most in terms of how I see what we should be doing with our lives. Maybe I will think of some better words in a moment, but these are at least a good start. On this subject, the great scholar Ernest Becker summarized my feelings probably better than I ever could. On artists, Becker wrote:

You see that the fabrications of those around you are a lie, a denial of truth—a truth that usually takes the form of showing the terror of the human condition more fully than most men experience it. The creative person, then, in art, literature, and religion, becomes the mediator of natural terror and a new way to triumph over it. He reveals the darkness and the dread of the human condition and fabricates a new symbolic transcendence over it.[6]

There were numerous sources on screens large and small that expressed dissatisfaction with the status quo. They were all on television or in the movies, and once again far removed from my actual life. I do think I had something in common with countless youth, though, who felt disaffected.

It is an overstatement to say that he was drawn to rebellion just for the sake of it. False bravado and posing as someone you are not is as sickening as spoiled milk. No, deep down, he was prideful of not putting on the costume, or a mask, as is often said, that others so eagerly wore. Still, I have forever looked for a greater authenticity than this poor version of life that chugs along as unquestioned normalcy. Or, I am sure it was there in places I did not have access to. Everywhere were Walmart, or K-Mart, or both, malls, the same fast-food joints, and the rest. This mission was lonely. There were no indications that any other human being cared for anything beyond who won the game, who killed what animals, and who did not show up at church on Sunday. I could not put on the camouflage with sincerity and without hypocrisy. So, I never did.

The young man felt drawn to comedy heroes who occasionally gave the world the finger. There was Johnny Carson, and he was good but not too revolutionary. However, David Letterman came on television after Carson, and here was a person who was quite possibly in the know about our secret: the world as most live it is not right. Furthermore, Letterman may have felt as uncomfortable in his skin as I, just maybe. He flipped jokes and turned them inside out because the punchline was the joke, and the joke was the world as constructed and accepted by the masses. Letterman cared less about rules and what the guests were saying, as it did not matter to the host or viewers whether guests were big names or engaging personalities. It felt like there was little to no staging going on as one tuned in for the show. There was the maverick Andy Kaufman who often appeared on the Letterman program. Kaufman's comedy came across as completely pointless, and that was the point. The young man watched Saturday Night Live more than Letterman, because on the weekends, he could stay up past normal hours. It would not be outrageous to remark that he was obsessed with SNL.

People are more apt to turn to music as a force multiplier of rebellion. Unhappy youth and those of all ages often find their dissatisfaction expressed by musical artists. Everyone knows how 1960s music became the voice of Americans frustrated with the Vietnam War, civil rights stagnation, and other issues, to offer an obvious example. There was a pervasive discontent in those days about various injustices, and the sentiment was broad enough to encompass many kinds of grievances with America and its institutions. The closest I came to that experience, musically speaking, was the 1990s Grunge explosion.

Bands such as Nirvana, Soundgarden, Pearl Jam, Smashing Pumpkins, and Stone Temple Pilots captured the bleak sensibility of Generation X. Grunge was also called "Alternative" Rock and was intended as a reaction against the overly cosmetic, superficial clichés of the 1980s' big-hair, big-arena rock. A carefree style characterized the Grunge look, and the associated attitude was a punk-like angst with undefined grievances against conventional society. I can remember plaid shirts were worn over a t-shirt, and this alone was enough to lay claim to being part of Grunge. Tragically, Nirvana's Kurt Cobain, the central figure of Grunge, committed suicide. In interviews, he said things that had crossed my mind, and he looked uncomfortable in his skin. I argue that Cobain was one of those born with the blessing and curse of realizing there was something wrong with the foundation of polite society. So, I felt some kind of connection there to overwhelming sadness and the frustration that the world would never change for the better. Or maybe it was a lament that: "Is this all there is to life?"

In places never exposed in public, I had an excess of disillusionment with almost every worldly thing considered normal and respectable. In a movie, Marlon Brando famously replied to a question asking what he was rebelling against with: "Whattaya Got?" I do not know if Grunge kids knew what bothered them about the world or what powerful entity they were railing against. I did not know, not really. I often felt outnumbered by the world, surrounded by real people who looked upon me with disgust. Everyone saw that I did not belong with the folks who had read the instructions. Almost every person was concerned with the unimportant and the time-wasting, boring aspects of living. Yet, that must have been what mattered to people. Part of that young man wanted to fit in and get along, and another part of him hated the blandness of everything. Yet, I had no self-esteem and was glad when anyone offered their attention, even for a short while. Almost all the time, the hero lived out his hours in solitude.

I cannot say I was a full member of any movement. People often told me I looked sad or angry most of the time, and that was probably right. I hated having my picture taken. It was more than a phase. By about eighteen years old, I had shed the baby fat and was slim, almost tall, and gangly. My clothes rarely matched, and I could not gather much energy or momentum. The world was a dissonant place. The youth shrank away from almost every opportunity for the spotlight and dreaded having to make conversation, because I had no idea what to say. There were people whom I wanted to be closer to but felt no right to partake in life as a real person. I often felt profound loneliness in rooms full of people.

Looking back, my mental illness did not allow me to notice I had a mental illness. Depression is not feeling down or having a bad week, and many of you out there know this. Almost complete disengagement with real life and people told me there was no hope, despite any positive words of encouragement. This disease kills a person's energy levels and willingness to take on the most minuscule risks, and makes most undertakings in life seem unbearably hard. Very little to nothing you can think of promises an enjoyable time. The excitement others have makes the depressed person sadder. Commercials may be the worst thing ever invented. Every single individual is trying very hard to convey how ecstatic they are with the world exactly as it is. Happy people were mocking me, giving the false impression that life offered anything to smile about. I concluded I was born wrong, not different. There is a gigantic difference between the two, especially in a young person's heart. The deadliest feature of severe depression might have been the assumption that life would not change for the better. I am talking zero chance in the mind of the affected person. Nowhere could he imagine a future outcome any different than the "Groundhog Day" repetition of rejection and unanswered longing.

He has a mental picture of one particular dreary day in class as a college freshman. This episode epitomized his entire undergraduate career, but it must have been just a little more frustrating than the average. Somehow, the image remains vivid. To say nothing of significance occurred is accurate and misleading, as it was the nothingness that I can recall as memorable. It was a distance learning class where the professor was not physically present, instead appearing on a large screen. So, you can get away with zoning out and much more if one has any kind of cleverness. There were mostly girls around, and I was sitting in the middle row, with approximately 10 to 12 people in total. Everyone was talking to each other, and I remember thinking, "This must be how you make friends, especially a girlfriend." I so desperately desired to be part of the conversations, to perhaps meet a girl, or at least learn her name, and have others realize I was not a mute stalker/killer. The proximity of real people doing real things, while condemned to remain an oddity and alone, wears down a person. It was as if I weren't there. There was no way to chip away at the awkwardness and reduce my silent suffering. The thoughts race and are unceasing, turning to frustration and then anger, and next, I am screaming in my head, but with that familiar, blank mask on display. I started writing poems and drawing, which have often been coping mechanisms.

With depression, it is a tremendous chore to slow down the near-constant merry-go-round of negative thoughts. Negativity feeds on itself and births a thousand doomsday scenarios in one's head. The wheel spins too fast to handle, and I do not know anything that can slow it down except for medication and deep meditation. He had neither. Even with meds, getting the right combination can take a lifetime to perfect. Bad thoughts negate the will to try, so I am defeated by running through every scenario before reaching out to engage with any person. In other words, I worked out everything that would go wrong before anything could go right, so it was likely no combination of chess moves would work in my favor. Imagine seeing the ending of each movie in your mind before you watch it, with each scene being unsatisfactory to you, and therefore you choose not to enter the theater at each invitation. Every actual conversation spins on the wheel, too, as I interrogate myself as to every mistake and awkward moment. The collective weariness I felt meant that reaching beyond my safe inner world to the real one was just not worth it.

As a down-and-out youngster, I often tried to articulate my critique of the world through poetry and idolization of artists. Always, everything was kept inside until it was all too much, but he did not lash out or get violent. He was mad at some unknown force that kept him pent up. Furthermore, anger disturbed him, as did loudness/shouting/bright lights/staring. Suppressed emotions must find an outlet, so there was a time when he thought in terms of becoming a poet. There was a certain image he identified with: the long-haired and well-meaning bohemian dwelling on the edges of polite society. But, in reality, I was closer to Zack Morris than Kurt Cobain. Even so, he wrote very dark poetry and wondered if the words were any good or merely rantings and complaints.

Most anyone paying attention has some conception of the starving artist archetype. Instinctively, there was an attraction to the sensitive, mad genius, under appreciated, passionate artist. Furthermore, he could understand and sympathize with the misanthropes of society who were too original, creative, or too something to fall in line with the rest of the sheep. He could see himself that way if he were a real, or a whole, if you prefer, person. Assuming the disposition and role of an artist was the highest aspiration one could hope for, at least from my perspective on life and what it should be about. Not feeling part of the crowd, that wonderful word transcendence called out to him. Great artistry promises us a certain oneness with "real," cosmic, spiritual sensations and emotions. Somewhere in the untapped part of my mind, maybe art was a means to become a whole person. Only now can I profess that art was missing from my life and was a medicine that could have tempered my loneliness and frustrations. Artists tended to be sad because creative types often carry a significant burden. How could anyone make a statement about life, and do the reflection that the pursuit demands, without coming out of it a very depressed individual? I learned to expect sadness from my artificial surroundings and kind of leaned into it, so all those clichéd ideals about art rang true in my thoughts.

Art made a brief appearance in high school, and I almost felt like a real person for a short time. That school was behind in virtually every way, including the arts. There was nothing of interest to participate in that was even loosely related to creativity. There were no clubs that I can recall, except for the boring ones that overachievers pretended to care about. However, for one time only, it was decided to create and publish a school magazine consisting of any written or drawn compositions. Here was an opportunity to do something, so Kirk wrote a couple of poems fairly quickly that the teacher decided to publish. One was mostly pessimistic but ended on a high note, while the other lamented life's rat race and the neglect of things that truly matter. Who knows, they were not bad for a teenager.

Most importantly, Kirk was recognized by his parents and even by the girl who was supposed to be his young love: Jane. She mentioned that she didn't know Kirk had any writing talent. Well, of course, no one knew anything like that because how would they? For one, I could not adequately convey any personal preference or opinion to another human being. This was allowable only for the real people, and yes, I believed this with all my heart. As one would predict, any recognition soon passed as quickly as most of the copies were discarded. Still, the heart of an artist never left me, but I buried it again after this momentary display. I liked that artists could be odd to the extreme and have the whole world applaud them. He or she cannot belong, stand out as unusual, refuse to run with the herd, and win awards for it all. There were times when I took solace in the expectation that suffering might lead to great art. For a short while, becoming a fiction writer greatly appealed to our hero. He learned about the eccentricity of many of the greats, such as Edgar Allan Poe and Ernest Hemingway, but still felt like an outsider. I guess I acted out the role of artist here and there, but nothing much changed as long as my mental health remained untreated.

A time of fighting against society's norms, declaring one's individuality, and putting on a costume of protest or outright rebellion, regretfully never happened when it should have. I have come to believe that human beings need to mature according to nature's design. Worldly experimentation should happen somewhere in your teens and consist of the behavior I have been trying to describe. To be more direct, I think it is customary and valuable for a person to find an identity by rocking the boat, questioning authority, and exploring alternatives. So, do not be so quick to put out those tempestuous fires of youth. The great folklorist and author Joseph Campbell believed in this very idea. He often remarked that it was a shame that modern civilizations no longer carry out those old rites of passage. In other words, kids need room and time to blossom as individuals, distinct from anyone else, even if it is a little awkward and concerning to adults.

There are a thousand proverbs that counsel every human that he or she must ultimately find a singular path and walk it alone. No two people navigate the same one. I needed time and space for self-discovery to become well-rounded and more satisfied as an adult. As they say, preacher's kids seem always to become more trouble-making than the average son or daughter. True or not, the logic behind this notion is that dictating to and sheltering kids, to an overwhelming degree, will later make a combustible and unhealthy man or woman. There was no rebellion, and that was exactly what a hero needed to blossom and become whole.

My social stagnation persisted, despite some people saying positive things about my sense of humor. I eventually became confident that, here and there, when all variables were right, I could make others laugh. I still enjoy comedy for the laughter but also as a student learning the craft.

No one understands how ridiculous life is most of the time, its inherent unfairness, and tendencies to reward idiocy over originality, more than a comedian. Life is patently absurd; that is the only honest assessment someone with open eyes and ears can conclude. Until the present, the man still struggles with social anxiety and the feeling of being judged at all times. In other words, I carried the weight of pleasing everyone and automatically thought I was at fault for literally any disturbance. One could say that humor was a temporary relief from my charmless life.

The questions and worries I had about life may have been extreme, but not without substance. They may have made sense in roundabout form. To try to say it better, I look to the past and see battles with mental health and a boy with real concerns about what life means, and not a young man who was wasting his and all others' time. Okay, to try again, I was sorting out my mental health and did not realize it. I was doing it inefficiently and poorly, but I was making an effort. I wish I had known that the big questions, for me, were imperative and inescapable. The alternative to not facing down eternity and my role in the big picture resembles forgoing life and taking part in some simulation. Existential musings, even for a clueless boy, were not meaningless games. From my perspective, pinning down the big questions to things more usable and instructive *is* mental health.

It is valid to ponder whether I was on the trail of something fundamental to happiness but was unaware of it. Therefore, comedy could have been a tool to some end not obvious to him. I have very often used satire as a means to make fun of people and things unfair, pointless, pretentious, stupid, unreasonable, overly popular, accepted without merit, and more. It has been a method to battle back against my fears and the people who rejected me without declaring a formal war. Humor is like walking a high wire with a safety net, for several reasons. Also, most people are more likely to accept something they disagree with if it is presented in a humorous context.

For some, humor is only a joking matter, and they cannot decipher anything deeper than a surface meaning. That is fine in some respects. For me and many others of the thinking sort, humor works as a kind of small protest against the stale contrivances of the world. And that could mean almost anything, like all those things we have to do, but hate: traffic, standing in line, taxes, putting up with the local idiot(s), and the like. Things that just are, that exist without being questioned, need to be mocked sometimes. Even worse are those terrible ideas and practices that human beings insist on doing despite plentiful evidence that they should not.

I do not know how to convey to you, dear reader, the burning in my soul to break free from the everyday and have a genuine exchange with another whole person. And it never happened. It was indeed frustrating to be closed off and shut out, unable to move past the superficial and have a heartfelt conversation. Comedy can neutralize awkwardness and essentially force everyone to laugh and agree that: "isn't all this stupid that we are doing?" Letterman had a habit of doing this, allowing the critic within me an outlet. I could offer several examples from Saturday Night Live, but the recurring sketch "Toonces the Driving Cat" comes to mind at the moment. It was a comically bad cat puppet who was always allowed to drive a car with human passengers. The catch, though, is that he was not a good driver and would crash, and presumably kill, the car's occupants every time. It was hysterical that no one questioned the notion of a cat operating a vehicle, just his poor driving record. I identified more with the writers of such things on television than with the people I knew.

My depression and whatever else at work in my head have always managed to force self-doubt whenever the opportunity for creativity entered my purview. I have never felt hip enough to be a contrarian, bucker of trends. There was this strange syndrome of idolizing others and putting myself down. Perhaps some can relate, but I can convince myself of almost any self-hating conclusion once it is systematically rationalized in my mind. It is kind of like solving a long math problem. My brain becomes so detached from reality that I might arrive at the belief that the sky is green and the grass is blue, especially when trapped in a profoundly melancholic state. So, any untruth can become true, and usually, my conclusions foster fear and pain. Whatever thoughts of protest, raising a voice of disagreement, or sticking it to the man, die unspoken. At least, this has been the state of affairs for the vast majority of my years.

Being a whole person has been hindered by the reality of always being in the public eye. Whole people are always acceptable, fit seamlessly into the local culture, are confident in themselves, are respected as having earned a seat at the table of life, have thoroughly studied life's book of instructions, and one or five more things. Certainly, the real human beings own homes and have children. They are coffee drinkers and enjoy discussing it. Surely, any real person has an easy smile at every moment where smiling is appropriate. No one had to teach me that every action, inaction, movement, and choice takes place within a framework of public evaluation. This is doubly true of the South. It is similar to the old saying: "all the world is a stage." As you may recall, Ritual Interaction Theory supports my claims. Therefore, my argument is that southern culture compels every person to live in the public square more often than behind the walls of privacy. With that said, I am not claiming that it only happens in the South. Nope, but ritual interactions are a mainstay of southern culture.

Most of the time growing up, I secretly just wanted to hide when forced into contact with others. I think I am not incorrect to call myself hyper-aware of my surroundings but curiously untutored in interpreting what I sense and feel. So, as far as what this meant, I instantly blamed myself for any awkwardness, anger, or arguments present in the room. I wish you could tag along, dear reader, as the "Ghost of Christmas Past" magically carried us back in time. It was quite a spectacle of intense, inhibited nothingness. At least, this is what the young hero radiated outwardly, interpreted by his poor mind. Each holiday, it became increasingly harder to respect myself for being all alone among every other couple, male and female. It was only natural to indulge in closeness with another around Christmas and Thanksgiving. Every seating arrangement and conversational prompt rewarded the couples and punished the loners. It became a fantasy that he could take his place among the rest with a female love interest by his side. This would mean he was fast-tracked to personhood for sure, as his name would be at the top in bold letters wherever that list was kept. Did he convict himself too harshly, in this regard? I am not sure.

In Alabama or anywhere in the South, one learns how to be judgmental. Therefore, there are real, verifiable cultural traits and historical realities that demonstrate this is a genuine problem. In traditional communities, conversations might not be as private as one might hope or think. Certainly, any meet and greet at the grocery store, or exchange while picking up the kids from school, or at the football game, or work, etc., are recorded, disseminated, and judged on a scale from normal to ass-whoop-worthy. Local standards of action and interaction, of course, also include what you wear and how you wear it, how you maintain your yard, and every other personal detail. From experience, I can attest that cutting grass correctly is a very serious thing. After grass is trimmed, it leaves impressions of how one went about their work, and there are right and wrong methods to this and all else. Even talking on the phone or having one-on-one conversations can easily be reported and gossiped about around town. I sensed I was being surveilled by men with binoculars strategically placed on the tops of roofs and other vantage points around town. Okay, not literally, but something resembling that.

Gossip is important for enforcing the "right" types of behavior and punishing those who transgress against the requirements of conduct. How one greets another, whether a person ignores a friend or acquaintance, acts either too detached or overly intimate, or if one addresses another in an unusual or disrespectful tone, are serious matters that can haunt the offender. So, a "how you doing?" is the beginning of a ritual and not merely something thrown around without care. One must "speak" to another when spoken to. To "speak" is to acknowledge that other person by a procedure suitable to the social status of each and the familiarity that exists between the two. The result was paranoia and fear of "just being"—living and reacting based on whims and desires unencumbered by rigorous evaluation. Mental health does not endorse my upbringing, in other words. To simplify my message, the environment of my youth forced a person with social anxiety to live as if a giant spotlight followed him around every day.

Dear reader, you may or may not be familiar with certain aspects of southern culture, so please permit me to discuss some pertinent stuff. The South has remained more traditional for a longer time than the rest of America. By traditional, I mean life as it was before corporations, interstates, big government, contracts, franchises, excessive regulations, wage labor, and other stuff. For my purposes here, let's focus on how public perceptions still matter more in the South than in different places. Once called into question, an individual or family's reputation may never recover. The conduct of one member always reflects on the rest of the family, anyway. A man or woman's descendants can bear the shame of his or her long-ago mistakes. Everything is a courtroom all the time, and sentences can be cruel and unjust. A man always carries the responsibility to be hyper-masculine, and these pressures tend to produce imbecilic results. The word "toxic" is being used frequently in the popular jargon. Without a doubt, what the community decrees as right and wrong can be a distorted mess. Yes, females play a part and can suffer from rumors and asinine community shaming.

Could we compare the public theater of watching and being watched to our social media-drenched environment today? My theory is that Facebook, et al., are instruments to spy on so-called friends and others, learn about their whereabouts and quality of life, in the hopes that each victim is suffering more than you. If not, and it is revealed that a person appears successful, then a weakness in the armor must be found and then brought to light via private messages and passive/aggressive public posts. We humans turn any useful tool into a poisonous thing. Facebook et. al. serves the same end as looking out the window to monitor your neighbors. Messages and posts take the place of phones and person-to-person communication. I hated it all because folks in their kitchens and living rooms were having a good time revisiting and mocking my unfitness to live among real people. From youth to maturity, I fiercely resisted the rumor mill and wished I could eradicate it once and for all. Even to this day, gossip remains an awful thing. His reasons for thinking in such a way are due to a tangled web of feeling inadequate, mental illness, hating the rules, not knowing them, wanting and failing to be authentic, and a determination that life was absurd and unknowable.

Some of his most severe, quiet meltdowns occurred at family gatherings or other large meetings that seemed to last forever. This is mostly the result of being "on stage" for an extended time, reading the minds and body language of all those in the audience. It is extremely tiring. He read every glance and shift, every eye meeting his, or eyes purposely not doing so, and every other indicator of someone's attitude. He dreaded what must be going on privately among these people, discussing his wrongs and poor imitation of a real person. His was and remains a secretive existence where little information is shared, and he constantly searches every environment for hidden clues of intrigue and intentions. There is a productive, insightful talent here, a certain skill that is in high demand, but with the con of being distant and guarded.

My approach to life was not healthy or sustainable. It did not promote shared bonds with other people. In all things scholarly, he had a keen eye for placing himself in the predicament of historical figures. The best historians walk in the shoes of other people, no matter how uncomfortable the fit. History is foremost about human beings, warts and all. He has a surplus of empathy toward others, as others have repeatedly told him. However, as the hero studied real people and tried to please and be like them, his heart was not in it. For reasons unknown, he was always highly attuned to the behavior of others. Yet, small talk exhausts his whole being and depletes his enthusiasm. He found no sharing of souls and no closeness at all with another person, and I finally gave up trying. Real people obfuscate and lie, talk in circles, and use fakery, and that is what he must do too. There was an inner contradiction that never got sorted out. He despised the maze of every social situation and figured it must be necessary to become dishonest to be normal, likable, and real. So, to be real, he must be unreal, if that makes any sense.

Remember Michael Corleone? He asked his mother if being strong as a means to safeguard the family could drive them away. In my life, the more real or whole the hero sought to become, the less honest he felt on the inside. To the young man, social interactions became clinical-like examinations to be studied under a microscope. Like a guy in a lab coat, the aim in social exchanges was to discover the solution to a problem through observation and analysis. Any interludes of self-expression and authenticity, and all work toward symbiotic encounters with another human, were secondary to cracking the code. There was no value in the proper processing and sharing of the hero's emotions. Yet, he was so emotional, and that drove him; a truth known only by the golden-haired child. So, it was safer to ignore his heart to preserve his mind, all while laboring not to do or say the wrong thing.

In classroom settings, people were less strident about the rules, and weirdness was more acceptable. The real world of whole people taught me to mimic the conduct of the well-adjusted and confident. Nothing of my own was worth knowing, showing, or keeping. However, academia is different from the real world and is many times more stimulating. At this point in my journey, now in graduate school, the hero was all work and no play. All kinds of intellectual theories and ideas from the many, many books one reads filled his head with endless avenues of inquiry. With how his mind operated, practically any idea was like opening an infinite number of new doors, each leading to a hallway, each with more doors, each with more hallways, and so on. His grades improved at every level of education because, as one moves up the academic ladder, there are fewer tests and fewer restrictions on the imagination.

He flourished in the realm of research projects where students choose their topics, sources, and thesis. Almost any paper idea can be relevant and worthwhile with sound thinking and skillful execution. What can be considered valid History is limited only by the mind of the student. History is the king of the Humanities because every other subject falls within its domain, such as Religion, Literature, Sociology, Psychology, Anthropology, and so on. Instructions are minimal, creativity is rewarded, there is no set value of x, and there exists absolutely no chance of being forced to build a birdhouse. People have History all wrong. It is not an assortment of facts; instead, History is a repository of stories to study and clarify using one's own experiences and perspective. Then the historian traces how the stories interact with each other. At least, that is how our hero came to understand History. Like a research paper, he hoped the problem of attracting a female could be solved if he just tried hard and used his artistry.

Now in his mid-twenties, Kirk prepared the best way he knew to fulfill his dreams of marriage and family. Overall, his life was not horrible, but incomplete. The first and primary thing, he surmised, was to become attractive. There had been people before who called him handsome, but he could not distinguish between empty flattery and genuine compliments. He felt certain of being overweight and had contempt for his own body. His disgust with his physical form meant that a diet was necessary. Growing up around great cooks made him appreciate good food, and so he waged a long war against the scales.

The young man devised a sustainable eating regimen with a strict routine and began the long, step-by-step process of building up to rigorous exercise. A few minutes here and there on the stationary bike evolved into light jogging, and eventually, it became almost daily runs of a few miles. He liked routines and had finally sculpted a lifestyle of fitness that lasted for many years. The hero was very skinny, or at least that is what other people saw. No amount of running could sway his skewed self-appraisal, which led him to believe he was not fit enough. No one will like me with imperfections, he admonished himself. Part of the operation was underway, and the next step was to identify and meet a reasonably well-matched female. How though? He failed and failed, almost like an inventor before he catches it just right and succeeds.

I wish the record of dating were different and better, but my words now fail to express such levels of ineptitude. It is funny to others, I am sure, if you did not have to live it. Reflecting on the past, I recall seeing couples out and about, and wondering how two people could meet and then go through the process that led to a relationship. So many opportunities for everything to go wrong, he told himself. I had no idea how that process worked and figured it must have come about due to rare luck. Yet, that could not be true, because relationships were everywhere and common. Not once had I ever sensed a proper opening where a woman would welcome my clumsy approach. Any kind of interaction was preordained to fail unless perfectly orchestrated, I was certain. Nothing had improved, and I still felt a wall, or a void, between my heart and the beautiful closeness and fun that transpired before me, as if in movie scenes. Every time there was a female candidate, I made things worse. This unfortunate reality was due to my certainty that any chance for my dream to come true could be the last one. I clung on too long and tried too hard. Every failed attempt at courtship left me feeling emotionally destitute.

The hero overcame social leprosy and indeed met and married a woman with hopes of starting a family. Speaking in front of others in class indeed helped him blunt some of his shyness. In reality, he had reached a level of sociability that allowed him to recreate certain attitudes and behaviors. He was thrust into teaching college courses at 24, despite being unprepared. Terrified but determined, the hero had no choice but to act the part of a teacher until he became a good one. And he did. Kirk knew that failure was not an option, and he felt grateful to be attending college instead of languishing in a soul-crushing job. Consequently, he greeted the prospect of lecturing as simply something necessary.

By the time of his engagement with Gwen, he had a firm grasp on his responsibilities and was waist-deep in the struggle of completing his dissertation. The year before the wedding was the best of his life, as of today's date. The love was real. The hero was preoccupied with her and doing everything right to secure a successful future. The career path that all his mentors were urging, along with the direction his work was taking, suggested that he would become a professor at a prestigious university. That was a logical course for his life at that point. Though nothing was more prioritized than his relationship, and ensuring that feeling of absolute congruency with another person would be protected at all costs. There was some promise that this life could become the fantasy long treasured in his heart. The wedding sure had the look of a triumphant event. The setting and food turned out to be top-notch. Kirk was in a surreal state of mind.

It turns out that my wedding vows had an expiration date of about three years. The ceremony itself was fantastic; professionally done in all aspects and well attended. She went away, though, and ended it all despite his desperate grasping at any means to prevent the d-word from happening. The young man had never considered that the d-word was even an option, as it had never entered his brain. He could not bring himself to speak the actual word. Religion and everything else suggested the d-word happened only among the bad people. It was as if the hero was hit by a train not knowing he was even standing on the tracks. At times, he was hysterical with grief at this unavoidable train-wreck he referred to as a tragedy. For certain, it felt like the permanent death of a fantasy rather than a dream deferred. The hero faced an insurmountable challenge just to get out of bed. Several factors contributed to the couple's demise, ultimately leading to the end of their marriage.

One of the worst parts of being d-worded was how it made the wedding seem like a ludicrous sham. Why would people gather to honor a commitment that could be canceled with less trouble than a fast-food order? What was sacred or memorable about such a union, and why would it be considered special enough to spend huge amounts of money, plan for months, and invite everyone you know? Nah, all marriage unions should be finalized under the cover of darkness. It is a rather disgraceful fraud to participate in, and people act out these shenanigans in churches, no less. No, that whole deal now became an obvious joke, and moving forward, the hero did not respect marriage in the least. But he did not move forward in any meaningful way for many years. He was stuck in the past. During the turmoil of those times, the drinking began.

Mental illness surely held him back with more force than if the tragedy had happened without it adding to his grief. There was a roughly two-hour drive connecting our old apartment to my parents' Home. Just about all the artifacts of our broken bond remained there, and it was my responsibility to do something with these unsightly leftovers. Breaking in and out of panic, I assisted in giving away as much as could be scooted out the door. Driving one day, alone, I began scream-crying at her, but really at life itself. I banged on the wheel and gave myself a headache. Anger had been pent up for too long. The only relief in sight would be taking a heap of the antidepressants that never worked. I did not travel down this path, but weighed the upside of taking a long and permanent sleep. I did not blame God, but was more unconvinced of his existence. I could only affirm that all life seemed to be against me, and no grand plans would ever work out. So, I made none. Those dreams of doing what real people do and attaining actual personhood died upon signing that wretched paper.

There were many pressures from within and without that defeated the momentum of the little (real) life he had pieced together. Out of many reasons that the d-word occurred, I want to highlight one that is central to the overall discussion here. To be sure, I approached the prospect of marriage with great effort and sincerity. However, I was only somewhat more worldly and well-adjusted than I had been as a teenager. I had not been treated in any serious way for mental illness. Also, I had not yet learned that it was acceptable to be myself, did not know who I was, and had little self-esteem. One clear mistake was worrying about and then trying to correct every little problem that arose. Now I can see that when someone is feeling down around me, I don't have to take on all the responsibility for their well-being. In doing what I could to make our life better, I was a smothering person. The thing about love, no matter how thorough and romantic, is that two people have to maintain separate and shared identities simultaneously.

Whatever feeling of authenticity was tied to this notion of being married—a husband—and it was that status that made me feel more like a real person and a grown-up man. I had worked very hard to be able to say I was in the club, and a great deal of self-worth was balanced precariously on the stability of my marriage. When this supposed lifelong bond hit the iceberg, I felt like it was I who was sinking into the depths. It is not a good idea to define oneself via the conduit of another person. It is also unhealthy to do so concerning your job, wealth, or social standing, of course. Anyway, that space within me had never been filled with any lasting selfhood independent of every person and thing. When that matrimonial condition was destroyed, like it never mattered, it was like being rejected in toto then slowly dying.

The only responses to the big questions of life were all about doom and gloom. There was no order to reality, because life was merely a random occurrence. Now, his mind mostly contained expressions of regret and dire forecasts of a bleak future without love. Many times, he pondered why love had failed him despite his dedication to it. He accepted some blame, but it was not all his fault, and his heart was always in the right place. Did he not put in the work? For sure, yes was the answer. There was no faith anymore for him. Every bond that he worked to cultivate was bound to be torn apart. Why try?

It felt like I had let down my family and many of the people closest to me. With Gwen, I tried very earnestly to secure a livelihood for us, as was customary for men to do. Perfectionism and anxiety often made me completely stressed and exhausted. The more I tried to achieve, the harder things became, thus the Corleone effect once again. I took on more and more, making no allowances or time for mental well-being. Financial concerns were the worst. Throughout my life, my inner thoughts have consistently confirmed that I must work twice as hard as others to attain genuine personhood. Strange, yes, but that is just how the world looked through my eyes. The permanent separation took me back to the earlier days of feeling unmanly, dumb, and a spectator of life. Stretched thin in every sense of that term, my personal and professional life was suffering. This all started around 27, while I was performing well in graduate school, with a plan to create the kind of life that includes a wife, family, and a home. Everyone would surely gossip about me and this unimaginable fiasco now. Now, doing anything at all was practically impossible, such as getting out of bed.

At this point, in his early 30s, the hero lived daily with the certainty that he had committed offenses that were simply unallowable and unthinkable within his small world. Part of that world included the church and its rules. I grew up regularly attending the Church of Christ with my mom. That meant three times a week, without fail, for many years. Our religion was very conservative. The COC does not refer to itself as a denomination, and any member will eagerly tell you why: it is the modern representation of the only Christian group first established by and in worship of Jesus. Christ did not intend for there to be competing Christian franchises, each meeting separately with slightly divergent practices. The COC considers Baptists to be too liberal, which many non-members often find shocking when informed. My church did say that the d-word was okay when adultery had taken place, but that was not a part of my marital breakdown. Religion added a layer of guilt to my daily sorrow. How can one go back to church? In small towns, everyone knows your personal life and communicates their disapproval with their eye contact. The southern phrase "bless your heart" really translates to: you are such a screw-up, aren't you?

I find the Church of Christ to be upfront and consistent, but not very emotionally uplifting. And it is not just this non-denomination, as that could be said of countless individual churches in every region of the country. Some would protest that the church is not supposed to be fun and should be more solemn; however, I disagree. Where we congregated did not have any imagery of Bible figures or even crosses, because they did not believe in anything approaching idol worship. There are no musical instruments and no choir, ever. Singing is led by whomever, and everyone else joins in on a very equal basis. Yet, singing talent does not grace each person to the same degree, unfortunately. Baptism is performed through full immersion and is typically done only once in a church member's lifetime. There is plenty of repentance or else preaching from the pulpit, but I do not know if there is more or less than in other churches. In his life, the hero gradually drifted away from religion, experiencing periods of disconnection until church-going became far removed from his plans. Many people seek out religion in times of crisis. Though the messages received from his religious experiences seemed quite prohibitive and not healing in nature. The hero was already well aware of all the bad stuff not to do. He did not do those things until he did.

In general, religion has alternated between an afterthought and an unsolvable riddle with him. The struggle with issues of deities, the soul, the afterlife, morality, and so forth is certainly common with people of all religious and non-religious backgrounds. In that regard, his unanswered questions and search for clarity were not unique. It did appear to the now adult man, though, that he contemplated these things, very essential to the big questions, more than most. As a youth, I followed the religious teachings and outlook of those around me. We are raised and come to believe the things we do largely based on the circumstances of the environment that surrounds us as children. Those beliefs form the basis for evaluating life and how we should live it, what constitutes righteous and proper behavior, and how religious worship should take place, among other things. These form a religious orthodoxy we inherit as youths, but that might be augmented or rejected as adults, of course. Some never investigate the beliefs bequeathed to them.

Religion makes many people feel whole, but I cannot say that has been the case with me. I should also mention that religious culture has provided me with some pleasant experiences and introduced me to several people whom I like, including a good friend. Throughout life, religion most often functioned as an obligation to fear and sometimes dread. These sentiments arose from the teaching that one must not miss church or risk offending God, which can be intimidating. The church functioned as a responsibility to check off a list more than a place of learning or a lightening of the soul's load. In other words, showing up was the chief responsibility regardless of what happened during the service. My church was not very joyful or inspirational, at least that is my assessment looking back. Anxiety made the whole experience a little more haphazard. Church activities never enlivened my soul, but I was very afraid of not doing the right things. All matters religious left me with an obsessive prayer mandate, entirely of my making, that I still adhere to. For years, I prayed in a particular order unnecessary to divulge. But it was strict, and I could not entirely stop repeating what was uttered inside my head over and over.

I think most people, if honest, would admit to some degree of doubt regarding their stated faith. In the Bible, some people are mentioned as questioning God, but I cannot recall who they are right now. If you are fond of Western Civilization and all its material advantages and respect for human rights, etc., you should realize much of that was possible due to religious freedom and the government's neutral position on spiritual matters. Without these, there would be no Western Civilization as we know it. And no matter what someone says, American founders were not looking to Christianity for help in creating the Constitution. Nor did they intend America to endorse any religion over another in its official capacity. In matters of government, those men most often consulted Enlightenment philosophy or English common law. Those exceptionally intelligent individuals, such as Thomas Jefferson and Benjamin Franklin, struggled with their fidelity to Christianity, to say the least. So, we should not feel at fault for contemplating the big questions and critiquing the religion appointed to us as youth.

There have been a handful of commonly held religious interpretations and practices that are beyond his understanding. Any system of faith worth professing can withstand the darts thrown at it by inquiring minds. Part of his hiatus from church-attendance had to do with a certain preacher's endless stories of heartbreak and suffering. The sermons were tough to take. It seems that religious gatherings should promote more happiness than sadness in this already agonizing world. Other thoughts have crossed his mind. The notion of being born a sinner just does not seem fair or reasonable. We would not apply this doctrine in different areas of life, condemning an infant for actions of long-ago family members. In general, if humans are naturally evil, why would you blame the product instead of the means of production? Many other aspects of religion do not make sense to him. He is aware, too, of how scholars question literal interpretations of what is found in the Bible.

Philosophical works of art have informed his worldview more than his religious upbringing. In the quest to understand himself, defeat mental illness/addiction, and capture some measure of contentment, the hero stumbled upon the opinions and works of William James. A philosopher and psychologist, the brilliant thinker wrote the classic *The Varieties of Religious Experience: A Study in Human Nature.* He wrote many books and maintains a broad legacy and influence. Living during the late nineteenth century, James was skeptical about traditional religion and often felt depressed when pondering the big questions. James fell into a dispirited crisis, worried that life had no meaning. He was not the first and would not be the last. The hero can identify with this.

James' findings in the book included a description and comparison of human beings classed as once-born and another he termed twice-born. The former category refers to those who are satisfied with life as it is, unbothered by injustices and world calamities, and who feel no serious desire to investigate their beliefs. The twice-born are the downtrodden and mentally sick, James related, because they do indeed reflect on life with eyes opened and a mind that processes the wrongs of the world. About these, he wrote, "their spirit wars with their flesh…their lives are one long drama of repentance and of effort to repair misdemeanors and mistakes."[1]

You might think that the recommendation here prioritizes the once-born as better, but you would be incorrect. The twice-born eventually boil over and reach a place of extreme distress, but afterward emerge feeling like a new person with a definite purpose. This is true happiness, according to Professor James. They reach a more profound level of existence than the once-born. James said, "The process is one of redemption, not of mere reversion to natural health, and the sufferer, when saved, is saved by what seems to him a second birth, a deeper kind of conscious being than he could enjoy before." Could I possibly be ranked among the twice-born?

That question must be answered later, but the truth is my religious faith has long been shaken. So many people out there are like me, as the data reveals Americans are losing interest in organized religion more so each year. I am a member of Generation X, and we may be the first true malcontent generation in American History. The X people have a dissatisfaction that does not necessarily stem from an obvious cause. It was not planned that way, and I have not greeted the loss of faith as a great boon for my mental health.

We are living in an era unlike any previous one. When it comes to religion, at least in America, we can pick and choose from basically every form of belief and unbelief that has ever spawned any kind of following. We modern people do not need to go further than the computer to learn about this and that flavor of religion. It is like picking from a large restaurant menu, in some respects. There has been widespread disenchantment with traditional religion and formal church attendance for many decades. Perhaps my favorite intellectual, the legendary psychologist Carl Jung, wrote more eloquently on this topic than almost anyone. Discussing twentieth-century attitudes toward religion, Jung described the average person of his day. He wrote:

> ...modern man expects something from the psyche which the outer world has not given him:Doubtless something which our religion ought to contain, but no longer contains, at least for modern man. For him the various forms of religion no longer appear to come from within, the psyche; they seem more like items from the inventory of the outside world. No spirit not ofthis world vouchsafes him inner revelation; instead, he tries on a variety of religions and beliefs as if they were Sunday attire, only to lay them aside again like worn-out clothes.[8]

\I find it necessary to mention how certain core aspects of religion can contribute to poor mental health. I think everyone understands that children are usually indoctrinated with some thought patterns or philosophies, ranging from positive to horrific, that stay with us well into adulthood and sometimes forever. Religion has a role in teaching people how to think, and unfortunately, that may also mean prescribing the doctrine of fear. More than that, religion instructs us that humans harbor some seed of evil within, and that we must worry about getting what we deserve lest we follow laws interpreted by other inherently flawed humans. Once a set of preferred interpretations becomes tradition, they must not be trifled with. There are religious matters I can no longer easily digest, and one is that humanity is not-so-great because a smooth-talking snake once convinced two people to try fruit.

No mental health professional would advise a patient to think of himself as a corrupted, malignant being who should feel guilty for being born that way. To my point, I lived many years believing I deserved no help, second chances, or compassion. My default state of mind had me feeling apologetic for my very existence; I was sad about failing to be perfect, and then I felt sorry about feeling miserable. It never occurred to me to accept and tolerate myself regardless of all else. Instead, I wondered what the hell malfunction had happened during the assemblage of my body and mind. Religion was by no means the primary cause of my misfortunes and pain. But I think religion, as I know it, starts the conversation about who you are, and what you should be doing—the big questions—from a place where every individual is born with insurmountable debts to repay. The emphasis is on what is wrong with us that must be fixed instead of our specialness and each individual's singular mission to brighten the world through inborn goodness.

Despite what I have said on religion, I have never once speculated that any great problem of mine was a "religious crisis." Even so, had any other human been acquainted with my various states of discomfort and confusion, he or she might have, maybe, used that term to define my state of mind. It would make sense, given how I have questioned what makes life worth living and whether there is anything out there for me that is not frivolous and shallow. These are just a few of the many big questions. Perhaps it is a peculiarity in the way that I think, but it is less religion than belief itself that is puzzling. Yes, you might be right to interject that there is little difference between that and a religious crisis, dear reader. That being said, I have marveled, at certain times throughout my life, how human beings can profess great faith in any person, book, set of ideals, or anything else. I have trouble believing in belief. This might not be a good characteristic at all. I have no idea.

My rumination on religion reminded me that I appreciate and have learned from the book of Ecclesiastes. It makes one think. The book is also full of wisdom, philosophy, and poetry. Of the many lasting passages, "All is Vanity," or "Vanity of Vanities," has stayed with me since first hearing it. The wise teacher's words suggest a man who is frustrated and possibly dejected. One way to interpret the passages is that life is meaningless. Well, dear reader, you can probably imagine how I relate to such a perspective. After the d-word, all my goals, and those cravings to take my place among real people, such as my father, and to sit at his table with pride, were flushed down the toilet. At some point, the years pass, and you reflect on your past life as a dream that never quite came to pass. And yes, it does feel like that person is dead and all matters related to the marriage were fantasy, or all those memories were about some other person you once knew. So, I consented that life was all vain just like the wise preacher stated. Then, all at once, he ceased being himself. Nothing we do matters, and if there is any entity arranging my life by some logical blueprint, it is not me.

Ecclesiastes also suggests that nothing on this planet has any permanence. Again, the word vanity arises. We human beings must be vain to think any accomplishment or any other beloved person or thing is not simply wiped away like dust. How do my wants even register among the countless people who live and pass away without notice? I'm not sure, but the author of the book classifies humans alongside animals because we are all subject to the same earthly laws of life and decay. However, human fools like me can fret about the big questions that, in turn, introduce distress into the world. And what does all that disturbance of the spirit produce? Nothing of significance. Will I be remembered? No. Even men and women much worthier than I cannot overcome irrelevancy, and the preacher reminds us, "There is nothing new under the sun."

There are a few directions one can go once it is accepted that all is vanity. Nihilism leads to nowhere. The biblically accepted view, as I understand it, is that earthly life is temporary, but God is eternal, and so is the afterlife. So, yeah, do not hitch your wagon to this cursed existence and do live in accordance with God's plan. This design is not something you will comprehend, so walk by faith. Indeed, a person is haughty to think otherwise or think too much. For my usual way of interpreting life, I might read the book as a prescription for depression. Or, I can empathize with the guy who reads Ecclesiastes and wonders, "If nothing matters, then I will do whatever I want."

Thus, why not hedonism? The hedonism club never adopted me as a member, but for several years, I unofficially adhered to some principles that might lead one to that conclusion. Something was driving my life, and whatever that was had nothing to do with the reign of the golden-haired boy. The drinking hobby became an addiction and then took possession of everything. And when that takes place, you are in some ways a hedonist. Addiction is rowdy and reckless by definition. So the big questions only mattered in that my answers were somewhere along the lines of all is vanity. There was no moral to my story. From where we are, life got worse before it got better, and the hero's journey turned very dark.

CHAPTER 4:

Darkness in the Mourning

"I am trying to rip open the inconsolable secret in each one of you—the secret which hurts so much that you take your revenge on it by calling it names like Nostalgia and Romanticism and Adolescence;...Wordsworth's expedient was to identify it with certain moments in his own past. But all this is a cheat. If Wordsworth had gone back to those moments in the past, he would not have found the thing itself, but only a reminder of it;...These things—the beauty, the memory of our own past—are good images of what we really desire; but if they are mistaken for the thing itself they turn into dumb idols, breaking the hearts of their worshipper. For they are not the thing itself; they are only the scent of a flower we have not found, the echo of a tune we have not heard, news from a country we have never yet visited."[9]

Long ago, the curmudgeonly yet astute Thomas Carlyle bemoaned humanity's disconnect with the natural world, as he wrote and philosophized during the early stages of industrialization. He called it the "Mechanical Age," and mourned that no longer could Western Civilization be called "the Heroical, Devotional, Philosophical, or Moral Age." We have heard this before, but it was back during the early nineteenth century, when these trends were brand new in the world. All of our good nature as human beings was devoured by the bottom-line-ism creeping into Carlyle's purview. He remarked that the godly virtues were no longer the prime movers of human intentions. So many others would follow in his footsteps that his words almost ring out as cliché, in the present.[10]

Mental health treatment has taught me that meditation, clearing one's mind of clutter, focusing on admirable goals, and seeing myself as good and unique are a few of the ingredients for positive mental health. Yet, our era is negative and superficial. Our mental health has been left twisting in the wind. Our leaders never anticipate how their decisions might leave us in a poorer state of mental health. What Carlyle saw was just starting, and it continues now and will never stop. I have always felt like we are losing something every day—that each new sunrise means we are moving further away from something pristine. To understand this, I must consult my own history of mental illness along with some of the ideas of people who have commented on modernity. I must honestly ask if living with eyes fixed on the past has hampered my life.

Solving the riddles of my life has been a formidable task. There must be a root cause of the sad and lonely hours and days. As a matter of habit, I tend to gaze backward for both answers and comfort. My lifetime pursuit can be partially characterized by a quest to understand the origins of "my stuff." We all have that, and by that I refer to the natured and nurtured outlook of each person. That includes everything in one's character, strengths and shortcomings, and most of all: mental health. Mental health defines a person, encompassing aspects such as belonging, wholeness, authenticity, identity, and some of your favorite words, too. I have used the hero's journey as a framework to encompass all the smaller stories, including everything I have been, no longer want to be, and what I hope to become. My education unearthed some valuable aspects of the hero that had been largely overlooked. And education continues to this day, as I can now clearly understand.

Art has been more instrumental to my philosophy of living than previously known. It might hold the secrets to achieving some enlightenment, or at the very least, having exchanges with others that run deep. Creativity of the organic sort has entranced me and served as a calming influence amid various storms. My worried thoughts that all is vanity, or something close to that, have probably emboldened my inner search for ways to express myself. Only in the past year or two has art reemerged, taking on a new form of powerful responses to those big questions. Is art the way to immortality? We shall see, but artists are the kind of rebels spirited by what I can envision as closer to what stirs in my soul. Sometimes I turn to stories, such as a book or film, to try to understand something about myself and then share a bit of wisdom with others. In reality, this is what storytellers, the best ones, strive to accomplish. Telling or listening to a story can be one of the most instructive and far-reaching ways to illustrate great life lessons.

I remember *The Wizard of Oz* coming on my television set at a very young age. I am not sure if the movie fits the mold of a hero's journey. Regardless, it is not that the film has been especially important to my life, but right now it is a logical place to turn and is very relevant to my recovery. The film is a story about a story. Well, one might say a dream, because almost all the action never really took place. All that aside, this is how I interpret it. It is folly to spend time wishing for things we do not have. Setting up idols to emulate outside of oneself must always be disappointing. There is always a man behind the curtain. As finally revealed to Dorothy, what we have is all that was ever needed if identified and harnessed for good. That is my favorite thing about this movie. I cannot say why these simple thoughts did not occur to me much sooner in life. Could I not hear it, or did no one say it, or was the problem a matter of a chemical imbalance in the brain?

The characters in *The Wizard of Oz* were lacking wholeness, but that was only an illusion. Each of Dorothy's companions pleaded that they needed something to claim their realness. Dorothy dreamed of the simple return Home, which turned out to be always accessible to her. I think we can add a theme of growing up to the classic movie's long list of good ones. Reaching adolescence and then adulthood requires more than just time and the body's biological processes. Embodying a whole adult person cannot materialize without the stories that build a history. Certain rites of passage are customary. Lessons are to be learned, and we are to reach maturity. An incomplete or misconstrued arrangement of history does not allow people or places to embody their authentic natures. It can lead to blind obedience to self-destructive missions, and the same thing repeats with every person. Stories are the instrument every group and each individual must use to rally talents, labors, and passions toward meeting some prophesied destiny. We must explain to ourselves what our actions in life add up to, and who we think we are, before we can let anyone else know. Surprises often happen. As most of us recall, Dorothy did not realize the shoes she wore would be so pivotal to her story.

People have a story, as do large entities of every kind: professions like the medical field, institutions like a church, even businesses, and towns, cities, states, and countries. What works in the big picture to explain a place or institution can also serve each individual as we tell ourselves the story of our lives. Americans of the past often preferred to view their history as advancing toward near-perfection. Not everyone, but in general, this has been the case. If the history of the United States were a graph, the lines would rise and fall instead of gradually charting upward, however. That is how most people experience life. There are twists and turns, starts and restarts, going forward and suffering setbacks, and rarely do our plans play out as we wish. I believe the story of my life is ongoing, of course, and I hope it is finally trending in the right direction. Things are different now, post-mental health crisis, and my flow chart feels like it is rising upward in a more predictable trajectory. However, there have been unexpected turns, totally unforeseen, and progress that seemed more like disasters. I do know this: it is not wise to let someone or something outside of oneself narrate your personal story. Sometimes, it only takes a reframing of the mind to change the meaning of events that have already occurred.

In graduate school, I began to see all texts, such as private letters, as stories of some kind. I am not the first to do that or anything, but simply using that word was different from the book reviews and other analysis-driven histories that passed before me. It was the simplicity, most of all, that attracted me to think in this way. When a person hears the term 'story,' it prepares them to be entertained or learn a valuable life lesson. We think we know what it means to tell or hear a story, and neither requires sophistication or advanced education. A story can be rudimentary or as "big" and epic as *Star Wars*. The greatest authors of all time tell stories, like William Shakespeare or Charles Dickens, but so does your uncle when he relates the one about the fishing trip. To learn about my family, region, or country, I might share a narrative with you. From this point forward, I am trying to tell my story from my perspective, without the old worries of failure that come with being a real person. We shall see, I am never sure in advance.

Storytellers who weave together characters and events that form a legacy provide meanings that individuals may interpret as important to their lives. That meaning can be simplistic, but that word does not equal unimportant. The substance of the story can matter just as much, even when partially or entirely untrue. If we listen carefully, we can deduce the purpose of the person behind the story and what they want us to know about the characters. Leaving out a sentence or maybe even one word can change the interpretation entirely. Every report on television filed under the category of news is a story that has passed through a trail of human scrutiny, involving many people, before it reaches the public in whatever form. The news is supposed to be unfiltered truth, but the reality is more complicated.

My story has been unceasingly biased, and I cannot say anyone deserves the "credit" for that except me. Others probably are accessories to the crime, I think. It does not matter, though, because there is only one person left to take the fall for the making or unmaking of an individual's story, and that is who we see in the mirror. With all my classes and conversations about history and identity, I gained only a partial understanding that I was on a search that led me to begin this book. Being self-aware is both a blessing and a curse, as it often enables one to see the big picture more clearly than the little things. In this chapter, the pain of living as an unacceptable character in my own life takes a devastating form. Yet, I am becoming more convinced that the pain might have been unstoppable.

I still believe that every person should see themselves as the hero of their own story. But do I? Sometimes, I am better at knowing what to do from an analytical perspective than I am at practicing the precept from my typically emotion-driven thinking. Most of my experiences either do not fit with or are hard to ascribe to particular phases of the hero's journey. Or, that could be wrong and just a result of my negativity. That makes no difference at all. Calling myself a hero is a literary device, but the work of authoring a genuine understanding of my past is difficult and time-consuming. Art has to be front and center somehow, and it is necessary to make peace with all those "what ifs" that have dominated these pages, casting the hero as less than a real person.

People have commented that dwelling on the past is useless and can hinder progress. I am sure this is a correct thing to say. There is even more to consider in my life. The idea that the good days have gone makes the present and future less clear. Let's think about the following example. A big-budget movie is opening for the first time with great anticipation. For some reason, the director decided to bury the climax, the resolution of the drama, near the beginning of the film. A viewer would naturally feel disoriented and less invested in the rest of the movie. Maybe a person in the theater would even question their good sense instead of blaming the way the story was told. In life, this might have happened to the hero of my "movie." It is plausible that I have stumbled through my days confused while doubting my perception of reality.

We tend to look backward for relief from our worries, and this is true of individuals and communities as a whole. I think the reason is simple: the future is unknown, and the past is comparable to a movie we have already seen. Folks relive the moments when characters should have done something else or when luck conspired to dismantle one's good intentions. Our plans go awry, and we imagine we can fix them with an "only if." This detail and that event would have made all the difference, we tell ourselves. And, of course, I mean the real-life characters in life as well as those from the movies we have watched. The past is known, and we think rewriting a script is less taxing than creating a new one from scratch.

Some choose to use the past to look for meaningful family heritage. On the micro level, the interest in tracing one's ancestry backward is just a form of storytelling. As you might be aware, the Internet has made genealogies even more popular and accessible. People want to take pride in some aspect of their heritage and desire a connection with something greater than themselves, or they may simply seek to share their family's background with others. Some make great efforts to advertise their descent from famous people who have long since passed away. If they cannot find a claim to fame in the historical record, they might invent such things. Every person, kinship group, community, region, and nation has an important story to identify and retell, over and over.

Thus far in my life, I have not explored searching for my ancestors. This has been recommended to me given my History background, so I make an obvious candidate to spend days and nights in libraries, on computers, scanning for information. Likely, I have not done so because of my unconscious assumption that I do not belong to any significant group or have any authentic origins. Being half a person does not meet the prerequisite to search out real people from the historical record. My inner voice, or narrator, said such things to me all the time. My instincts are the off-spring of a well-worn negativity I have carried with me for so long. With this in mind, I have always wished my life to be linked to something of lasting value or interest. Still, that boy in front of his grandmother's television had no shortage of stories in his head. My chronic non-belonging, as might seem rather obvious, has always led to this secret hunger to place myself as a key character in some captivating drama. So, my beginnings are important, as they are to every story of any depth.

Stories that explain the origins of almost any person, place, or thing are inseparable from the process of identity-building. Let me amend that more confidently and express that origins form the foundation of building a person. Now, I have gained some insight into my origins, but I still get very frustrated with the lack of firm answers. Primarily, my journey is about the emotional, non-material aspect of living, which, to me, is the most important part. Students of the Humanities or curious thinkers will surely find that all kinds of people and cultures strive to locate a reliable source of how everything important came to exist. There is such a thing as a "usable past" if you choose to learn more about this, dear reader. An origin can be sacred or secular, but must contain at least preliminary answers to the big questions: Who are we, and how did we get here? Once these have some preliminary exposition, then people can proceed to solve the next step: What should we do?

History is a great canvas for experimenting with identity and for redrafting or inventing one's origin story. Many people fail to realize that history can be used as a tool to skew toward one's favored interpretation, and that it is not an unassailable ledger of facts. Until I studied history for many years, I might have been one of those. What we carry with us as the "truth" of history changes over time and according to what people want in the present. If we look at individuals and their stories, rather than textbook History about nations and empires, then that record of things that came before us is even more readily made to bend to a person's will. It is not that difficult to accentuate one part of our ancestry and dismiss other parts. It has become fashionable to suddenly assert one's Native American identity due to some link found to a close or distant family member. Also, someone might overnight become Italian, Scottish, French, etc., for the first time in their life. Where the historical record says little to nothing, people can adopt favorite theories to fill in the blanks. I am saying that history is there for the taking. It is not static. All one needs is a little effort and access to research.

The malleability of history is not always a good thing. As it has been repeated in various ways, the group or class who controls the narrative of the past can direct the course of the present and the future. Such a group can convince the masses to participate in egregious conduct that results in the vilest behaviors imaginable. This has happened, of course. However, the selection and dissemination of origins also have the power for good, and can serve to link or unify individuals behind a common purpose. The reason for all of this is that most people, when considering the nature of a thing, look toward the beginnings of the thing. This offers the promise of excavating the original intentions before the thing inevitably becomes tarnished. Some pay homage to an original purity that is gone but could emerge once more. In my opinion, the collective aim of every project eventually reaches a forgotten or unintended condition, and someone or a group will announce their intention to restore a place or thing to its former glory. Then, stories play a great role in representing the ideals of a thing, such as a nation or a human being.

Control is a crucial term to consider in the context of this discussion. In totalitarian governments, a dictator typically owns the past of the masses. He at least tries to accomplish this. By doing so, he informs people about their history, how it came to be, and dictates what their aims should be in the present. We have seen the literal destruction of primary sources. As a result, history is falsified to control people and get them to work under a tyrant's goals. In which direction should I look for that mean bully who authored my story? There is nowhere to search except within, as far as I know. This person, whom I often refer to as the hero, must have betrayed Kirk. Until a few years back, all that I collected as my life was formed out of bad materials, driven by mental illness, and a very poor attempt at editing. I am not sure I ever took the responsibility seriously, but maybe now that is exactly what is happening.

Being unaware or inaccurate about my history, or yours, can function like this example of the dictator and the duped population under his authority. So each of us can fool, misuse, and even debase the person we are by misleading ourselves about our history. This may come as a result of a huge variety of circumstances, and that includes all that we are: our mental health. Also, another person can scheme to give us a fabricated personal story, and this is a form of manipulation, abuse, and/or gaslighting. Our culture oftentimes convinces individuals with past trauma and/ or mental illness that they are a diagnosis more than a person. They are made to distrust their history, and this causes them to denigrate themselves. Dear reader, you have read how I did not think I was a whole person deserving of happy endings. I have been listening to and watching a biased story in my head, one meant to portray me as a weird outsider.

Who created it, my mind? Did society play some role in this? I am not sure I have the full answer.

In most cases, history provides numerous sources for analysis, including letters, newspapers, diaries, and other primary documents. In my life, there are fewer pieces of evidence and a memory that is not that reliable. So, patching together something that makes sense is very challenging and perhaps unrealistic. Despite that, I must try my best. It seems a cruel thing that we have the least recall about the most impressionable years of our lives. I had no sense of self while battling insecurity and isolation growing up, nor when older and trying to forge a new life for myself. Oh, I tried on a few hats, but none of them fit. Now I can attest to the importance of self-confidence. There is no replacement for this invaluable life tool. I believe most people now have a sense of loss that is largely due to forces beyond our control.

Needless to say, as people and members of whatever community you belong to, we can undergo little self-reflection without some vague idea about what came first. The greatest, most expansive, and important origin stories aim to uncover the essence of all that matters: the emergence of life and existence itself. Every known civilization pondered these particular big questions and provided some kind of answer(s). At their core, I believe people of all places and times share more commonalities than differences. Anyway, it is not unusual for one civilization to promote more than one story of creation, and one also finds that those narratives might contradict one another. Some postulate how the whole world came into existence, while others might only pertain to the emergence of a particular people.

Most origin stories that are handed down and/or written in some form are classified under religion. Certainly, the Garden of Eden in Genesis is a prominent example. Genesis emphasizes the blankness of the world before God populated it with every form of matter. Other narratives from around the world engage us in a likewise manner and include a passage like this one I made up: "In the beginning, everywhere there was a great blackness on the earth." The great filmmaker Orson Welles believed that looking backward toward some Eden-like existence formed "the central theme in Western culture." The "lost paradise" was an ethos revisited again and again in stories, he said. We learn a great deal about people based on their version of an origin story. The Roman Empire told of two brothers raised by a female wolf. There is a strange commonality around our planet of brotherly conflict leading to some founding. Anyway, another reason I use the word 'story' instead of 'myth' is that when people read a myth, they assume what is to come is untrue. Stories do not carry this burden.

Those interested in national identity focus on the beginnings of America to define and proclaim what it is all about. But, exactly where and when do we look for the opening scene? Does Christopher Columbus play a role or not? The Pilgrims and the Mayflower, Thanksgiving, Native Americans, explorers, and all that must be front and center, no? Most Americans claim some knowledge of George Washington, the Declaration of Independence, Thomas Jefferson, and other figures on the currency, as well as the Constitution. That is, those people whom we can count on to recall something about the distant past. Black Americans might focus more on the Civil War and the end of slavery, when the founding principles *began* to be more fairly allocated to all.

I believe the study of history can be likened to one's journey of discovery. For me, researching history is akin to foraging within my soul for clues. It may not look as such from another's point of view, yet I find the universal in my singular exertions to produce some synthesis of my life. If the United States were a person, we share questions in common and a modern shrug of the shoulders that asks, "What is authentic and untarnished that I can lean on?" Could we call this an identity crisis? America did not suffer through the Middle Ages and has no ancient past in terms that most people recognize. Therefore, we can confidently surmise that the supernatural and mystical causation has little to no place in America's founding lore. There is no magic, no Camelot or Merlin, no dragons or demigods, embedded in the catalog of American heroes. We know George Washington was just a man and even have images based on his appearance. Therefore, Americans will have to be content with the story of Washington and the cherry tree, Paul Revere's Ride, the Pilgrims as freedom-loving refugees, and those patriotic portrayals of America as a "melting pot."

Generations of Americans have crafted a narrative that has shaped their history into a unique and remarkable outgrowth of all the accumulated wisdom and advancements of humanity's most prominent civilizations. The genius of Egypt, the Greeks, the Romans, and Europe all coalesced in the land of the free. Many in the country and around the world have historically regarded American origins as a sanctuary for the best of human values. The people and principles of its founding made America into a "city on a hill" for the whole world to envy and emulate. After criticisms mounted and became too unsightly to ignore, the notion that America is exceptional is no longer a politically correct viewpoint. Defenders of the old story have been backed into a corner. We now have a problem with locating the materials that make a distinctive American character in the present. The best of what many see as American virtues are somewhere in the past. This coincides with how I have interpreted much of my life.

If the greatest country in the world cannot get its story straight, then I must feel better about mine. Americans have not come to terms with the revised interpretations of their history. The Democrats and Republicans are like two storytellers on a stump, each coaxing the audience to embrace one story that, somewhere, diverges from the other. Detractors now have no faith in any story, and for others, the climax of the American "movie" is too near the beginning to make sense. Those faithful to the founders are looking backward with confidence and forward with delirium. This is what one finds if we only notice cultural trends and think about what we see. Even with Americans who never invested in the exceptional narrative, the present and future are concerning and uncharted. There are inherent issues with storytelling and its longstanding ability to cull a usable framework from the nonsensical world. As you might have guessed, what happens in big stories about nations might also occur with individuals and their histories. I have sought out my origins to improve my mental health and locate some time or circumstances that can reveal what went wrong in my life.

To this person now writing, the golden-haired child lives as a kind of perfect splendor that probably will never be restored. There is beauty attached to this lone image that is timeless. There is something about that moment and memory that reminds me of innocence lost. I can attach almost nothing else tangible to the picture that has become nearly mythical. Additionally, the most engaging aspects of the story, which are still unfolding, are presented at the beginning instead of at the end. This is a great barrier to the rewrite under development and to the man still living with a heart bleeding for the past. My story needs reworking, and so does the one about American History. Thankfully, I only have to concentrate on telling my own life properly.

If origins are crucial in creating a group identity, and if identity is necessary to flourish or simply be okay, and if aspects of the current world put the identity in peril, then the group will somehow suffer. All that applies to an individual's mental health also applies to that of the community as a whole. Part of my hero's journey has been my efforts to locate or invent a sense of belonging to feel like a real person. But, there is scant evidence of the modern world that entices me toward transcendence of the common and ordinary. It is easy to see my life as all vanity and concede that the big questions can only take me to a place of depression.

If a place can act like a person, then a community's history must have growing pains, adolescence, maturity, and more. America's teen years probably started after the War of 1812, but what about mine in this elaborate schema of my invention? There was no rebellion to take seriously in the hero's life. Therefore, growing up, learning the ropes, and advancing to the next level remain shrouded in mystery. America surely grew and looked like a fully-formed, independent nation, but I have only regrets and failure. This author-hero has yet to reach that point in his story where he achieves wholeness and stands confident in his identity. Where is his specialness, and where is the proof that the hero exists apart from every other human being who walks the earth?

Education must be to blame, right? Is ignorance bliss? My college education introduced ideas that revitalized my desire to find myself, but also sparked a questioning of practically every fragment of received wisdom. Now, and for a while, we have been filled with doubt about every story from history. America provides a great example of how history is contested among people living in the present. There has been a very noticeable conservative backlash against criticism of American principles and some of its early leaders. As many complain, we no longer look up to guiding stars such as Washington, Jefferson, and James Madison in the same way. I will not even test your patience with Andrew Jackson. Christopher Columbus is more reviled than revered, largely due to the Spanish treatment of the Natives in the Americas.

The fact that we are alive now, rather than during some previous era, matters to our mental health and outlook on history, as well as our personal histories. We have been living in an extraordinary period that broke from the customary pace of historical change around 150 years ago. In the last decades of the nineteenth century, there was a rapid advancement for mankind driven by the ill-defined concept of modernity. To attempt to explain what happened, imagine a person who lost weight that you interacted with daily. You would not be surprised to see a slow change that occurs gradually and is often imperceptible. That was how the world worked forever. Now, envision a scene starring someone you had not encountered for a year who lost a massive amount of weight. Suddenly, you two crossed paths without a warning of how he or she transformed. The change would come rushing at you with jarring abruptness, because in your mind, the weight loss was not gradual but all at once.

That was how the world leaped, and we are still living with the legacy. Without much time in between, human beings were introduced to the telegraph, phonograph, telephone, electricity, motor vehicles, motion pictures, airplanes, and then a little later still, nuclear weapons. Also, modern transportation and industry gave rise to mass production and the kind of big-city environments that are now commonplace. The steel and oil industries fueled vehicle manufacturing and city infrastructure, which in turn contributed to travel that necessitated restaurants, hotels, and gas stations, ultimately allowing for suburbs and beyond. Only forty-nine years separated the horse-bound Civil War from the tank-and-trench World War I. Think about that, dear reader, if you choose. It might be fair to say that the world has undergone a widespread nervous breakdown.

We were born and still reside in an incredible time that has engendered brand new levels of psychic disturbance. Considering that the world has been gradually losing weight for so long, our sudden surge in shedding fat is unprecedented. Therefore, we are still coping. Every really smart man or woman I have read agrees that modernity plays mean tricks on mental certitude, as it pertains to purpose and identity among billions of other mammals. I mean that mental health disorders are mirrored, and to a degree caused, by the unstable ground we are thrown onto by the consequences of modernity. What afflicts the community also affects the individual. Practically all believe that mental illness has never been a more comprehensive plague than it is right now. Regardless of who thinks what, I believe history has played a part in my depression, anxiety, panic disorders, phobias, and other more hidden ailments of my mind.

I want to turn to Jung again to contemplate our society's collective mental illness. Jung wrote the passage below to contrast the mentality of the Middle Ages with that of the modern era. First, let me make it clear that I have no wish to set the time machine on a course for medieval Europe. No, there are too many reasons not to do that. Having said this, Jung and many others have noted what has been lost in terms of spirituality over the past hundred years or so due to the characteristics of modern life. The idea here is that the world today misses something crucial to humanity's well-being, while simultaneously gaining modern conveniences, cures for diseases, and more which I need not mention. The great scholar and teacher wrote:

> How different did the world appear to medieval man! For him the earth was eternally fixed and at rest in the center of the universe...Men were all children of God under the loving care of the Most High, who prepared them for eternal blessedness; and all knew exactly what they should do and how they should conduct themselves in order to rise from a corruptible world to an

Jung helped explain the mind problems associated with living that most of us greet with unquestioning submission. In 1933, he wrote *Modern Man in Search of a Soul*. By this time, Jung had formulated some questions and answers about what mankind was to do and feel in the face of the modern menace. As you might guess from the title, Jung speculated about how humans would cope, find meaning, and perhaps discover an ultimate spiritual authority. He related that the truly modern man was a rare type. Here was a person who had become fully conscious of every implication of living, then, in the twentieth century. The age we still live in perfectly suits a psychologist, as he or she may be the best armed to diagnose the neurosis that accompanies mankind's ability to destroy the Earth at any given time. He brilliantly anticipated mental health issues that have taken shape over the decades up until right now.

Jung wrote that the modern "stands upon a peak, or at the very edge of the world," with "the abyss of the future above him."Further, he has stumbled his way up before the void, "leaving behind him all that has been discarded and Outgrown, and acknowledging that he stands before the Nothing out of which All may grow." It was necessary to break from the herd mentality of the masses, and of tradition, by "voluntarily declaring oneself bankrupt…" and accepting that "nearly two thousand years of Christian idealism followed, not by the return of the Messiah…but by the World War among Christian nations with its barbed wire and poison gas."[12] This is very perceptive and poignant, methinks. Therefore, an enlightened person carried a burden with him and was likewise very troubled, having "suffered an almost fatal shock, psychologically speaking, and as a result has fallen into profound uncertainty." Yet, the astute author also claimed that modern man was the most likely to call himself "old-fashioned," due to a kind of psychopathic over-compensation for his avowed break with the past.

If we concede that standing before the "Nothing" is inherent to the modern condition, staring into Jung's abyss, then I subconsciously sensed something of this kind in childhood, long before I had heard of Jung, William James, or any intellectual. There is emptiness in Western Civilization where self-confidence once held court. I am not immune to obsessing over my story, and I have come to realize that I can be counted among those born with the instinct that the world is not as it should be. What is wrong, and the solutions to repair our world, come much harder. There are at least two different ways that "we" experience distress, because we can refer to a group or the individual. I am standing behind the notion that we, in both regards, lacked a centrality of identity in my lifetime that can be interpreted as mental illness. Did modernity create mental illness? No. As you know, mental illness is part of being human and has always been there. However, Psychology itself does not predate the modern era. Also, the world as it came to be over the last few centuries made mental illness more visible, and that fact should be much more than a footnote in some mental health textbook.

Although neither religion nor family heritage gave the younger me much to cling to, education alerted the young man to a universe of possibilities. Then, a second education in mental health clarified the problem and presented some preliminary answers. When I look back, I see how a terrified and sensitive young man turned to education to help him make sense of his confusion. The hero felt a pull toward the past to better cope with his present woes. He was like Indiana Jones, exploring every corner of the world in search of his treasure, but his object of fascination was the book that contained the instructions within. Yes, perhaps it was on a dusty shelf that he might learn about in class or as a result of his research. Thankfully, he was introduced to some people who asked the same questions about origins and what life was meant to be.

I read the criticisms of the world from smart people like Jung and others. I could "meet" the great thinkers now every time I visited the library. Therefore, I found myself dismayed by those who appeared heartless and careless, unconcerned about the big questions. It seemed that the whole world had lost its childlike wonder that Wordsworth wrote about, replaced by something unknown that was callous and uninteresting. Everything about the boy and the young man prioritized the past over the present and future. He was a searcher for lost things and for causes that made the world so confounding to him. The nineteenth century was important to the young scholar; he somehow understood this. This is when the Industrial Revolution collided with traditional ways of living.

To clarify what all this means, I think the childhood film *The Never-Ending Story* can be interpreted as a meditation on the "fatal shock" and "uncertainty" we must navigate simply by being alive and of the thinking sort. Watching this so long ago, I sensed that the film engaged the big questions somehow and unlocked something mysterious and vital. Even those words, "never-ending story," weighed on my mind. I needed to know more, but I could not fully appreciate a film more sobering than one would expect from a so-called kid movie. I did not decode the various messages here until much, much later, while deep in thought at a place I was forbidden to leave. However, I am unsure if others experience this reaction to art, as I do, when we like a particular thing but cannot quite put our finger on why.

The story unfolds on two levels of fantasy and reality, beginning when a young boy named Bastion discovers and reads a book that serves as the narrative of the film. His life and reading of the story sometimes interact with the fantasy world contained in the book. The setting is called Fantastica and is ruled over by a child empress. Her kingdom is in crisis, and the young warrior Atreyu answers the call to adventure, just as in other classic tales filled with harrowing conflicts and fairytale creatures. Most of us remember the flying, endlessly lovable, giant dog-like friend of the protagonist. But, I digress. The villain is not a diabolical person or a monstrous beast, but is instead known as "the Nothing." Formless, the Nothing threatens to overwhelm the idyllic Fantastica forever unless Atreyu and/or Bastion save the day.

The popular book/film is about many things, and perhaps everything, depending on how one interprets the story. The Nothing is the absence of hope and imagination. At least to me, it symbolizes the encroachment of the real world on the one of our aspirations and the end of unjaded curiosity. It is not modernity here, but perhaps that moment of accepting the world in all its ugliness that replaces innocence. Also, the Nothing could represent when each child realizes that their father is not the toughest or wisest man in the world, or it can be compared to a consciousness of evil's existence, a lack of faith, remorse about the big questions, and more, I am sure. Most importantly to me, the Nothing is the despair and lack of interest in everything called depression. The Nothing is not the same for every person, I think. In the midst of depression for all my days, a nothingness reigned over me like some kind of tyrant-king, dictating that my life amounted to very little and decreeing my story was inconsequential.

You are right to wonder if I feel that the Nothing threatens us, has for a long time, and that we lack enough weapons to fight back. However, I have more tools to defend myself, such as counseling, self-directed learning, and medication. You are also probably on the right track to think that the Nothing of modernity and the kind indicative of this hero's story are tethered to each other somehow. For all time, religion is the primary instrument humans use to protect against hopelessness. It is the ultimate answer for all of the big questions. Why is there suffering in the world if God is all-powerful and all-loving? Religion does reply and makes efforts to ease our minds, but the answers are not sufficient if they are some version of 'God works in mysterious ways.' For, in my interactions with religion, there are a whole bunch of questions that are resolved by not resolving them. That is, religion often obliges us to find peace in relegating the unknown to an inaccessible wisdom held by the supreme power. Then, we must be gladdened by the frustrating and forever non-answers.

It is no coincidence that around the turn of the twentieth century, religions and their promises became noticeably under attack from intellectuals. As the dehumanization of human beings increased, traditional means of repelling it grew less effective. It was the world in the midst of the Industrial Revolution, after all. Friedrich Nietzsche was one of the small cadre of intellectuals who shaped the modern mindset of the twentieth century. He was brilliant, original, and provocative. On this matter of infidelity to religion, Nietzsche wrote in 1882, "God is dead." Controversial for sure, but he meant that religion was no longer the axis on which our lives twist and turn. Christianity specifically did not hold a monopoly on the truths of our existence, and people were turning from God as the source of authority in their lives. By any measure, he was right. Though there had to be some force to which people would turn to avoid the Nothing, right?

I did not read Nietzsche or any other philosopher until much later, but I felt unmoved by religion as I knew it. My memories of religion are not wholly happy or sad. I clearly can think back to sitting in those long, uncomfortable pews scarred with penciled graffiti decorations, with Bibles and songbooks staring me in the face. They were not bad times at all, but I wished for faith and happiness to seize me and override all my doubts. Why did it not, I wondered? There was an emptiness that I avoided and only admitted to myself over these last few years. All this added a few more pages to that story in my head, where I was the hero from nowhere who refused the heroic journey. So, religion could not substitute for the things I had been unknowingly searching for.

In graduate school, thoughts from intellectuals like Henry Adams opened my eyes to a reckoning with my lack of faith. Texts like his deepened my wrestling match with the big questions that likely will never subside. Adams famously described a general shift away from religion around the turn of the twentieth century. He wrote *"The Education of Henry Adams"* as a memoir and account of lessons learned over a long and accomplished life. The part-time historian included a long section in his book called "The Virgin and the Dynamo." The Virgin stood for religion, but especially a passionate and ever-present kind of medieval faith. At the same time, the Dynamo represented the remarkable technology/scientific world of wonders of his present, best exemplified by the giant electric generator. Adams posited that one world, where he was now an old man, was giving way to some new one just barely taking shape.[13]

Both religion and technology had what he called a "force" of attraction, but religious zeal was being replaced by a confidence in science to explain the past and future. The faith people invested in Christianity, which once persuaded Europeans to build stunning, awe-inspiring cathedrals, was now directed toward the creation of a forty-foot-tall generator. Adams proposed that we trust science much like the committed Christian espouses belief in the Cross, because people cannot comprehend how the technology works. Both religion and science require faith, in other words. Force was the key word, because Adams did not judge people for being attracted to technology—it just was. Adams provided a glimpse into the future that one would have to admit contains much truth. Do we put as much trust in our religious rituals and prayer as we do in electricity to work or in medicine to cure? The answer seems a clear no. I believe Adams was commenting on humanity's unrelenting will to advance through its inventions. One sensed that Adams was not altogether pleased with this transfer of faith and passion. It was coming, though, irrespective of our wishes. Technology, however, has never been that holy grail of my imagination.

These are extraordinary times, and as I write this, there are robots, called AI, that act and do things as if they were human. We assume this is only the beginning and accept a future of unlimited potential for man-made machines to do, think, and who knows what. Those futuristic stories from decades past have come true without most folks noticing. Like Adams standing before the generator, we calmly receive this as: "it just is, oh well." The ultimate God-like achievement is the power to create life. Yet, we have been prepared and trained to read about the next remarkable scientific achievement, such as the person who witnessed her friend's weight loss one pound at a time. A truly scary future may be hurdling toward us faster than we can stretch out our arms to slow it. It is valid to wonder if we should or not. Although I am not good at predicting the future, I can now make some sense of my past and the hero's journey thus far.

For every technological accomplishment and for every new age of living at greater ease, there is an irretrievable loss of some kind. Our lifestyle today can only exist by conquering and displacing what came before, and this description pierces right to the heart of what modernity feels like to me. The world's present state has supplanted a less sophisticated but not necessarily inferior style of living. Professor of Geography Bruce Braun put it like this: "To be modern is to mourn."[14] No definition of life as we know it, to my knowledge, is so in accord with my sensibility on this subject and aligned with what I have felt but never articulated. If we claim that we are modern, we "live in a permanent condition of loss," but "this is an unrealized mourning in the sense that it remains unconscious." On that last part I am not convinced and believe we are quite conscious of what modernity gives us and takes away. Until finding the work of Braun, I could not link together a dull, aching loss within my spirit, my childhood, and the mental health/addiction struggle. Now it's clear, I have been in mourning. What is not plain to see, however, is gauging how healthy or unhealthy this is.

I believe I must be guilty of the sin of living in the past. In my case, there is no need for a trial; we can proceed directly to the sentencing phase. What is it that pains me so much that I miss it and grieve? Wordsworth also professed his mourning, as evident in his writings about the wonders of youth being replaced by adulthood. When does warm and breezy nostalgia stop, and when does a more sinister longing for the long-gone take over? It does not matter the era and whatever obstacles faced, as the passing of every chapter tears away at my soul. This is more than the tactics of the normal person who is a bit nostalgic, in my opinion. There is the positive side of my sensibility and then those regrets about my history that led me toward addiction.

Finally, I combined so much of what has influenced my life, and then realized how my career and mental health hurdles are both about mourning. I have been on a personal odyssey, where I found only unfulfilled expectations and an ever-increasing dread of the future. Some call that depression, or we might even define depression as the permanent state of mourning. Something was not right, and that young boy knew it. Even now, my incomplete childhood and stifling teenage years haunt me. In history, I followed the calling to study how people create identities while learning about the shifting landscape of modernity and how it can be unsettling. It must be that mourning comes naturally to the hero of this story. I believe I devoted myself to history because that was the only legitimate place to look for my future. The answers must be there, and the golden child must be involved.

It was my instinctive searching for meaning that led to an important new word: saudade. This is very recent. One could combine mourning and nostalgia and get somewhere close to this wonderful Portuguese word. Saudade is much more than my meager comparison, so I will try to focus on why it holds meaning for me. I can relate to thinking back on a part of my story that has passed away and mourning its loss. This is a significant aspect of who I am; at least, it is a big chunk of what motivates me. On a more abstract level, there is no English equivalent for the fear that something I yearn for is missing or was there but is now buried. It is sort of like a worry that the best things have already been handed out, and I did not show up for my portion.

I have always wondered how many people can sympathize with my innermost, guarded, and possibly weird thoughts. "Maybe the whole world is corrupted somehow, and it is not that you are just defective," I almost thought. There must be more out there like me; this was a very logical and sensible conclusion. For some, discontent probably washes over barely realized if at all, and for others, the "condition of loss" is more palpable. Jung said the "notion of modernity-as-loss that can be traced to the level of society is repeated at the level of the self." Now, we are talking about mental health. One result of modernity is the separation of "alienated" people from external nature and their inner nature. Then, following this logic, "what was needed was the recovery of the core of selfhood—the degree zero of the self still existed, timelessly residing in the unconscious."[15] So, the human quest to experience a return to nature before humans corrupt, pollute, and alter it is not unlike the reassertion of a core self, whole and attuned to our origins. I feel that the masses might share the same sentiment, and I simply cannot estimate how many relate to these principles.

What Jung wrote on the state of the world, I believe, applies to my journey and correlates with Braun's commentary. The great psychologist and master of the humanities noticed the effects of disappointments and disasters on the anxiety-ridden mindset of the twentieth century. Jung's conclusions were set against the backdrop of world events, with great wars and revolutions front and center in his mind. Jung attested that "the upheaval of our world and the upheaval of our consciousness are the same. Everything has become relative and therefore doubtful."[15] This basic observation has been stated many times, but it is particularly relevant to Psychology and mental health. Jung spent much of his long career discussing that information and those perceptions just beneath our ability to recognize them. Some can access that stored material more readily than others. So, mourning can be submerged within us with a few bubbles here and there that reach the surface. Alternatively, it can be more pronounced, depending on the individual and the circumstances.

I believe that what plagues the lead character of this narrative is, in some way, universal. Mourning is a term that describes my inner life, and we all know that what is inside eventually spills out with mixed results. Someone cannot endlessly trample down uncomfortable feelings. And the following is a true statement, and one that feels unhelpful to ignore. In another example of events-as-of-late coincidental, or seemingly so, Phil Collins' song "Take Me Home" is playing in the background. A computer program arbitrarily chose it, and not I. Now, so many meaningful and emotional songs come to mind that allude to the "back to home" idea. Ozzy has one, Blind Faith's "Can't Find My Way Home" is very good, and I am a fan of Edward Sharpe and the Magnetic Zeros and their song "Home," and there are many others we know that are not necessary to list. Inherent in this kind of artistic lament is a theme of mourning. Yes, without a doubt, either the creator or the listener (or both) must feel that grief. Very often, the artist hints that a return home is not possible, but desired even more so because of that fact. Alternatively, returning home is conceivable but arduous, as is the case with the hero's journey motif.

Returning home does not necessarily refer to the act of a human being physically going back to a specific location, of course. The allusion to home can be interpreted in a metaphorical sense and/or serve as a reference to reuniting with a person. I heard that saying "you can never go home again" from some early source and hoped this old saying was inaccurate. That breezy day, walking through a neighborhood, reappears now, and how it consoled and sparked a flirtation with belonging, origins, and roots. I still have a mournful spirit, and it continues to raise its hand, reminding me of the desire to rewind to my early childhood. It has to be a symbolic return, I suppose, but even so, sleeping dreams and frequent thoughts will not allow my imagination to forget the concept of time travel. Regardless, I presently cannot conjure any idea, and no single word as more representative of my mental health journey than mourning. I am downright romantic. And, while I have sorted through enough of my "stuff" to feel proud of this declaration, being romantic or nostalgic could work to my detriment.

I perpetually wish to return to what has been lost. It is safe to say that I have the romantic disease that I imagine many of my artist heroes also suffered with. No time in my life is safe from the romantic impulse to remember and mourn. Some people fear change, but to me, change is a form of tragedy. No part of my life has ever felt complete enough to move on like healthy people are supposed to do. Perfectionism plays a part, as I sense that each era of my past could have been something greater; however, the feeling is much deeper and profound than your typical 'could have's and' should have's. This is why I look for something like saudade, which is a better representation of what constant mourning feels like. Maybe I am foolish. Even so, this push and pull of loving and regretting my romantic DNA may be what makes this person a hero. In other words, all this might compose an identity I have been looking for.

Until recent years, I had not synthesized what I learned from the greatest minds in history with what I know about mental health. As a teen or close to it, he did not have ready access to the big ideas that later enthralled him. In his family setting, there were few books, no Internet until rather late, and even cable television was not possible for a long time. In nostalgic interludes, I recall visiting the store to rent both a V.C.R. and a movie to put in it. Anyway, it never occurred to him to read. Perhaps this state of affairs caused him to develop a rich imagination. Those youthful thoughts led to an unremitting conclusion that something about this world was just not right. He lacked the resources to relieve the troubling feelings. Simply put, he did not know where to go or what to do.

The longing to attach his soul to the transcendent consistently led to a sense of disillusionment. Once good music was found, the machine-created radio sounds hit his ear like nails on a chalkboard. Simple sing-alongs are alright for campfires and proms, but should not be confused with music that invigorates, haunts, and even saddens. These are all genuine reactions to living with humanness. Without trying, he noticed that people did not engage with one another honestly. Most everyday everything hinged on some fallacy, lie, or insincere agreement. The rituals of human meet and greets of every kind were just charades performed for the benefit of…who knows who or what. It probably did not help his popularity to be a deep thinker, and he can always remember being that way.

He is confident now that mourning played a role in wrenching sadness and then the excessive drinking. There was a thing he was looking for that he could never grasp. And, the more he tried to capture his grail, the more defeated he was. Not only did failure occur, but I could not envision any change making any difference. From this headspace, it is not unreasonable to reckon that living is no longer a thing to look forward to. This path could only lead him to a dark wilderness, indeed, even if his consideration of the big questions cleared a route to academia. I would like to include some passages from David Foster Wallace that are particularly illuminating. He recommended removing our self-interested obsession with the unimportant and reminded us of whatever we have lost in the modern world. Looking back, I believe life would have fallen lighter on my shoulders if any of this wisdom had been present. He said:

> The really important kind of freedom involves attention and awareness and
> discipline, and being able truly to care about other people and to sacrifice for

I do know that harboring feelings for a lost something, possibly an identity unearthed from the past, remained on his mind most of the time. High school cool never came his way, and he felt a distant separation from all cliques, large or small. His interests were always different. No one else residing on his planet cared about the few things that he did. Trying to introduce a teen to Muddy Waters was like teaching a person a new language for the first time. Video games were just games back then, not the alternate reality, life-consuming things they are now. There were no clubs (the kind you join) he could remember, except ones that probably had something to do with birdhouses. He had many heartaches, and still that enormous hole inside was left unfilled. More than wanting something, he was cognizant of the things he did not: almost everything he saw as the norm. The mundane grind of a nine-to-five life held no appeal. For the first half of his life, the hero leaned on academics to provide some sense of self.

What I am trying to explain is similar but not identical to what Jung called Individuation. It is a potentially lifelong process that requires hard work. It has been said that Individuation may never be concluded, and in fact, cannot be, due to the constant change over time. Individuation may be a continuous push and pull that forms a circle instead of a straight line. It is about becoming one's true self, including the dark aspects that linger in the unconscious known as the Shadow. To become whole and achieve the greatness within each person, someone must make peace with repressed feelings and, in my interpretation, unlearn what they have learned. By this, I mean do not settle for languishing in mediocrity, and do not choose a path that someone else has decided on for whatever reason. This could be too simplistic a summary, I realize. Spirituality is somewhere in there, I think, and so is identity, belonging, and mourning. I would like to include something from Nietzsche about shedding any skins that have been placed upon you, that you no longer want, and becoming your self. So, here it is:

> Any human being who does not wish to be part of the masses need only stop making things easy for himself...Every young soul hears this call by day and by night and shudders with excitement at the premonition of that degree of happiness which eternities have prepared for those who will give thought to their true liberation. There is no way to help any soul attain this happiness, however, so long as it remains shackled with the chains of opinion and fear... There is no drearier, sorrier creature in nature than the man who has evaded his own genius and who squints now toward the right, now towards the left, now backwards, now in any direction whatever.[17]

I needed schools of higher learning to begin learning about what made me unique. College work allowed me to think beyond the limitations of small-town life, where I had come up dreadfully short, and see the world with a wider view. So, like many folks, my fascination with the past was partially driven by a search for identity, which essentially boils down to asking: Who am I? The journey to find an identity began where most people initiate such things: wherever you are. Location determines a significant portion of the attributes and patterns that make a person who they are. This place and this age then constructs part of the culture that builds the identity of every person. The more I think about it, the clearer it becomes how history has become my professional calling.

Both history and my history must be consulted and compared to figure out "my stuff." The same goes for you, dear reader. Modernity produces mourning. I am convinced of this and hope to encourage you to believe it and reflect on its impact on our well-being. All kinds of movements and causes support my contention that our souls crave more than the ordinary. Whatever the soul is, I could not lie and claim it is not part of mental health. There are positive trends in food production, as well as a growing preference for organic eating. There is a very noticeable fascination with handcrafting. With a large portion of the population, old-fashioned methods of production are practically worshiped. All of it presupposes that, once upon a time, the products and necessities in our lives came to us via a more natural and pure way. Many people now reminisce about well-worn ways of doing things that have been supplanted by the cheap and easy. In my younger days, I don't recall much hoopla over antiques and worn-out collectibles. Some of the qualities that have always been missing from my life, such as fearless individuality, have drawn others to what I call romanticism; others might prefer a different name.

True romantics often use a keyword that registers in my life, yet one that is fraught with complexities: authenticity. People desire to eat naturally as a means to reconnect with a more authentic experience, which they suppose was once more common somewhere in the past. Sure, it is verifiably healthier, but the heartfelt motivation is the unspoken faith that organic equals pure, and pure is authentic, and that, yeah, this all amounts to healthier living. With everything, there is an origin. Take almost every interest, and there is an undiluted, authentic-ness to reclaim. That is the perception but usually the reality, as well. When asked to choose, I guess that most people opt for authenticity or profess that it is preferable to inauthenticity, because the latter evokes the word "fake" in our minds.

The greatest intellects have discussed the concept of authenticity many times, using varying terms and methods. It is a wonderful word, but elusive to capture for oneself. Because who knows what is authentic anymore under layer after layer of worldly obligations? After many months of reflection on topics like these, I concluded that I had pursued authenticity from a young age. Casting my vision backward to find some missing piece of myself is a very familiar thing. The failure to find it meant having no identity, wallowing in negativity (pessimism), and allowing the Nothing to take firm hold of my life. We who partake in life as it is currently constructed have the advantageous luxury of visiting romanticized worlds without having to stay there permanently. Most people would not repeat the undertaking of the transcendentalist Henry David Thoreau, who chose to live alone in nature for two years. He famously wanted to leave civilization to comprehend the meaning of life in all its authenticity.

I can mourn all I want while enjoying electricity, air-conditioning, and refrigerators.

Just because some demur at the threat of being classified as a Romantic, does not mean they are not exactly that. My father would never have consented to such a thing or understood what I meant by it. As you appreciate, dear reader, he represented the manly arts in actuality as part of his real life. Yet, I think he was a romantic. I know this because one thing that we could do together was watch old Westerns. Oh, and some I viewed many more times than I desired. However, I enjoy them too, and his favorites were not the revisionist, morally ambiguous Westerns, but rather films that, you guessed it, romanticized the West. On the TV set at Home, *Lonesome Dove* and the *Outlaw Josey Wales* were two that he always put down the remote for.

Like many modern people, my father subconsciously found fault with the present and looked to something that reminded him of a better time. I believe most people locate a nostalgic time in their history, or History as a whole, and try to reconnect with it somehow. Therefore, people are in mourning in different ways. Everyone I know has a grievance with the modern world and imagines that people were more authentic sometime in a previous era. For my dad, Westerners glorified a lifestyle close to the land, where men roamed free of most laws and regulations, and virtues like justice and loyalty still mattered. Classic Westerns promise a world where good men are brave and common sense prevails in small communities. Cities and desk-bound work are, by definition, excluded as inappropriate for a real person. Villains are individuals or institutions that disrupt the natural order, and they ultimately lose. My dad was more emotionally invested in these things than he ever made public. So, his interest in Westerns went beyond enjoying a story, and my fascination with history was more than academic. We are both romantics, like many people in the modern world, and we share a sense of loss. As a person familiar with History, I know that no time was as great or as straightforward as we sometimes prefer to think, but my emotions often rule my mind more than logic.

My father probably would not have liked a film that is almost perfectly illustrative of my romantic mind: *Dead Poets Society*. Like *The NeverEnding Story*, there was an attraction to the film's themes and messages before I could articulate why. Robin Williams (Mr. Keating) plays the type of teacher I wish had taught some class early in my life. He is the main character who ventures to a very strict, prominent, uniformed school for boys. Williams shined brightly in this kind of role, and I think he was made to play it. Keating brings unbridled enthusiasm and an outsider's willingness to bend the rules for the sake of those in his classes. We see that another person is leading the class before Keating arrives, who is gruff and stuffy, instructing the kids about poetry as if it were building a birdhouse. He is completely by-the-book and commands that students assign a ranking to poems using a numbering system. It is overly scientific and boring, viewers quickly learn. However, the new teacher is the opposite of this old, balding one in every way. Poetry is too personal and expressive for some emotionless rating, Keating tells his class. He urges the boys to rip out the pages of this lesson from the textbook. The boys initially look around the room in shock but then follow the instructions. Everything about this class will be experimental, and Keating challenges the system repeatedly.

The film is both about romanticism as a movement and expresses it through the characters and storyline. Keating does not mind that the boys sneak out at night, very much disregarding the rules, and read poetry to one another. The clandestine get-togethers are the "Dead Poets' Society" of the title. Most of all, students learn about poetry from the Romantics and are encouraged to create and recite their own. There is even a reference to carpe diem (seize the day) that figures prominently in the plot. The leader of the Dead Poets' Society is Neil, who aspires to be an actor. Neil lands a lead role in a school play, but his domineering father forces his son to forsake the arts in favor of becoming a doctor. The dad does not care at all about the frivolous world of self-expression. Keating, of course, encourages Neil to chase his dreams.

Ultimately, Neil commits suicide because he is forbidden to live in accordance with his heart, and the cranky headmaster fires Keating. Before leaving, all the students stand on their desks and recite Walt Whitman's poem "Oh Captain! My Captain!" Romanticism wins and rigid formality loses. Inner-discovery wins and material success loses. Emotion wins and logic loses. It must be stated that suicide can be a very romantic thing, *symbolically*, when it is portrayed in art. Romeo and Juliet taught us that long ago.

I am not Neil, and my life was not his, but I have often imagined a different childhood for myself. There was never a Mr. Keating around who might have pushed me in the right direction. This movie can be grating because it is told so purely from a wide-eyed romantic's perspective. Many moons ago, I desperately needed some inspiration to experiment with the unknown and tap into my artistic side. It would have helped if someone had simply told me it was all right to be different, original, and myself. Perhaps I could have learned about my hero's journey earlier and known what things to pursue and what to ignore. In the story I was living, there should have been some major revelation that set a young man on a course toward greater peace and confidence in his purpose. I'm unsure whether I have a deficiency in accepting reality, or if I try to avoid it, or if neither is true. Certainly, I do not want to dismiss the inner calling of these things, intellectual and artistic, which are crucial to my existence. I wish to no longer be at war with myself, which is what Neil's father was asking him to do. Maybe Neil did not want to mourn being something he was not for the rest of his life. Like I have done, he did not wish to live miscast in the story of his life. I believe I must continue to indulge these parts of myself, whatever the cost.

Learning about myself, mental health, education, and really bad experiences brought me to a place of greater self-consciousness. It seems finding out who you are is so vital to revealing you to you, and me to me, that identity must be considered an invaluable aspect of mental health. As now seems obvious, I want to attest that a full-person approach to healing is necessary for all human beings. My holy grail might be good mental health, free of addictions, for now and forever. And in my non-humble point of view, this must be done by restoring the soul of the man or woman. Knowing myself, the usual coping mechanisms are good but will inevitably fail. My constant and primary hope every day is that knowledge will lead to enough contentment to ensure my story is not a tragedy. Happiness? Not sure if it is possible.

For whatever reason, while still young, the hero felt certain indescribable things that needed a means of expression. Looking to the past for some sense of self merely worked halfway. Only recently have I come to realize that my historical interests were more than just curiosities about old things. A longing for answers to the big questions greatly affected my studies and my teaching career thus far. I should inform you that I labored over whether or not to include the last two words of the previous sentence, as adding those words presumes that there is yet more of a career to come. More than anyone understands, I hope this is true and not false optimism. You should know that my life took a terrible turn, and I made some great mistakes that endangered my career. This is still true. In general, I avoid this and want to right now. Everyone is in mourning in our world. I think this is a permanent condition, and I cannot imagine how a mentally healthy person can avoid it. Maybe the key is harnessing it.

The commentary in this chapter, which wrestles with rewriting my life story, became possible only after a grave crisis. The wrong road, the road of excess that brought me right up to the brink, I called "The Darkness." And I honestly did say those words out loud or in my head, daily. Those words were reassuring. I must confess it was a guilty pleasure, mind and body numbing, and a high. There is more, but that is enough for right now. I like that term "the brink." Many scholars have used it or something similar to symbolize a transformation that carries a person to the edge of nothingness, only to emerge as something new. Looking back now, maybe reaching the brink was necessary to advance to a better place. I love what Ernest Becker wrote here, and hope any passages from my mind compare favorably to this:

> Man breaks through the bounds of merely cultural heroism; he destroys the character lie that had him perform as a hero in the everyday social scheme of things; and by doing so he opens himself up to infinity, to the possibility of cosmic heroism, to the very service of God. His life thereby acquires ulti-

> mate value in place of merely social and cultural, historical value. He links his secret inner self, his authentic talent, his deepest feelings of uniqueness, his inner yearning for absolute significance, to the very ground of creation. Out of the ruins of the broken cultural self there remains the mystery of the private, invisible, inner self which yearned for ultimate significance, for cosmic heroism. This invisible mystery at the heart of every creature now attains cosmic significance by affirming its connection with the invisible mystery at the heart of creation. This is the meaning of faith... The truly open person, the one who has shed his character armor, the vital lie of his cultural conditioning... is absolutely alone and trembling on the brink of oblivion – which is at the same time the brink of infinity.[18]

My brain sired these words: The Darkness, as a term representing drinking at night until I was not able to consume any more. Much of it cannot be remembered but lasted with a few stops and starts for roughly ten years. It was an everyday (night) occurrence. Once past sundown, no other person was awake to judge or criticize. It was quiet, and it was my time. There was no light at all, except for the dim kind from a computer screen. No matter how downtrodden I felt, embarrassed and thrown away after the d-word happened, there was something to look forward to. Oh, the pain or disappointment might be unbearable right now, but no matter because "I have The Darkness." I didn't dream at all, and blackouts marked most nights. Waking up was never greeted very happily. If enough of my favorite time of day were left, I would start again in the dark. Even then, I was trying to control time. I have always been unhappy when the night turns to morning.

In my childhood days, there was nothing to tempt me toward the dark side. My parents never smoked or drank anything except sweet tea and diet cola. At any place where family met, for any reason, one could bet on the absence of alcohol. Drugs were never mentioned. No person I recall talked about anything that was not family-friendly. It was almost as difficult to find the wild side of life away from family gatherings. I remember the rare occasion when a schoolmate invited me on a journey across the state to a basketball game. Of course, I was hesitant, but I gathered the courage to say yes, thinking I might be part of something more fun than the normal blahs. Sadly, the boy driving the car was not approved of by the rulers of my household, and the potential trip was vetoed. I did not go. Perhaps that was right, but at the time it left the young man very frustrated. He knew this was a chance to do whatever kids did to have fun, and part of that rulebook explaining how to be a person might be revealed.

I never found that book, but eventually some kind of "medicine" will find each of us. I mean, people can only carry sadness around so long before something is sought to lighten the load. The beginning of drinking was not like a Hollywood movie or what many people imagine as the norm. Culture repeatedly transmits this idea that stress or trauma drives people to the bottle. Can that happen? Certainly, though my stress seemed to have no start and no end. All the various negative feelings were always present, as if they were inherent from birth. No special incident or upsetting memory set the stage for the alcohol problem.

I never needed much of a reason for doing what became like a ritual. Getting to that state of intoxication made me free, and I am not sure I had ever felt that way before. My mind slowed until it reached a state of comfort, so why wouldn't I continue reaching for that tranquility as often as possible? In the mid and latter stages of addiction the calm begins to fade a little and then the excuses start for prolonging what addicts do to themselves. And, all addicts can relate to what I am about to say. A good day deserves a celebratory drink or three, and a bad day needs the same prescription to mitigate our woes. Holidays and special days of every kind require us to pick up that drink or whatever the substance might be. I knew this was true, having seen such things in movies and on television. Weekends, too, must be thought of as the perfect time to forget about working hours and enjoy one's favorite spirits. Soon enough, every day is a drinking day.

I graduated to severe levels of drinking without wasting much time. A little was alright, but the warm glow one receives will end, and the hero was afraid to lose it. So he learned a really simple trick to maintain it: overwhelm your body with huge volumes of booze. And, beer was fine and tasted good, he realized. Although the harder stuff does the job more efficiently, and who cares about taste in this kind of pursuit, anyway? The quest to connect to something beyond day-to-day trivialities, to immerse my being in something intense, and to escape unhappiness and worry, was found in The Darkness. At least, it was the best and closest solution discovered so far. Once his body was saturated with a drug, it was exceedingly hard to stop and comparably easy to maintain some in his system. Once he stopped all at once and hoped to sleep. Instead, his mind kept jerking his tired body awake, again and again, until morning. Ending my commitment to this substance was simply inconceivable.

Shame is a factor that motivates the use of strong drink and also is a consequence of it. Alcoholics Anonymous lists resentment as one of the strongest inducements to start or continue an addiction. It seems that I resented myself much more than I had negative feelings toward another person. It is similar to regret, and I have plenty of those as well. To summarize, I have never forgiven myself for not being a whole person. Shame has always been there and begins to accumulate in the aftermath of the myriad of drinking-related incidents. So, the more shame I felt, the less I cared about it. I know some of my peers find it necessary to frequent a variety of liquor stores so as not to appear to have a serious problem. In other words, making purchases at one place of business twice in one night, or on successive days, or occasions close to one another, loudly announces the unmistakable impression of alcoholism. Some care about that, but that concern got worn out and discarded somewhere along the way. As I said, one can get numb to various embarrassments once gone far enough away from the normality of polite society. To make the point in a slightly different way, having no self-worth (self-resentment) prompts a person to discard the things that once mattered.

Resentments of the past could not be contained and raged in my mind and soul. It has taken until now to assess the hero in this way, so he has mostly been operating without all the facts. His misery had a source that goes a long way toward explaining his Otherness. Even to this very day, there is some part of his mind that replays the what-if questions. He mourned missed opportunities that, like with Dorothy and her friends, were always there for him. One day, he woke up and felt old, as if he had not lived, with time itself opposed to him. Why the drinking? Why all the wasted days? Now I can say that the "hero" had not faced his real enemies. He was hiding away from disorders of both the mind and the spirit. The first part of restoring mental health is knowing thyself. This did not occur and is still ongoing.

Dear reader, I want to devote a little space to explain the lowlights of what it means to be addicted to alcohol and go without it and/or try to cease drinking. Withdrawal from drinking is possibly the most dangerous among all the drugs, and every one of them has its distinct wrath. You can die from alcohol withdrawal, quickly and easily. I would put a couple of gallons of liquor in my system every two days during The Darkness. So keep that in mind, and also please be aware how I lacked all understanding of withdrawal when first suffering its effects. Heavy drinking shatters the body's natural sleep modulation, and I routinely went days without any rest at all.

Trying to recover from The Darkness was like healing from being hit by a car, and it took a few days. Both inside and out, every inch of my body felt dry, and nothing but time made that improve in the slightest. My hands felt as if skin had been replaced by sandpaper. My insides cried out for water, yet drinking water made me feel worse. I was also hungry, but eating anything caused severe nausea. I did not feel good lying down, often in urine, but felt much worse in any other position, so I stayed mostly still staring up at the ceiling. Hallucinations can be terrifying. The worst of them were the voices and scary faces. I recall demons and monsters that manifested on the wall, dissipated back into the wall, changed a little, and then reformed again in cycles over hours. I might hear singing or chanting. One awful night at a mental hospital, some kind of pep rally was underway with a band playing right outside the walls. I have heard and seen things all my life, but nothing at all on par with fighting through addiction. Amid the worst of it, I had no idea if I had slept or not, because how could I tell if this was happening or was a nightmare? This is some of the worst stuff, but there is much more.

There was a several-month-long period that I somehow survived while believing all sorts of things that were not real. The following all took place while tending to my classes. I did not have a real bed, and the man now cannot understand why he felt undeserving of this basic privilege. So, I was trying but not succeeding in sleeping on a cheap (the cheapest) mattress on the floor. Every night, an army of bugs attacked him, mainly his upper body. There was endless scratching every night, all night. I was so bothered by this as to scrape the skin on my arms up into an ugly, bloody mess. It looked like the outcome of an animal attack. Also, I was certain that bugs were inside my skin. Seeking advice on how to neutralize these pests, I found the strongest kind of insect spray which promised to be effective. I sprayed everything on my mattress and bedded down before realizing I would be saturated with whatever pesticide chemicals. So, that caused me to burn in many places. While out and about, tiny spots on the floor began to get up and walk around, and there was other stuff along these lines. When driving, I couldn't tell if it was a garbage can, a man, or one of Satan's mercenaries. As you have rightly deduced, dear reader, these things were all products of my unwell mind.

My next statement may not be popular. Non-addicts cannot know what it means to feel irredeemably addicted. It is not a matter of intelligence or effort; it just is that way. In the population, there is an abundance of both the sympathetic and the other crowd who see addiction as weakness, and I cannot say which group is larger. You will meet many more than one person who will wonder aloud or silently: why can't you just stop doing that? Like, just don't anymore. I have a preferred illustration of addiction for those who want to know more. Imagine that you are a sick person who is in severe pain and in the hospital. Doctors are treating the illness using methods that are not working well enough. They tell you over and over to be patient. As you lie crumpled in the hospital bed suffering, you notice a bottle of medication just beyond your reach and somehow are aware that it can end your pain. It is not a cure, but it will almost instantly turn down the dial of your suffering until it reaches zero. That healing medicine is effective for a few hours to several days. The only thing is, the doctor and everyone you know agree that you should not drink down the medicine under any circumstances. Yet, there it is, you can easily see it. If we are talking about drinking specifically, then you might say your medicine is available wherever you go.

In the addiction/mental health community, the misadventures, accidents, anecdotes, and troubles that come as part of using substances are called "war stories." Perhaps others use a different set of words, but it was introduced to me this way. Depending on where you are in life, a story might cause laughter. Generally, that is not the correct approach. So, to think about it, I suppose when former airplane pilots get together, they can chuckle over mishaps that were quite dangerous. That is an example, but addiction is not a profession, and war stories cannot function as in the case above.

So, yes, I have war stories, but for now, I prefer to limit how many I share. Few, if any, may be told, and I do not know yet. Among addicts, and I do not care what your addiction is, there is an unspoken understanding that stuff done in the name of your drug causes suffering. The longer it goes on, the more stories one has that end somewhere between embarrassing and tragic. Therefore, there is no need to ramble on or even mention most of that. Once using started to put me in uncomfortable situations, the self-imposed restrictions for what is tolerable lowered, and then fell again each time. In other words, for some, what is acceptable to go through changes as one encounters each shameful incident. A person thinks, hmm, might as well keep rolling downhill. This way, a good person can slip to the bottom.

What I am doing now, the act of reliving and writing about harrowing times, is not easy. I consider this one of the hardest undertakings of my life. I was a teacher concurrently with most of what I have been telling you, from the age of 24 onward. I functioned for a long time and managed to do my work very well, and everyone said so. But an addict can function fine until he doesn't, and that stark reality comes calling for one and all, eventually. Being an addict with any kind of normal life is like living on borrowed time. The clock begins to count down, the sand through the hourglass, and one has a finite amount of time left before the bomb detonates. A drug is the ultimate liar, making you promises it cannot keep. A drug, or any addiction, such as shopping, eating too much, too little, and the rest, is rabidly jealous of every other thing not like it. Your addiction will not stop until it removes everything else except what it loves. Then it will end with your end.

For what seemed a very long time, The Darkness was the hero's most trusted friend. While pretending to be far less damaged than I was, I went on reenacting the same scene with similar results. I can now see how The Darkness stood for much more than a time of day. Indeed, it was a life of giving up and giving in. No longer did I resist any aspect of the drug's call. It had me in the way that many of you are familiar with. Whatever your "Darkness" is, when you are fully submerged, you are owned by some invasive thing more expansive and powerful than yourself. It is like a reverse spirituality, one that turns all the hopes and good-natured parts of humanity into lies. If there is a devil, I bet he schemes to invert our inner world, or the soul if you prefer, to make us see the good as the bad and vice versa. I certainly did not know why I was doing all of this except that a d-word had left me ripped open and very hurt.

I was mourning in this way, but in other ways not then apparent to the hero. Yet, relationships end every day, and some people do not even mind and are happier as a result. There was much more. It was a grudge with the world that I had never confronted and never made peace with. Nothing made me feel like a real person. That was the real enemy at work. The Darkness was bound to come, as I am convinced that it would have arrived anyway, wearing some costume. There was rebellion in my system, unused and impatient. I had this creative side, so elemental to who I am, yet it was never developed or even taken seriously. Everything took a toll on my mind. Like happens every day, darkness arrives at a prescribed time, then slowly intrudes, then creeps ever blacker until one is enveloped by it.

It finally occurred to me that I had been gaslighting myself for so long, having told myself a false story about my origins and identity. I was looking for something in my personal story that may not be there. In place of something heroic, I reinforced the notion of being an intruder among the ordinary, real people. Still, the search continued. History was the first outlet found that might supply me with an identity and purpose. There were promising leads, but ultimately, it was all disappointment. My holy grail was still far from my reach. I believe that when this happens to a person, they will try to fill the giant hole in their life with something else. It may be a temporary solution, but it will never last forever. A new sentiment arose in my head, only in the years of crisis and recovery, that I must destroy myself—along with the remnants of poisonous habits—to create something better and new. Maybe it was time to tear up the old script. However, I would just become like Dorothy, the full expression of the person the universe intended me to be. I wasn't there yet, though. Much more work and pain had to take place.

CHAPTER 5:

Dreams

"Almost anybody can learn to think or believe or know, but not a single human being can be taught to feel. Why? Because whenever you think or you believe or you know, you're a lot of other people: but the moment you feel, you're nobody-but-yourself. To be nobody-but-yourself — in a world which is doing its best, night and day, to make you everybody else — means to fight the hardest battle which any human being can fight; and never stop fighting."[19]

My vision was blurred, so I couldn't recall everything clearly. I know the feeling of something urgent and serious gripping me and propelling me forward. There was some unrealized reason we were not to tarry and move swiftly toward some important place. What? Where? I did not know these answers. There was a gravel country road.It was somewhat curvy but not overly so. My sister and my mom were with me, and they were equally convinced that hurrying was the right approach. There was a flourishing green forest on both sides of the road and nothing else. I also know that there was very green grass, about a week away from needing to be mowed, on the ground. We traveled in some kind of vehicle, but I have no memory of it at all. I am certain, though, that the car broke down and had to be abandoned. So, for a while, the three of us walked at near-top speed toward something significant.

This went on for a while, and then we arrived. It was an old, distinguished church. It could have been a cathedral, and I am not able to say why, but it was historic and worthy of some special status designating it was not just another church. We all had the same sensation of arriving at a destination that had called to us, as we approached the front door. Then there was a surprising twist. I am not sure if the door had a cross or a name written on it, but thinking about it now, it was most likely the name of the church. It was crossed out with a big red X, resembling graffiti done with paint, in a way that made it impossible for me to read what was underneath. Above it, and I assumed the role of leader at this point, in big red letters was written: Hannah. Stunned and fearful, I figured a red X meant that some evil cult was at work. Most likely, it was a satanic group. I informed my companions that it was time to leave. We ran away. Very blurry now, I noticed some hoodlums straggling about the area, and then it was over.

This dream stayed with me as none other has in my life. At the time, I did not know how memorable and still possibly influential it would become. All my years, my dreams have been more than the norm, but I really cannot say for sure. As far as I know, highly involved, strange dreams might be so common as to deserve no mention. Yet, my gut feeling tells me that, based on my experiences in this world and conversations with people, my dreams have been especially indelible and rare. Dreams are such that words fail to convey what you felt and made perfect sense while dreaming, so it is hard to talk about them when awake. Many events and people reminded me of that dream for roughly one year after it happened. I am still waiting to see if the dream has any more to tell me, now. Other dreams, too, have left me stupefied, as I try to figure out what they reveal and why they recur. Not all dreams come to us while sleeping, as well.

I'm not sure about you, but I have never been one to have much interest in signs and prophecies. I have never had faith that life unfolds according to a plan and that things happen for a reason. But faith is something that had to enter my life for it to get better and become closer to who I am. I had never paid attention to horoscopes until the last few years when

I realized I am an Aquarius. This sign seems to kind of fit me in that very vague astrology kind of way. We have all heard that when a person tells their story, it can be understood as a pattern leading to something great, once viewed from the end instead of the beginning or middle. Inspirational over-comer stories tend not to be inspirational for this guy.

The reality is that I can see a pattern in most things and make sense out of terrible life events once they are past and I'm living in the good times. I bet you can too. So, I guess I don't pay attention when someone expresses a belief like this. The classic debate of whether life is random or ordered is one of the most profound questions. It has many other related quandaries, such as the one that considers why bad things happen to good people. It seems to me that tragedy can enter your life without any apologies, ushering us toward some outcome that was "meant to be." Life doesn't have to make sense. Yet, I can see very easily why human beings want to believe that it does, especially the bad stuff we endure.

Perhaps I can believe that mistakes, disappointments, and great losses can all mean something if we choose to see it that way. I have been told over and over in the mental health system that we can pick how we feel and respond to undesired circumstances. So, perhaps it is feasible to believe that I can assert meanings out of whatever life's roll of the dice offers up. For now, I think this is alright to feel. By now, you know I am pessimistic, and to that, I will add being one of the ye who have little faith. What I have been doing is piecing together a story worthy of a hero, one that spans many years of ups and downs. But, you know what? I now see evidence of dwelling too much on the negative to the point of being blinded to the life that was transpiring in front of me. At the same time, I had a very limited capacity to handle life until I received the proper kind of treatment. Recently, there have been instances that, when taken together, may add up to make sense despite the presence of a lot of negativity and pain.

Out of many realizations bordering on the profound, one has been recognizing that I have lived life backward, My revelation highlights how serious, responsible, and studious I was as a young man, and then the trouble in mid-life, which has now given way to a more useful and unproblematic approach to rebelling. I did not revolt in any meaningful way as a teenager and was unaware that it was possible and allowable to be myself. That knowledge came very late. I am convinced, without needing any peers to evaluate this, that it is essential to helm life's stages correctly and in order. One should be energetic and risk-taking, as well as doubting and world-weary, at the appropriate times. Another way of stating what I mean comes from a Bob Dylan song, where the singer proclaims, "I was so much older then, I am younger than that now." I always enjoyed those lyrics, but now I realize what they mean to me. Another effect of living backward is reacting to life's milestones with inappropriate and confused emotions. That is similar to expressing regret for not appreciating moments as they come.

In 2011, I walked to the stage for my final graduation, but not with the exuberance one associates with such an occasion. Certainly, earning a Ph.D. is a dream for anyone who first undertakes such an intimidating task. It was hard-earned and well-deserved, as I made straight A's in graduate school. My parents were there, and so was my academic advisor and mentor, Dr. Phelps. One must wear specific regalia, such as a cap and gown, denoting a doctorate recipient and not a person receiving a lesser degree. I had not walked in any graduation since being forced to at the end of high school. These ceremonies are dreadfully long and boring, in case you did not know. There is a speaker who makes clichéd pronouncements about how we can make our dreams come true and have the world at our fingertips, and so on. There I was, sitting next to my major professor, who had been there from the beginning of graduate school. My name was called after several hours, and of course, I made my way to the stage. This should have felt like the pinnacle of my educational career and a reward for the countless hours of work I had put in.

I felt relieved, but not proud or celebratory. It seems as if there should have been a party or something, but I cannot remember even telling anyone about it. I think impostor syndrome was at work. Kirk was unable to feel worthy of such an honor and downplayed its significance. This was a notable example of him not giving himself credit, feeling he somehow was not good enough to deserve it, and silently predicting there would be bad things to come. What was next, he wondered? In hindsight, the reaction was strange. He did not feel fast-tracked on the highway of success at all. It was depressing to attain the goal, like a letdown. The hero had trouble describing exactly what was going on at the time. The best he can do, right now, is to relate his disappointment that the culmination of such a lengthy student career was an emptiness that, well, that is all there is. Maybe an expectation was there that a wave of answers to the big questions would somehow flood his mind. It is possible the hope was there that some sage or even Phelps himself would reassure him that "now, you are part of the club, we can tell you all the secrets of the universe." If you are saying to yourself this was a very odd thing to think, the hero understands. It must be a sign of poor mental health.

My identity should have been set in stone: a scholar and teacher of the Humanities. Let me make it known that I have an extremely high regard for the Humanities and its teachers. Over the last two years, this admiration has grown, and I can only think of a few professions more vital to living. Yes, the reality is the opposite of what those who disdain the impractical arts, such as History or Literature, believe. We need such things to be whole. It may be this very respect that prevented Kirk from considering himself a part of the intelligentsia. So, I did not look upon myself as one of the gang of very smart and thoughtful teachers of the collected letters, books, poems, speeches, theisms, political commentaries, etc. of the world's greatest minds of all time. I should have. But those folks sound smarter, grew up smarter, and probably were smarter, I told myself. It would have been true to remind instead that: "your colleagues are smart in ways you are not, but you are smart in some ways they are not. There is plenty of room at the table." Again, a time machine would be useful.

Once, a person in the scholarly arts told me I should lose my southern accent to advance in academia. Then, I calmly considered if this advice had any merit. As of today, I hate that person and everything the rec-ommendation represents. Having spent most of my life in Alabama and

Mississippi, I have come to understand that a stigma is attached to that region. Many people I met were sons or daughters of professors or had backgrounds that privileged them to pursue an intellectual life. Yes, to some, having no accent sounds smarter; it is true. I no longer care or have any Fs to give. One must be proud of their heritage, and I am surer of that than of most other things.

For the sake of the story I am telling now, it must be explained that a university is like an island of liberal thought. And I attended a school in Mississippi so the island analogy might be even more apt. No matter the location, a university or college represents a sanctuary for ideas and opinions that might not be safeguarded the minute one leaves school grounds. And by liberal, I mean classical liberalism and not any current set of political preferences. To provide a more helpful explanation, I should explain that an area, county, state, or region might be opposed to free thought and even dangerous to those points of view that are freely expressed and protected on campus. In such an environment, the hero excelled and learned a great deal about ideas and people from foreign lands previously unknown to him. He liked it even though, admittedly, he could be uncomfortable in this or any other setting.

Dear reader, you should also know that he always had a divided self, being partly an intellectual and also a common-sense, southern boy. To be honest, I enjoy being the person who my immediate company finds most surprising. Whatever the case, he lived in both worlds, going back and forth between them and not always with ease. I suppose the main objective here is for you to understand that I never truly felt part of either crowd. I am always too much for one thing and not enough for another. For some reason, this revealed itself more than ever at the moment he departed graduate school. In the hero's journey, with his mission complete and triumphant, the hero is supposed to bring back a gift or power to his community of origin. Although, I do not feel this took place at that time.

Things were falling apart around him during the very days he completed graduate school. The weight of the world was already pressing down on him. Three major events happened around the same time, and the other two were not good at all. He wishes he had assumed the identity of a doctor, one that rightfully belonged to him, but that just did not happen. A historically disastrous tornado outbreak occurred in April 2011. It was very scary. No need to say much other than he was near the center of the storm but did not sustain any bodily injuries.

The disaster of all disasters was the beginning of the end of his marriage, which struck the hero like a guided missile soon after his graduation. The decline and termination of the paper-thin binding that holds together modern marriage took roughly a year to reach completion. He was informed that this was going to transpire regardless of his opinions, and he tried everything that came to mind to forestall it given his limited experience. The hero was turned inside-out as his closely-guarded secret, of having an internal wounding, was exhibited for public display. Nothing could be held in. Final execution was delayed but could not be prevented. He had no appetite for eating or for life at all for many years. It is not accurate to say the d-word brought out the worst in him, as the real culprit was not getting help for his disease over such a long time. And the disease has many names and dwells in him in multiple forms.

The hero was becoming an addict, as his world was collapsing around him. I use the word addict, even though various other people in the addiction community disagree with me using that word. In response, I couldn't care less. I am an addicted person by nature, and through the convergence of whatever causes and effects assign a person a package of parts composing the total. Addiction is not a thing you have, it is a thing you are. The addiction exists beyond and separate from the urge to consume strong drink. I never saw it coming my way or wanted it to happen. You may or might not be aware how addiction sneaks up and overwhelms a person until that person wakes up one day and says, What the ###!? Addiction lays claim to victims using a predictable set of tools, but plenty of elements are distinctive to my experiences.

I believe marriage took place too soon for the highest chance at success. He was extremely stressed all the time, attempting to balance a personal and professional life, teach, earn an income, and complete his full-time job of dissertation and degree work. Our situation was neither stable nor well-planned. He was not well-armed at all for this fight, and you could say he was totally unprepared for the coming war. In his dreams, marriage sealed the deal on happiness and guaranteed him all that had been lacking. Once enacted, I felt it was okay to put a huge check mark next to marriage with a nice, bright ink pen. As someone once uttered too soon: "mission accomplished."

No imagined scenario existed where marriage was to condemn him to further privations. Before the disaster became unavoidable, the student, in his mid-twenties, learned that drinking was alright and just part of the world of professional adults. It was fine to happen socially, just as it was allowable to go out to places, preferably with friends, and have drinks and a good time. It happened once and then again, almost as if it was expected. There was no condemnation of drinking, and it was not a signif-icant issue. This was far removed from the mentality of his young training, when drinking was odd, immoral, and conspicuous. The downfall of his dream did not help matters, as is obvious.

In the public arena, there is a wink and a laugh that goes along with drinking that does not exist concerning other drugs. At least, this is true of the public, professional, intellectual, and worldly lifestyles of the modern era. A different kind of sensibility permeates the villages of the Nowhere, South. There are people primarily led by a conservative religious ethic and others who watch the stock market and know, and can pronounce, the different varieties of sushi—and the two groups do not agree on the amount of acceptable sin. Yes, this is an oversimplification. Anyway, the young man's experience with drinking at first was somewhat endearing and typically occurred during social outings with friends.

Intoxication and what comes with it is not memorable among the sushi crowd. Falling, passing out, and even causing a scene are alright at the beginning stage of addiction. He was not mean or boisterous. He did not turn into a monster and get angry, at least with over-amounts that are still fairly reasonable and sane. Rather, the effect was to slow him down, numb him, and make him very forgetful of all things unpleasant.

Unfortunately, the hero had numerous unpleasant thoughts and real-life concerns during the period of approximately 2010-2011. Drunken episodes make good stories. These stories are necessary for familiarity with the manly arts of adulthood. With certain professions, it is a given that you drink, and the only question is: What kind of liquor do you prefer? Someone may or may not inquire if you are a beer man or have a preference for the hard stuff. Both are okay, but the hard stuff will likely increase your status among groups of professional men.

These were new rules from the handbook of life that he did not know existed, and he began without practically any information about drinking. So, he had little experience with late-night, bar-carousing and was uninformed about the differences in the varieties of alcohol, and so did not know what he was doing. It was the equivalent of falling into the pool headfirst, eyes closed. When people casually discussed categories of alcohol, name brands, kinds of mixed drinks, tequila, liquor stores, and such, he nodded along and hid his ignorance. "Oh yeah, of course I know what Scotch is," he might have said. He had alcohol before as a teen, but these dalliances were few and child's play compared to the coming storms. It happened as an undergraduate once, and the hangover was so bad he swore not to do that again. By the way, oath-making and breaking grew commonplace later on for him. With all this said, he would learn enough of the places and practices of drinking to be a professional. Having never participated in the fun college phase of life, he entered young professional-hood as a neophyte, unarmed for both the good and bad times.

For a time, alcohol was a fun and experimental thing. I at first limited my consumption to the weekends. When one crosses that barrier, it serves as a mile marker and can be the start of a downward spiral. I was not one for most bars and clubs (the kind you go out to). As more or less a hermit, it is not shocking that these places would not feel welcoming. There was a lot of noise, some dancing, and incomprehensible social interactions. In no way could going to the club produce any result for me other than loneliness and embarrassment.

But I was married now. Since I had no personal life previously, gaining one looked like a normal and even positive development. There were most often people known from graduate school in attendance, and Gwen was always there. She knew these rules well enough. I should mention that Gwen was neither from the South nor ruled by a conservative religious tradition, and she knew a great deal about every kind of sushi. She was my chaperone, companion, and interpreter. Therefore, this period of going out was filled with plenty of harmless fun and endless stories. Of course, a strong drink loosens up an inhibited person. But, I did not care that much for socializing, so the novelty of that did not last long.

What comes next might be familiar and repetitive if you are a veteran addict or know something about the life. That covers most human beings. I hope it is not just the same old' story, as I do not wish just to stack more regurgitation on top of the pile. No one wants addiction, and some cannot see it coming. I did not, whatsoever, and never even thought of the possibility of becoming an addict. Much like with the d-word, it was not on my radar. I am the type to believe that if drinking feels good every time, and I partake in it part of the time, why not do it more and feel good all the time? At this point, there were mixed drinks, beer, and a wide variety of liquors. Going out was novel and promised good times. This was the first time in Kirk's life when socializing was a consistent and innocuous activity. This is what real people did, and he was aware of this fact.

I think George Carlin said something in the ballpark of what I am about to write, but I am not sure. Some people begin drinking and reach a point where the pain and sickness that follows alcohol surpasses the good feeling, and these folks quit. Then there are the smaller but still substantial numbers of people who walk or crawl through hardships but do not quit. As you might know, the bad stuff gets worse and worse, but addicts keep going while thinking: "Well, I have gotten through the worst of it." So, I am one of those people. I began to learn certain realities of drinking as well as the taste and effects of different liquor store options. Vodka was not for me, as it seemed to leave behind sharp headaches. I never learned much about wine and ignored it. I turned away from sweet and fruity drinks and toward Bourbon. There was no beginning of my fall that can be firmly identified. It was the gradual and sensuous seduction that formed the personality and appeal of most drugs. My body and mind told me I needed it every day, and realizing that came too late. My body rebelled against me if I did not do as I was told.

The near-imperceptible, gentle embrace of the drug was made more palatable by my strong physical health before The Darkness set in. I approached my marriage and family dreams with order, steadfastness, and discipline. By the time of the ceremony, I was about 6'3 and 175 pounds with almost no body fat. I had turned myself into a cardiovascular machine like never before or since. This was due to the hatred of my physical self and the belief that I was not lovable unless super-skinny. Even then, I only saw someone overweight in the mirror, when in reality there was nothing but skin and bones. I figured out what to eat to maximize metabolism and minimize calories.

I started my fitness routine on a stationary bike and then graduated to jogging. Although no records were set for speed, my regiment was consistent and very successful. Once established as a routine, I can perform almost any task repeatedly with an obsessive preoccupation. As for drinking, I could engage in all-night sessions and run the next day. Even early in this disease, I could complete more miles than most people each day while drinking every evening/night. Hangovers were not as bad as you might think. So, the exercise reduced the most severe and blunt-force damage associated with drinking. At times, I would use all night, get an hour of sleep, and then play basketball for three hours. This state of body and mind did not last forever. One of the many costs of desperately clinging to my long-sought love, amid the falling apart, was the demise of daily jogging. Much more than once, I felt like Henry Hill during that paranoid montage of drugs, desperation, and helicopters in the movie *Goodfellas*. My energy reserves eventually emptied. Life was beginning to be a different kind of hard and fast-paced, but there were still inner voices claiming that this lifestyle was commonplace as a fledgling member of the sushi class.

To be clear, there were many ups and downs during this period of my life, multiple times of quitting and a small number of sober intervals, from roughly 2010-2021. I was teaching at almost every point on this timeline. Thus, I guess I proved to be adaptable and stubborn, as well as somewhat resourceful, as one has to be juggling the contingencies of extreme habits. This is not ego-building, as my admission here is more about trying to understand and explain how all the using could coexist with the professionalism and hard work that never went away.

Fear and perfectionism played a major part. I am proud, I guess, but that is a good thing, right? In the sense of being a professional teacher, yes, methinks. Though in terms of asking for help, or confessing to my mind that life is no longer sustainable, pride is not your best ally. My avoidance disorder can be a barrier to self-awareness. There were many firsts in my life and almost unbelievable situations, and most of them were also the last things I wanted at the time. Yet, I was, and I am, a good teacher, and there has been undeniable proof to confirm this. I can no longer be as humble as I was back then because downplaying my worth morphed into self-harm and sustained poor mental health. Despite all else, I appreciate how professors sparked my interest in the big questions, and the facts suggest that I have inspired others as well.

Reader, you may or may not be aware that substance abuse and mental illness should be but often are not classified under the same umbrella. I have been talking to you about mental health, which encompasses all the disorders and diseases. I interpret physical ailments as also being mental and vice versa. Body and brain cannot be separated, and the "mind" is not some immaterial cloud floating in space. Every respectable doctor and healthcare worker understands addiction to be a disease, and if using a drug is not a mental illness, then there is no such thing. This is also mostly understood, yet all the time people are forced to be one or the other, with mental health and substance abuse centers separated. I know within the system, some mental health leaders are discouraged if not ordered to abstain from mentioning addiction. This is not always the case, but it is very real. Steering addicts away from considering themselves mentally ill is deceptive and probably deadly. The whole person must be treated, and the mind is the only thing that represents the entire self. You are mental health, and I am too.

Given my experience, I have the ability now to compare the treatment one gets in mental health with the places and people who help folks with the addiction disease. I will proceed as if you are smart but are not familiar with rehab or mental health facilities. I learned that there is a difference. All the people along my path, with only a few exceptions, wanted to help my comrades and I. There are different forms of mental health treatment, but I have been to a few clinics attached to hospitals (with one or two exceptions) called Behavioral Health. Most likely, you have heard of the distinction between inpatient and outpatient treatment. When one agrees or is forced to seek inpatient treatment, in most instances, the stay is for a few days up to a few months. There should be no stigma, but of course there is. Many people benefit from a brief stay and then go back to the "normal" world and a productive life. Many more should go but are wary of being labeled as crazy. Sadly, the living arrangements can be uncomfortable for some reason. And that reason has to do with not giving anyone sick a possible weapon to hurt themselves or others. Chairs are extremely heavy and hard to move, pick up, and throw, for example. Also, chairs may be safe and appropriate for other purposes, but sitting in them is not one of those.

Mental health and addiction centers share many commonalities but a few harder-to-notice differences. A new guest's shoelaces resemble a cord, wire, or similar material—and so they are confiscated. Very few outside materials are allowed, and that means none of your favorite foods. You will find that meals can range from awful to good, all depending on where you are. There will be early mornings regardless of your preference when to wake up. Throughout the day your time will be pre-planned, but there will always be hours of boredom. Some, but not a majority, of the other fellows and ladies might be enduring acute symptoms, which can be scary to be near. It is greatly misleading to ignore, dear reader, the truth that one will live in close quarters to some who are delirious and overwrought with pain. Some have a deep, stinging wound to the soul. There is much more, but let's stop for now. Essentially, I find the distinctions separating the two to be in how help is provided to patients, clients, or other relevant individuals.

In rehab, the good folks trying to make you better often assume you are not trustworthy and, at that very time, are scheming to find trouble. There are reasons for it, sure, that I do not need to explain to you. There is an assumption of guilt until proven innocent. Further, I found rehab to be less responsive to my particular kind of neurosis, or diagnosis (maybe), and more concerned with "by the book" solutions to problems. But I am not a problem, just a person. There are some creative rehabilitation strategies or philosophies available, but most utilize the twelve steps as their guide. There are endless pages of analysis one could outline on religious-based rehab institutions. I have never been but have heard plenty that is not good. For instance, I know of one that prohibits medicine and persuades addicts to pray the disease away. That does not mean I am characterizing all Christian rehabs as bad news. How could I have never been to one?

The hero lived for a time at two different rehabs, with the second one being a much more rewarding stay. This latter one was less glamorous in comparison to the richer one, but it had more common-sense people and solutions and was less fraternity-like. Oh yeah, if you are thinking about booking a vacation at a rehab or mental health hospital, get ready for lots of classes. For him, this was a welcomed development. The hero knows all things school: sitting and listening, taking notes, and sorting out the gist from the unimportant details. So, while every other person grumbled and whined, classes offered the man, now in his early forties, a morsel of normalcy during extremely harrowing times. He got the impression that the people who worked at Bynes Rehab cared and were trying. By the way, those folks make very little, and a prerequisite for this kind of job is a concern for others with the addiction disease. There is no other reason to work for pennies and tend to the very sick and occasionally hostile. Sometimes, he misses the people he met there. For the uninitiated, rehab facilities tend to be fiercely protective of the separation of males and females. This logic may not need to be explained to you. By the way, Bynes and most rehabs are nothing like the celebrity money-pits that one might associate with television shows and commercials. More resources and higher costs does not necessarily mean better.

At no time in his previous life did he ever consider a future with rehab as a part of it. Rehab was for the bad druggies who lived out there, somewhere, far from his circumstances and anything the least bit familiar. It was something for rich people and criminals addicted to multiple kinds of illegal drugs, he occasionally thought, somewhere in the back of his mind. Nothing about sharing rooms, bathrooms, and dinner tables with strangers appealed to the private and shy man. How did he fair, among the folks he found there? From the vantage point of the graduation, when they called out his name and degree, Bynes did not exist. He could not see it as a potentiality in the worst-case scenario. At times, when it came to being in these places, the hero removed himself and only watched as someone with a striking resemblance lived each day on its terms, cried alone, met with his counselor, stumbled, got up, and survived.

But when some light managed to brighten his dreariness, and the slightest shred of hope entered this battlefield, the hero realized an ability to withstand more setbacks than he had assumed possible. On the whole, life was up and down just like on the outside. He felt incredibly alone half the time, unable to find any synergy with his peers. So that part of the ordeal was like the rest of his life. If he were to be honest, now, the hero felt like he was too abnormal and injured for life outside the gates, but not damaged enough to be a full-time mental patient. At least, this was the message he received. Thus, the lack of belonging again.

I must devote some time now to an overview and appraisal of personal experiences with Alcoholics Anonymous. At the very least, I am striving to include some potent and essential elements, and so I know there is much more to the story. With that being said, your average, upstanding Americans have heard of A.A. but have scant real information about what it is like. It is widely recognized and understood to be some type of get-together about alcohol, and the name might be thrown around in casual conversations and in office humor. A.A. is part of our popular culture. Certainly, its exceptional reach and influence are not rivaled by any organization with a similar mission, and meetings take place a stone's throw away from wherever you are at any time. A.A. casts a shadow, overwhelmingly immense, over almost every rehab, and I say almost rather reluctantly. You may be familiar with this and have seen a depiction or parody on a television show or online content. There are endless offshoots, including those for narcotics, eating disorders, excessive shopping, and on and on. Each A.A. group is autonomous, even those with few regular attendees. One can easily walk through the door and stay a while at most meetings regardless of who you are. My introduction to A.A. came in 2018. After that, it has been an on-and-off irregular part of the hero's life.

It is necessary to comment on and critique certain aspects of A.A. to enhance the narrative that has been unfolding. I suppose more than anything else, it was frustrating to see how A.A. supporters were reluctant to stray from the script and entertain thought-provoking, non-orthodox ideas. I can tell you that free-thinking is not always rewarded. I meet those all the time who credit A.A. for saving their life when nothing else could. So, people treasure the steps, and that might be a little shocking at first. It is easy to notice the tendency for A.A. leaders to provide one solution, and one only, for any "failure" to endorse any part of the program: read more, read harder, in the A.A. literature. Of course, I am trained to analyze all information, and that is also my natural inclination. In academics, nothing is taken as true just because. I should add that honesty is not always acceptable at meetings. I have felt uncomfortable, as if Big Brother was monitoring what I said, with the threat of reporting my non-compliance back to A.A. headquarters. Thinking back, it was as if A.A. anticipated every addict's shortcomings and prepared a chapter and verse on it. It was all there in the book one often hears, but I have my doubts.

A more disconcerting reality is that too much time at meetings, and after and before, is used for graphic descriptions of drug use. Yes, I am talking about war stories, if that term helps to clarify. There is a reminiscing of using a drug or drugs, how one did so, who was with whom, the trouble that one might have found, the kind of high associated with each drug, comparing one drug with another, the sensory experience of taste and smell, and that is quite enough. There is a troubling glorification of addiction that may or may not be intentional. I do not need that and exercised my right to skedaddle. There are those occasions when any meeting of human beings could use a leader of sorts to call out and shut down. People should indeed expect to discuss drugs at a gathering all about not taking drugs. Anyone can see this as common sense. However, there is a way to approach recounting and telling your story, as well as how you package the specifics. I never need too much exposition of the wrong kind. If a person in recovery reaches enlightenment, drug stories are no longer amusing hijinks. I do not seek conversations that evoke the sights, sounds, and smells of a life I am trying to flee.

It is essential to provide a thorough yet fair assessment of this influential and life-saving organization. The twelve steps have been unquestionably beneficial to numerous suffering individuals over the decades. I am in favor of any institution that can come close to making that statement true. Yet, A.A. is not as perfect as its hardcore defenders prefer to believe. It is also not enough, alone, for many people looking to break the vicious cycle. The handbook is referred to as the "big book" and contains A.A. principles and triumphant personal stories. Since humans wrote it, it makes sense to remind that the big book is not infallible. That is logical to most people, I believe. Too many times, I have witnessed peers treat it like a holy text, refusing to abide by any reasonable questioning of a single paragraph or sentence.

Yes, A.A. can function as a kind of religion among its most steadfast adherents. It is not a cult, as I have heard people say. The religious overtones of Alcoholics Anonymous are impossible to miss and represent the most debated aspect of the organization. To be direct, many addicts would rather not feel obligated to make religion part of their recovery, and A.A. doctrine makes it extremely hard to do that. Although officially there is no affiliation with any church, as meetings unfold and especially with what the steps and creed outline, religion (Christianity) always looms in the background or foreground of discussions. The authors made that clear, and that is great for you if it helps defeat this hideous disease.

There is more that needs to be discussed regarding A.A. The group claims to advocate spirituality instead of religion as a prescription for recovery. Many actual members of A.A. do not appreciate that blurry line. After all, real people direct and form the rank and file of membership. Whatever high-minded ideals exist, they do not dictate the meeting, determine topics, or provide testimonials. Things are pretty informal. The majority of the content in any meeting is comprised of whatever people choose to say, unfiltered. To remind, my assessment here is dependent on those assembled at whatever church, college campus, or community center and cannot characterize every group. With that being said, I have many times felt afraid to speak up in any regard against the hallelujah chorus that can take hold of the meetings. Yes, I and others have discerned a hostility in play at the mere suggestion of slowing down the overtly religious-overtones.

At one of the A.A. groups, every week, a gentleman seized his opportunity to speak. He reiterated to all that his long-term sobriety owed to Jesus alone and not to any earthly powers. Furthermore, this older man loudly proclaimed that all attempts to get better were futile unless one came to Jesus Christ. That was great for him and his conquest of addiction, so I think we can agree with that part. Has the atmosphere of meetings regularly turned into a kind of Church of Christ revival, or at least an ordinary Pentecostal Sunday morning? Yes. As I hope you can discern now, reader, I aim to discuss and provide a prescription for the complex business of healing a whole person, rather than just a disease or disorder. Sure, for plenty of people, religion is exactly what the doctor ordered. And we could say that man is harmless and is simply stating his truth. Or, we could examine his rhetoric and wonder if it might be the spark that prompts someone to leave the meeting and never return. To add to this, consider that addiction is progressive and will end in only one outcome without help.

Your hero participated in many A.A. meetings and led a few, and the word 'spirituality' evoked both hope and consternation for him. It did for numerous others, as well. Unlike the word religion, spirituality is hard to fault, and it does not immediately create mental imagery of pews and preachers. Essentially, spirituality is often considered safe and politically correct, which can make it vague. The concept of spirituality can now be endorsed like never before in history. A.A. wrestles with mentioning God so often while also recommending spirituality rather than religion. What does that word mean? In the language of the addicted, we seek a higher power of one's choosing, so that is the start of one definition of spirituality. This sounds good and is good.

A person inquiring about spirituality at a meeting will be advised to seek and create a higher power, regardless of what it may be. There is no A.A. at all without spirituality; it is indeed that indispensable. So, I must work on this project, and others have explained to me that anything can function as a higher power; A.A. itself can be that for you if necessary. As has been said in all seriousness, we are told to look around the room and spy any object as a placeholder for your higher power, implying that hopefully a better one will reveal itself. This was ridiculous for my peers and I, and it simply will never work. To be fair, I understand what is being communicated: just stay with the program no matter what, and have faith in something. Dear reader, you know I am an over-thinker and must delve deeper into the conversation to find any remnants of spirituality available to me. A plant or eraser and such will not do.

Spirituality is still a work in progress. At least, I hope there is positive momentum, because eventually a thing can't just be in the process of becoming but must be. In other words, to benefit him, the hero needs to discover answers to the big questions, more than just think about them. I became envious listening to enthusiastic A.A. stories, specifically those with an "aha moment" of clarity, when a higher power seemed to reach down and put her healing finger on a poor sufferer. He is not a total cynic at all, but rather a pessimistic romantic. Thus, he wanted to have a spiritual instillation of truth and wisdom not from this dimension, but could not think of any instance of such a thing. So many have and let others know about it.

I have heard similar sentiments from other A.A. acquaintances who wish for the unexplained, transcendent good. I have made significant progress since about two years ago, when I pondered whether an inanimate object could be my higher power. For a while, he thought in terms of the collective will of humanity to invent, transform, and survive. It was almost like making the collective unconscious a higher power. Because, as anyone familiar with a little history will attest, people have remarkable abilities to overcome. It is less the collective unconscious and more Humanism that represents this sort of higher power. Certainly, the talent that human beings possess is greater than that of any single individual, so perhaps this fulfills the requirement.

Dreams, though, set the hero on a new course, revealing a promising avenue to believe in some metaphysical good active and working in his life. It started with just another dream that turned out not exactly that, at all. For him, going to sleep is a chore, and he wakes up every night, every time, after a dream. They tend to be vivid and lucid. These can stay with him, but the one with the church door, the red X, and the word Hannah is the most remarkable dream of his life. The last part of the name is the reason why. The hero cannot recall any name featured this way during his sleeping hours, ever. Besides that, he did not know any Hannah other than a few faces in class from the past who came and went without any affiliation.

The messages started while I was at Bynes, but they meant nothing at first. This was until I interacted with a new guest, and his name I really cannot remember. He was very earthy and drew pictures. His look was that of someone beaten up by life, which is not unusual at rehab. Soon after the dream, standing next to him in the food line, he struck a conversation about music, and art, and his brother. He volunteered out of nowhere that his brother's last name was Hannah. This other person's surname was not the same as his, it is worth stating. The hero perked up, not expecting this at all, and from that day forward he pledged to solve his dream riddle. Later, the hero and his new, temporary buddy found common ground, and that included an interest in songwriting. The two made some poor attempts at creating a song, and that was it—the unnamed fellow exited our living quarters and treatment, never to return. This last bit was not extraordinary at all, as people appear and disappear due to the exigencies of hard living.

Another out-of-the-blue occurrence brought my attention back to dreams shortly after that episode. I cannot offer the precise length of time between the two incidents involving Hannah. However, it was no more than a week. In every rehab I know, there is a common room with a television, and the room where you sleep is unlikely to have one. Watching TV is limited by the day and hours, as well. The logic behind the big room is to encourage and teach interactions and bonding with others while discouraging isolation. Addiction is a mental issue, and to say someone has a mental problem is really to say that someone has a problem with existence. Therefore, many folks in rehab need repetitions aimed at being whole and relating to others as that whole and not stunted person. I never had control of the remote, which was akin to being king for a day. He is non-confrontational, after all, and there were almost 30 people here, each facing different levels of discomfort. Entertainment choices were rarely in accordance with what the hero preferred and were likely to be movies with explosions, dragons, or exploding dragons.

One day, a film about scientists and aliens grabbed his attention for a little while. It was not bad, but he caught only a portion of it. After tense scenes about how to communicate with alien life, and what they were saying, and stuff of that nature, there was a big reveal at the end. I think it was the main character, and it turned out her daughter was someone called Hannah. This was not a minor plot point you see but mattered and came at the climax. I did not view long enough to determine why it mattered. So, maybe another coincidence, but no, he did not think so. For the first time in his life, he committed to the possibility of being part of an unfolding sequence of events set in motion by design.

He wishes he could have solved the dream mystery right there, but his time at Bynes did impact him for life. My father had been sick for roughly a year. As I said, all he knew was physical exertion in work and play (sports) all his life. True to form, he continued working until the very last day he could. It became very hard for him to eat solid food, he became extremely weak and struggled to walk a few steps, but my dad retained a sound mind. I received the news one day at rehab that my father was near the end of his life. He broke down that afternoon while sitting in his counselor's office and wondering the how, if, and when, of going Home. You see, at places like this, the powers-that-be are not eager to allow the guests to leave for any reason until the term is up. The doors are locked, and people are discouraged or forbidden from lingering outside, which is particularly important for those who are court-ordered to serve some dictated term. Thankfully, they let me go home twice at sad but opportune moments near the end. I was present and watchful as daddy's pace of breathing slowed, and then stopped altogether. A few hours before, I spoke a few words, believing these were heard. At least, this is how I interpret it, and this will not change. As I said, his disease had slowly taken control. Where I lived at the time was a former hospital and the very location where my father was born.

Time made an impression now like never before, even though he had long been fixated by it. To be more exact, he was concerned with how to control it. In the very old days, he stayed up as late as possible before the TV screen fuzzed over to watch Carson, Letterman, and then whatever entertainment menagerie. He always wished that the night would not end, and was quietly excited when another show came on one of the three channels. While drinking, he also sought to stop time and remain in that state of numbness all night and forever. I reckon I tried to suspend logic or something like that.

Even when daddy grew increasingly worse, the hero did not allow a thought to form of a realistic timeline or one at all that ended in death. Holding tightly to time was a way in which he combated anxiety for all his days. And it was the night where he found anxiety could ease, as the hero stole his life back from prying eyes, gossiping tongues, and all the people who he did not understand and who could not understand him. More than ever, his father's passing made clear that stealing time could only go so far, and there was none of it to waste. It was the child still present in the man who hoped closing his eyes and wishing could make something good last forever. He knew it was not logical. But you might call it a previous stand born of desperation, overwhelming anxiety, and disassociation with the infuriating real world that was his only recourse throughout years of abject sadness. In addition, the boy's and the man's nighttime was a way to take back control from the modern randomness.

At rehab, he did not have to face the day or night in the same way as before. Dear reader, that is not to say it was easy; it was just different. Like a university, a rehab center is an island surrounded by streets, houses, and businesses filled with "normal" rules and people. Even the language can vary within those walls. We do not minimize mental disease and that word crazy has no place, ever. It is a given that every person you meet is mourning and possibly devastated to the core. There was his anxiety, but a team of counselors, therapists, and the like help maintain a constant and predictable calm. At least, that is the goal.

This last word, predictable, is essential to life in these confines. Every significant thing happens at roughly the same time of day, and the nights are short. He adapts well to this sort of thing. The rules of the clock ensure that medicine is distributed without fail, which is crucial. Without medication, but especially strong sleep aids, the terrible feelings would toss and turn him during the dark hours. I gained a reputation for taking large numbers of an array of strong, nighttime meds that would have incapacitated a "lesser" depressive. So, sleep was not as hard as it would have been. There were good-hearted jokes and laughter about this, I fondly recall. The rehab reality is meticulously planned, and there are forces at work to decrease anxiety as much as can be.

At rehab, the hero learned many valuable lessons and believed they could be applied to lead a better life. As you can probably tell, dear reader, the man likes to learn, think, analyze, and form solutions to abstract issues. For all his days, he believes that any situation can be made better if given creative license to interpret and solve. In the classes, one learns about coping strategies and triggers, among other topics. A coping strategy, and please forgive me for telling you what you might know, is a plan of activities and behaviors to protect against using a drug or thinking about doing so. Counting backward, going for a walk, exercise, meditation, writing anything, watching a funny movie, and…you get the idea. These are drilled into people's minds.

Once an addict leaves the island, it is comparable to a bird leaving the nest, and every single old foible, and every former, unfortunate, malignant person, will be waiting for the baby bird. Wherever you go, there you are. Yet, the hero felt stronger and wiser than before, and he was something of a leader at Bynes in his own quiet and unassuming way. Still, there was the shortcoming, or whatever it should be called, of failing to feel a casual closeness with others. There was the well-worn and very tiresome old story among his peers when class was over. He met a sad reality about rehab every day, and that was that his cohorts talked about drugs more often than any other topic. He knew, though, the gates would swing open one day and force him back into the bewildering "real" world. But would he be a real, whole person this time?

Triggers were a frequent subject, and he felt no confidence about having a firm hold on them. In any mental health setting, a trigger is an idea, a person, a place, or a thing that spoils progress and drags the healthy back to the illness. For addiction, this is called a relapse. Good-meaning people reinforce the importance of knowing one's triggers and being well-prepared to battle them. Triggers are endless. It might be a trauma, a particular house, certain old friends, or even a song. Mostly, the hero concerned himself with emotional triggers rather than physical ones, knowing himself well enough. Yes, for him, his head is his world, and how he feels dictates what he does. That is a problem, as non-material triggers that you cannot touch or see are harder to combat than physical triggers, such as flesh-and-blood people, tangible things, and places. As you can figure out, anything that can be touched or seen can be avoided—one can drive a different route, not attend certain events, and keep away from certain people. When it comes down to it, the hero feared but admitted to himself this reality: any situation can trigger him, regardless of person, place, or thing. Lately, stuff on the TV or Internet blindsides him and makes him cry, to give you some idea. Certainly, daddy's passing was emotional. He clung to his avoidance tactics along that path, and they failed him.

With triggers and all related concerns, I have learned the importance of self-honesty and sincere reflection. With that comes certain facts that cannot be pushed aside. From 2021 to the present, your author has had to sit in many uncomfortable chairs, listening to advice and general information focused on mental health. This includes classes and individual therapeutic sessions. Add to that a good amount of reading and thinking on my own. Many things that must be said now, for my words to have meaning, are tough to relive and write down. In the course of sitting and listening, I have learned that using can come due to something painful occurring in someone's life, but there is much more. Using is not necessarily a result of a direct cause. Nor does it have to be how someone finds relief due to a long-ago trauma. These are triggers, certainly, but no reason is reason enough for someone like me.

I have grasped the reality that drinking to alleviate a particular upsetting thing cannot represent the whole picture of my addiction. Existence itself is a trigger. So, a bad day might elicit a reason to drink, and coping skills are meant to help with that, and all of that is true. Though, as I uttered one time in a group setting, what if you just like to drink? The simplicity of it is terrifying. And, I have to ask and answer it, too, because one has to give your enemy a name to wage war against it. I must enjoy doing something a great deal to repeat acts that are very likely to end in costly miseries. The disease can be too much to handle. It is a constant danger, lurking and inviting, and perhaps you comprehend the cruelty of the cycle. The enjoyment lessens, but the habit continues, and the consumption increases as one chases the promise of a quick payoff. Still, the amounts are uncontainable, and then the guilt is overpowering, and the urge grows again, and around and around we go.

The cycle of guilt, promises to stop, taking more of the drug, guilt again, then the want to instantly change your mood, is real for all sufferers of addiction. And this goes for all, too, who are not substance-addicted. Those things I uttered about never again consuming more of my favorite substance were meant. Those letters that formed the words, and the words that built the sentences, were not thrown about carelessly. Realistically, I cannot fault one for thinking this very thing. As the disease went on, adjusting as it does to the ins and outs of your life, and taking over every time, I fiercely held on to the will to make addiction all mine. It was not allowed to touch other people. Here was an oath directed toward the ones I love, and I had no tolerance for putting those people at hazard, ever, in any way. You know better, dear reader. Any secret truces negotiated with the drug were violated without exception. You might ask: why did you continue to sit at the bargaining table with this notorious deceiver, and then buy into the deception? Not sure I can answer right now. When the sky has already fallen in your life, you might be apt to say "no more, not again." I was sincere, but the drug turns all of us into liars.

I wish he had addressed more of the questions that bothered him and had adhered to his recovery plan. I was glad to leave rehab behind, but I was also sad to go. You may have felt the same about something in your life, dear reader. Well, he did seek out A.A. meetings and went to them every week. A great question haunted him, and that was: what pressed him to need so much alcohol to feel "safe" and not exposed to the invasions of the Nothing? Addicted people need the assurance of having the drug close enough so as not to suffer going without. It is like a child's preferred blanket that cannot be misplaced, ever. For me, why was that so much, and from what place came the desire to increase my consumption each time? There were mornings, or afternoons, waking from a stupor to find I had drank way more than humans are normally able to and live. Yeah, one indeed develops a tolerance to the drug over time. I had the feeling, though, that there was more to it than this.

Time was on his mind but not his side, upon leaving a three months stay at Bynes. It was December 2021. Shame is a terrible thing to take on, but it was truthful. Drinking was solitary and not intended ever to affect people, but it does. The harder he tried, the worse the repercussions—the

Michael Corleone effect. At this point, he desired stability and sobriety, to be Home, around his beloved mother, the rest of the family, his dog, and attempt to relinquish the bad feelings such as shame. He had lost time involved in this nonsense with police, and rehab, and places he should not belong but did. Making up for time became the chief concern, and he tried. Sadly, there were not enough usable answers to the big questions, and the dream and his dreams, now, that so much had changed, were puzzles to him. Like always, he did not seek to portray the role of a problem.

The old habit persisted, and just a little turned into too much before he was even cognizant of what was happening. When drinking, I lost the ability to moderate or even know when I passed the point of no return. From getting that warm, comforted feeling to the blackout phase was like instantly going from standing still to rushing down the road, super-fast, in a sports car. That is, it was so rapid and unnoticeable that I woke up in the sports car and couldn't recall getting in, much less reaching the maximum speed indicated on the speedometer. There was no buildup, nothing gradual, and the ability to gauge smaller amounts versus enormous ones no longer existed. They say addiction is progressive, and they are right.

He remembers his last night Home, somewhat. It was the beginning of the end of a phase that started with The Darkness. Unbelievable events had taken place, once again despite his desires to the contrary. He took the route of remaining numb for as long a time as could be guaranteed. I am not having this pain just sitting here on my chest, which is entirely unacceptable. Looking back, and he does not want to, life at that moment was surreal and took the form of delaying the inevitable. Maybe it resembled how a condemned man acts in his final moments before the execution. Our hero was all alone in every sense of the term. It was not the golden-haired child but some kind of frightened boy who took over control of the man. He now preferred to think of every day as The Darkness with no one able to shake their finger in his direction, and that meant cutting off communication altogether to sources outside this world he was in. A common concern in this condition was running out of supply and even though there should have been plenty, the decision was made to get some more. Our hero was more afraid of running out than not consuming more drink, and I am not sure non-addicts can understand that. The television had cut off due to lack of activity, but it still flashed upcoming movies and shows as advertisements. The one that kept cycling all around the screen at this point was something titled "Hannah." Again and again, because that was how our satellite system was designed to work. That name was the last message from Home.

If addiction never entered his head as a youth, and rehab was never thought of as a potential destination, jail was even more of a shock to the system. The hero heard plenty about it at rehab and other mental health hospitals. He found himself there again. Among the guests, he was not too afraid and found the other fellows to be alright. Everything else, though, was a nightmare piled on top of endless other nightmares. And this was the kind with no definite end and no method of waking up. He wants you to know that it did not last more than a few days. Sleep was very unlikely with the cement floor or hard bunk as the only options. The floor was littered with garbage, and it was evident that cleaning had never been introduced to these quarters. In the lone shower, the floor and walls were covered in black grease and dirt. One would not become clean, but only dirtier, and no soap was present at all. There was a cruel joke: one working toilet in the pod with roughly a dozen people. The food was not edible unless forced down with water.

One perception became clear: no person working at this forgotten space, nor any individual in the county, nor a single senator or representative from the state, cared about the people interred here for even a single second of their lives. Sleeping away the hours was the only protection the boy had here. So, to help toward this end, the hero completely disassociated from himself and reality. It had never been achieved or even attempted in such a comprehensive way previously. He closed his eyes and pretended.

Although, his eyes had been opened to some harsh realities. After this second stint in jail, he understood how people can get lost, caught up in an indifferent system. By 'lost,' I refer to how troubled individuals cannot prevail over the police, judges, and parole officers who are always on their trail. The law identifies individuals who are high-risk and potential repeat offenders, not to lend aid to them but to target those who are vulnerable. There are the inherently bad apples and then the majority who could use some education and redirecting, and are willing to make positive contributions to the world. Only the bad apples flourish in jail unless the process of incarceration turns the healthy apples into rotten ones, which it can. What about the problems of the redeemable fruit? Drug addiction is there as probably the primary roadblock. Other than that, there are lots of mentally ill people without access to treatment, and, namely, proper medicine. There are a few themes in this thing I am writing, and one of them is how life taught me the fallacy of over-generalizations. The bad people and bad places are more complicated than that, he has learned.

To say the least, the tribulations of this period of the hero's life brought forth the lowest, most dejected and depressed state of mind. He almost succumbed to the body blows, one after another. He was ready to submit. There was nothing left for him in the world, and his dreams were dead. In the hero's mind, there had always been a woeful deficit of self-worth along with that old perfectionism. Well, whatever this was, it represented the opposite of perfection. The funny thing about perfectionism is that it causes a person to quit. This may not be a well-known fact, I'm not sure. The inevitable failure to achieve perfection leads one to renounce all effort. There is no way more second and third and fourth chances at life will be granted, he assumed.

Jail has no interest in helping you once your allotted time is over. The car was somewhere else, and wherever that was, he could not get there. This predicament came during January 2022 but lasted a little past that. Christmas had been nice, just as he had planned during those months in rehab. That was temporary, and that time was lost as if it had only been a dream. He now existed outside of time, as there were no routines, obligations, or distractions to contend with. Avoidance of everything could be entertained as if it were a job. There was no day or night, just The Darkness at every hour and moment left to him. What he had were a few clothes, a suitcase, and a few notebooks. At rehab or mental health facilities, the hero enjoyed writing and drawing to pass the time. He had written on the cover of one writing pad the words "Leaving Las Vegas." He was unsure but felt it likely that very few would get that reference. There were the words "no turning back" that repeated in his brain.

He also secured with him the preferred drug of choice and plenty of it. You should know, dear reader, a little about the surroundings of this area. The hero was a country boy if you recall. The towns are small, with little life and few places to stay, such as hotels. And hotels were all his mind could think of, but I only knew of two or maybe three. As it turned out, he would visit three in total. They were sparsely located across this county he did not like, and it did not want him there. Any addict becomes a Ph.D. at getting by, finding a way, and relying on the kindness or credulity of strangers, whichever comes first. So, he managed to secure a means of transportation to a hotel. By inhabiting this new headspace, separated from time, nothing else mattered outside the activity that would likely happen around the clock without fail. Nothing beyond that was thought of or considered, especially once the drug wrapped its arms around him. Whatever this was would be permanent, he reckoned. It was very cold then, he does remember.

The hotel stood mostly empty on the edge of the town, at the start of what could be called the "Las Vegas" stage of addiction and mental health collapse. Mostly, the rooms were empty. If it were 3 a.m. or 3 p.m. it did not matter to him, and he did not regard time as most people did. It was akin to being in a Las Vegas casino, where there are no windows and no clocks. It could be Monday, or Saturday, or who knows. Drinking went on almost uninterrupted. The consuming only ceased due to involuntary and unavoidable sleep that hijacked part of the day, every day. And, he devised all kinds of methods not to sleep, as that only ruined the intoxicated state. Food was mostly avoided, too.

He had been seeking a more thorough, exhilarating kind of intoxication, and he felt certain it could be done with the right variables in place. You see, one must eat enough not to get sick and vomit up all that hard work that was accomplished. At the same time, anything other than the drug in the system slowed down the effects of drink and wasted liquor, so too much food was also the enemy of that warm feeling. One had to strike a balance, and he at least made an effort. He refused to water down his drug with any other substance, and he did not need a glass or cup. It was swallowed down straight, and there was no whiskey burn after reaching that disaffected level of drunkenness. Some of you might understand. Once started, it behooves the addict to maintain at least a moderate degree of the drug in the system. If I let too much time lapse between drinks, then the man slips too far out of drunkenness and closer to all that must be avoided. Then, reengaging drinking is a challenge and tests one's talent at getting the stuff down and into the system until that time when the warmth takes over. Ideally, the hero partook of his drug of choice quickly and consistently, as if he were a real person doing something normal.

Much of the memory is blurry, but he cannot forget the unwelcome visitors. Even here, the maid comes around every once in a while, and they are persistent in getting hold of your dirty towels. I am sure someone tried to do this, but he did not acknowledge her visit. There were no dirty towels, anyway. The police were pests, and there is no mistaking that distinctive knock. How many visits did they make? His educated guess is three. There were a few trips in a police car and two stays at the Behavioral Center that was informally known as the mental hospital.

Once, there were two nice people, a young man and a woman, who showed up to escort him to a different mental health facility. First, however, the hero checked into the regular old hospital for a few hours. His blood was very unhealthy. When that IV is rolled in and begins to pour into your veins, there is a short-lasting, very good, refreshing rush in the body. He was shivering, lying on that fold-back chair one finds in most clinical rooms, and he began crying out of nowhere. Whatever that substance was, it altered his focus from Las Vegas to other, sorrowful things in the real world. That young fellow pretended to enjoy talking about history with the lonely and disoriented patient. It was a bittersweet and pleasant trip. After hanging out for a while, there was no place to go, so it was back to another hotel and reviving business as usual. He was glad to be out of the real world, and time, enclosed in his private world where pain did not live.

Life characteristic of Leaving Las Vegas could not guarantee a hassle-free existence, as the damned people and places of reality kept intruding. Some people were persistent and highly annoying, and a judge was involved for reasons not explained to him. Each successive hotel was lower in quality. He has a handful of clear memories of the second one, and it had the worst décor of all time. It was very old, and the design and color scheme appeared to be a mishmash of several failed renovations, all side by side.

There is more. A guest was forbidden to enter the office and was forced to interact with the employee on duty via a device resembling an old bank drive-through window. As he was later told, his stay on these premises was cut short after he failed to open the door for the cleaning ladies. This must have occurred repeatedly. Police arrived from nowhere and encouraged him to relocate to a different part of the county, or anywhere else.

The last hotel of the Vegas escapade had the aura of a bloody stain on a busy yet desolate highway. It emanated the kind of indifference that made the hero believe he might be able to survive here for a long while. It was a motel, whatever that means. Such a place is a good hideout, as there is very little concern to offer new towels or to inquire if guests need something. Just make sure you are paid for. In all of this, the hero understood how the Vegas lifestyle would eventually end. He hoped life would not enter its final act soon, and tried not to think about it, but had accepted the outcome. Besides, all dreaming was over now.

The Nothing had fully swallowed him, as obnoxious invaders showed up for the last time. There were no thoughts of the future or hope. The room was quite cold because the door would not fully close. But that part was fine. The television was never turned on because the remote was never found. That did not matter, either. He had become on the radar of local law enforcement, and again, there was some kind of business involving a judge. All of this is true, although he never left the room, or caused a stir, or broke any law. That knock again, and one knows without fail the police have arrived. They never visit to cheer you up or for any reason other than bad news. He cannot be sure how many days were spent here, but it had to be at least four or five. He was fully intoxicated and had been for the whole Vegas experience. It was increasingly more difficult, though, to get that warmth or any discernible high anymore. These individuals were not nice at all and did not even let him gather his belongings into the suitcase. So, they left this scene, and he had some idea of where this road was taking him. Certainly, it was not Home or any place he would choose to be. Also, the destination would not be one where friendly faces would welcome him.

It was the second and last visit to the WBU mental health hospital. Before checking into his room downstairs, there was an overnight convalescence in a reserved, small wing of the hospital. It was kind of like a detox, but not really. Readers, in case you do not know about this, a detox is where an addict is housed for close medical supervision until he or she has recovered well enough from the worst aspects of withdrawal. Thankfully, detox centers always offer strong medicine to sedate the patient, alleviate the most painful symptoms, and cause sleep. However, remember that this was not that. Instead, he believes this place was used to evaluate whether a new guest would be dangerous or not, and then a decision was made on which side of the soundproof glass they would temporarily inhabit. To make a long story short, he was not given any medicine at all in this agonizing opening act of his hospitalization. There were brief interludes featuring mini-cans of Shasta cola.

There was no getting comfortable in the hospital bed. He alternated between believing his aching head was the worst of it and thinking his painful, churning stomach bothered him the most. Additionally, there was a lot of shaking. He had ice water. He would drink a bit, which somehow made things both worse and better, and then pour some on a rag to wipe his face. It was impossible to get comfortable in that hard, inflexible hospital bed. The hero can relate to you that there was a nice man there, a nurse? Maybe. For the first time in what seemed forever, he watched the changing of day and night through a window. This was a horrible time, one of the worst I've ever experienced. Then, he was told about and then taken down to the room. He began to awake from his malaise, and there were card games, crying, meals, card games, an outburst or two—stuff like that. His birth date came and went without comment. He recalls being horizontal on that iron slab that reminds no one of a bed, on that day, staring up at the overhead light. You see, that light never goes off. He was a dreary wreck and made a vow never again to have this kind of birthday.

The WBU was not a good experience, but it was likely necessary for him to advance in his hero's journey. Now, he did not think of himself as a hero then, nor did he feel that any logic or future good was taking root. It was the opposite. He received the medications needed to be able to sleep and wake up, eat, walk here and there—navigating the small confines and attending group. One young man was inconsolable and weeping, and we would cross paths again. I could relate to his pleas to return home. The hero was annoyed and scared, unable to assemble a single thought of optimism. It was a very limited space, and of course, people there with him were largely depressed, too. The powers-that-be made him show up in the conference room and play childish games, and most of the staff seemed preoccupied, except for a few. It was clear to him that the impatient staff worked in mental health but personally had not lived with mental illness. Facilities like these contain all kinds of people, either with diseases that are hidden or those that are obvious and unnerving. So, he means that you encounter all situations, and people are not "crazy" like the uniformed public imagines.

A couple of memories stand out. There was an undying thirst and yearning for something sweet. There are medical issues there that help to explain his urges. The shower head trickled water straight down, and there was no shower curtain. It was cold unless I pressed myself up against the wall. No steam. No warmth. Also, there was a young woman who radiated more brightness than the situation warranted. We talked a bit and played a card game called Rummy. You just pass the hours as best as possible in a place where there is no comfortable spot to sit, lean, or lie. Between us, there became a friendly banter back and forth, as he was weaned off of stronger medications and onto moderate ones. She left first. As I was readying to go, someone informed me of her name: Hannah. She was never seen again in the hero's journey, as is usually the case, despite promises and alliances one makes here.

Unlike the hotels, the steps toward recovery found him in better facilities along his path. Dr. Aften was the head honcho of the whole system, and before leaving, gave me the "option" of continuing treatment at another, more tolerable mental health lockdown. This was the promise, along with better food, but the hero had no idea what it was and unsuccessfully sought information about this place called the CRC. It was never really optional, either. In any case, the amenities could not be any worse.

The CRC was a medium-sized building designed for patients who were ready for a next, less-restricted step. It was less clinical-looking but was designed to offer a more homey atmosphere. The people who worked there strived to promote a carefree, positive vibe. Surely, any person who landed here requires a break and a smiley, bright, uplift. Yeah, the food was miles ahead of the previous stop. It was plentiful and kind-of home-made. After all, this place was small, with about a dozen or so patients at any time, and sometimes with as few as three or four. The most cherished selling point, though, were frequent smoke breaks all day long. As expected, the day starts before the sun does and is filled with pre-arranged activities and meals. Oh, he had a private room with a regular-sized bathroom and a shower that accommodated an adult human. Mostly, he ate, attended classes, and took breaks outside. Weight was gained. There was some outdoor recreation, but not on most days. The people who worked here were kind and attentive. So, despite arriving with great trepidation, life was at least better than expected.

At first, he was simply glad to be somewhere decent without the threat of a sudden upheaval weighing on him. Gladly, the staff here did not startle you with that dreaded knock. It was people-friendly, concentrating on the person rather than an old book or even a diagnosis. I must say, this kind of treatment — literally watched and cared for around the clock —

should have been what the doctor ordered long ago. For example, it could have aided my well-being, say, before having a breakdown before heading off to college. This is not your prudent author placing blame. It did not happen that way, so that is that.

One of the friendly faces who picked me up and drove the short distance to my new residence turned out to be the manager of the CRC. I did not know that at the time, as I felt quite overwhelmed with the newness of everything. Over a few days, as we discussed the logistics of getting the suitcase delivered and other necessary items, and getting acclimated to the new environment, we spoke frequently. One day, while sitting in his office, I noticed the nameplate on his desk. The manager's last name was Hannah. Now I was convinced that some higher power was trying to inform me of something or leading me somewhere. Mostly, I decided it was the latter. Even for a glass-half-empty, romantic-pessimist, there was too much evidence to disregard all of it in my usual manner. Here was a pattern that transcended the superficial norm, and perhaps, taken together, constituted a spiritual experience. It was not believable, but undeniable. Yes, the person sitting here is mostly convinced that spiritual is as good a word to use as any other. At the time, that name, following me to the CRC, gave a beleaguered man a shred of optimism.

It was surprising but really should not have been, how bits and pieces of belief that disparate scenes in life are part of some aggregate plot, one leading to another, can sustain a person through rock-bottom depression. This notion became a possibility in his mind, at least. Could we even say his story started to make sense? Not sure. It was fortunate that classes were part of the weekday routine, though weekends were dreadfully boring. Just as before, classes enlivened his spirit here and there, and certainly he felt comfortable in that environment. One thought often flashed in his mind: I can think of some topics and methods useful to these classes. They can be improved, and he began to feel strongly about it. At first, my game plan was only to suggest ideas possibly helpful to people like myself.

This marked the beginning of something that is still unfolding: an interest in mental health, Psychology, and all things related, both for self-help and to instruct others. I learned from the classes that aiding others with mental illness and my well-being had an indefinable, necessary relationship. I had no idea that I could teach courses in mental health, but this began and continued. It is strictly voluntary, but my classes get a very positive reaction. As for my overall story, or hero's journey, it is difficult to relate just how crucial this part has been in terms of transforming a Vegas-bound ending into something better than that. I still have whispers of self-doubt, though. Those inner voices persuade me to think that the therapists, doctors, and all others were just trying to make me feel good. I currently question those voices more often than I believe them.

My stay there lasted a long time, almost five months. I know people say this all the time. But it felt like maybe a year or more for a few reasons. In this place, family could visit once the Covid curse lifted. I got to see my family for the first time in a long time, then on many occasions afterward. I had not visited with my little dachshund until then. Big questions are only fulfilling if the family situation is sound, after all. It is worth repeating what you already might know, that people are by far the primary reason your mental health treatment is bad, tolerable, or helpful. Most of all, the poorly paid ladies who did so much of the work, and with whom we relied on and interacted constantly, played an integral part in making my CRC tenure very positive. I call them the CRC girls, and in my mind they represent some mental health superteam, like Charlie's Angels.

Also, your hero began to contemplate the big questions once more, and he came to a few conclusions. Whether they were just doing their job, who knows, but the staff listened to the hero pontificate on subjects that most often were psychology and philosophy. I was not merely luxuriating in thought because I could, as his main objective was to solve the riddle of himself. This had long been an earnest desire and perhaps was his holy grail. It was basically the same mission as when he chose a university subject. What was the origin of his origin story? He wanted to know the reasons for his vacant childhood and the melancholy adulthood, despite being something people aspire to. He had Dr. in front of his name, after all, but had portrayed himself as a wannabe. Then, he literally just forgot about the PhD for years. That could not happen anymore.

It was at this facility, one of the last stops on this chapter of the journey, that he began a healing process that led to any possibility whatsoever of writing a book. In depression, there is no forward thinking and no big plans. One cannot take on the world when you are barely hanging on to this "real world" on the ledge, with your fingers slipping, and with The Darkness beckoning. Dr. Aften met with me throughout each week, asked questions, and I tried to honestly reply. This intensive treatment was new for me and very important. Taking medication, previously, had been like an appetizer sampler that changed on the menu several times each year. Thanks to the doctor, the meds make sense and work together.

Some in our world disparage the use of good drugs to help your mind or to end dependence on the bad drugs. Do not listen to that. Only now, with roughly a year as a sample size, can I see how mental health medications are meant to alleviate the worst stuff. To be more specific, previously to now I could not tell much change from life without to life with prescribed pills. I do not think I will ever be acquainted with joy, but contentment and optimism may well have entered my life as reasonable things. So, let me try to be clear, again. That what I just said was not possible without the right medications. Yes, there is more to the equation than just the pills. To summarize, I would say medication does not allow my cup to go dry, as it maintains enough to be either half-empty or half-full.

His stay was extended past the norm, and he really was afraid to leave. Here, there seemed a purpose that needed to be served. He mourns each atmosphere when forced to depart because time under those very specific conditions is forever gone. The same sadness of finality occurs inside the man after every class that expires, for the same reasons. He hopes to have a purpose now more aligned with how he actually feels about life. What I just said there is very aligned with Individuation. Time and again, he took for granted that others thought at least a little about the big questions and why these were so instrumental to living in this world. All the hero's life, mounting evidence should have steered toward the opposite conclusion—that most human beings need a push, and some inspiration, to be sensitive to the big questions. Hmm, who could provide that? A teacher of course. Unfortunately, one encounters so many liars in life before having enough wisdom to be properly armed. He was misled by our society and its mindless followers, who taught the hero that teachers did not matter much. Therefore, his self-esteem was lacking.

Our modern world communicates to us its values by who and what it pays. We must trust in athletes and celebrities to be the leaders and the wisest, then. Now, I understand the valuable gift of having great teachers to society and the individual. He had some. So, at the CRC he chose to take up the cause of teaching in a new way beyond academia. People are thirsty and cannot find a source of water. More than that, modern humanity is not conscious of being dehydrated. So, he did not know where he would go once past the password-protected doors of the CRC. People treated him well there and offered a reason to care about getting better.

There were not that many options at this stage of the story. Just thinking about leaving was very emotional, because it suggested the possibility of never going Home. These things in his mind made his arms and hands shake and turned his stomach round-and-round. It made him cry at those moments when his mind could no longer support the weight of accumulated, avoided, probabilities. He was fully institutionalized at this juncture and pretty naturalized with this little place. Oh, and he does not like change. One inducement aided Kirk during this time: I might be doing what I am supposed to. Add to that, a wavering consideration if every trial functioned as a successive scene in a worthwhile story. The dream surely supplied whatever faith he had. So, there was a decision to make, but it worked out much like the Dr.'s so called "optional" proposal to continue treatment at the CRC. In actuality, there was no decision: only a confirmation to travel down the path a bit more.

Mental Health is a large organization with many places to live. Ultimately, our hero left the CRC after a very long time and agreed to live in an apartment, with a roommate, and according to mandates more strict than a rental in the real world. Here were more strange things to adjust to.

At the time of this writing, there is no car but mostly free access to travel to walkable places. During the first week here, management discussed various topics, including guidelines and key individuals to know. One of those was someone named Hannah, whom the hero has never met. He is not exactly sure of her role. That does not matter, as here was another nugget of encouragement for the pessimistic romantic to keep truckin,' even lacking his truck.

Other dreams play a role in the story. Lately, every night I go back in time. My parents and siblings are always there, some extended family, and oftentimes acquaintances from childhood. Reality resembles a video game or something recorded such as an old VHS tape. This is impossible to translate in mere words. I seem to be the only character who has the self-awareness of being captured in this game-like life. It is delightful, as I get a second chance, a rewrite, and can socialize with people long gone including some who died before my birth. Although, things often began to go wrong right before I wake up. In many cases, the game is a project I created, and I have to go through each stage, much like a test, to reach a preferred destination in the future. This sought-after place is not a physical location but rather usually refers to my mom or my mom and dad.

So, in the dreams that I can only inadequately compare to a game or recording, I try but fail to inform other folks that these events have already occurred and it all will be alright down the road. Thus, I attempt to let people in on the secret that the hardships of the present allow my story to reach resolution. In a few dreams, I tell my family about my troubles to come, how I figured out why I had them, and to not worry about it. There is a happy ending, but my character is never able to convey this. Also, while dreaming I am certain all of it happened, but then upon awaking realize none of it did. The dreams sometimes are crystal clear. I think I have some conception of the relevancy to real life, but I honestly am not convinced. But the meanings in the dreams are in there somewhere, and I hope you refine and define the dreams for yourself.

Another dream is worthy of attention, and it stands out from the ordinary. This one actually came to me during the early hours of the morning, only a few nights ago. It was about 2 a.m. when I awoke and disappointingly found none of it was real. This one was of that variety that you immediately want to write down the details as not to forget. I believe the setting was in a mall or shopping center, maybe. More specifically, the major action revolved around a big table at an Italian restaurant. All five of the family were seated, along with my grandmother, each reviewing a menu. Yes, I am certain enough the restaurant was in a mall because of many storefronts on either side of the center. Suddenly a few celebrities showed up, including a young Tom Hanks. More importantly, I was again a child, and this time there were only good vibes and no mixed feelings. Instead of worrying about advancing to the next level, my young self sensed that all was well without need to hurry, worry, or inform anyone of my shortcomings.

In the dream, I thought to myself, this peaceful existence will endure permanently. In other words, there is no going back. Like in other dreams of this last year, my addiction entered into my head and threatened to erase the harmony and replace the young me with that guy who invented The Darkness. I will not choose that path, said the… man or the boy? I am not sure, but likely it was just a dreamlike combination of both minds at once. Why Tom Hanks? It probably owes to his movie *Big*, which recently came up in Kirk's life for reasons possibly pertinent. In this film, Hanks plays a child who switches into the body of his older self, overnight. It is the reverse of all the images and drama that have been flooding my dreams. But, the story is close enough? I will let you decide, and the film is great, fyi. Oh, and *Big* was the first movie Gwen and Kirk viewed together.

I have some idea of the major messages conveyed in this and the other ones that are closely related. There is an intense desire for me to apologize for all that took place, including that lost time of not belonging and the failure to be counted as one of the real people. The young man did not provide his parents with games to attend and sporting moments to brag about. Then there is something far worse. He did not make a Home and a family, meaning grandkids, as real people do with very little effort. So, there are none of those games either, and no Christmases, proms, and whatever other coming-of-age rites. I have never been real enough to send out Christmas cards with the wife and kids in front of my Home. In dreams I work to explain how mental illness killed my real dreams of being a whole person. Furthermore, I am trying to convince my parents that it is okay, that I figured it out in the future, and there is time left. Now, I am not sure that I believe that when I am awake.

The last two years have been very enlightening, from late 2021 to the present. Many of the lessons learned are included in the next section, the Conclusion. The discoveries are what now supply a well of strength, perhaps for good, in addition to the people who help in my recovery. The Hannah Dream cannot be disregarded as nonsense. In fact, there were more random appearances in real life of that name, I just cannot recall them all well enough to put down in writing. All I can do now is to propose one likely reason for Hannah and a few other best-guess theories. Hannah was like a lighthouse in that great old gospel song; a light to guide into safe harbor. Or to be more frank, each reference was a sign I was meant to be in that particular place to fulfill my purpose. This was enormously useful, necessary methinks, to crawl out of the lowly depths of despair.

Then, a couple more thoughts on Hannah. In the Bible, she remained a steadfast character who withstood public mockery before God blessed her with a child in old age. This was a patient person. She birthed the great prophet, Samuel. So, maybe, the golden-haired boy had something right that the man forgot. I am thinking Hannah alludes to staying true to who you are in spite of this modern world that works everyday to chip away at your singularity. I would like to use the same quote from Ernest Becker that appears in a previous chapter. It must be read in total to capture the major portion of what I am trying to explain in this section, just as much to myself as to you. He talks about heroes, and how every person can be one. Again, Becker wrote:

> Man breaks through the bounds of merely cultural heroism; he destroys the character lie that had him perform as a hero in the everyday social scheme of things; and by doing so he opens himself up to infinity, to the possibility

of cosmic heroism, to the very service of God. His life thereby acquires ultimate value in place of merely social and cultural, historical value. He links his secret inner self, his authentic talent, his deepest feelings of uniqueness, his inner yearning for absolute significance, to the very ground of creation. Out of the ruins of the broken cultural self there remains the mystery of the private, invisible, inner self which yearned for ultimate significance, for cosmic heroism. This invisible mystery at the heart of every creature now attains cosmic significance by affirming its connection with the invisible mystery at the heart of creation. This is the meaning of faith… The truly open person, the one who has shed his character armor, the vital lie of his cultural conditioning… is absolutely alone and trembling on the brink of oblivion – which is at the same time the brink of infinity.[20]

So, according to this line of reasoning, men seek to be heroes but are forced into a prefigured mold chosen by the community of one's origin. Of course, we do not select what society into which we are born, that is simply luck of the draw. As you know, I think of myself as the hero of my own story, and you should too. However, I must speak loudly and demand that I be the hero of my design in the story I am directing. Who that person is, I suspect the golden-haired child understood long ago.

I reckon most do not seek the road less taken and set loose that inner heroic self, for fear of the "trembling" Becker spoke of. Dear reader, you may or may not remember what Carl Jung wrote about the modern man—his staring into the abyss. You might call it "The Nothing." Or, you can choose not to, because, yes, I am throwing in lots of references never before or again to appear on the same page. So, I am not suggesting anything other than my heartfelt reaction to these words and how they apply to my mental health experience. To me, that word "cosmic" signals anyone to meditate on the big questions. Staring into the Nothing is what I have always been doing. I just had no idea and inaccurately supposed I was aberrant, weird, abnormal, etc., and that I did not belong. But the big questions are so integral to existence that I now refuse to cast me as the strange one. Most of life is a parade of lunacy at best, and a tragic waste of our lives at worst. In fact, I am declaring now that the lead character of this story is beautiful in his peculiarities, rare in his talent, and heroic in his purpose. And that is the last word on the subject.

CHAPTER 6:
Conclusion: The Palace of Wisdom

"I overcame myself, the sufferer; I carried my own ashes to the mountains; I invented a brighter flame for myself. And behold, then this ghost fled from me."[21]

As I see it, William Shakespeare was strangely right on the money. Dear reader, I confess that I am not an expert on the subject of Shakespearean literature. I do know enough to comment on the content of those classic plays as it pertains to this writing. What little I remember and interpreted is that those stories depicted humanity as cold-hearted, self-serving, devious, selfish, and dishonest. I think Shakespeare captured the dark hearts of human beings and how people work to secure what they want by near-constant scheming. The most intelligent individuals know how to manipulate others, regardless of whether it involves friendships or family relations. Now, it is not that Shakespeare presents bare-bones, everyday reality, but I realize how people and life can appear to be as he described. And that is the knowledge that escaped me almost all my life, through the self-hatred, lack of belonging, and yearning to become a real person. To live in this old world, one must accept that Shakespearean drama is not only possible but often true. People tend to focus solely on their interests and sometimes seek to undermine everything that does not serve those interests. Once this is realized, I can then begin to see the good. It is not an all-or-nothing blame game when humanity is involved.

To be more direct, I learned that I have been disappointed with people and life from a very early age. Recognizing this fact has led to my being better equipped to work on my mental health. And this simple thing, which might be obvious to you out there, took me forever to learn. You see, all those experiences that racked my brain, trying to understand why I was rejected for my differences, stemmed from an unrealistic expectation for everyone and everything. Why did he tell that story, so obviously false? How does she say one thing now and do a remarkably opposite thing later? How can that one in my life be disloyal to another, remain close friends, and not like, care for, or reward my sincerity? This is what people do.

Recently, another related aspect of the puzzle captured my attention: most people are flawed and afraid and do not live by honor codes or authentic impulses. Human beings try to get by and are doing some level of work (almost said best) just to remain free of the torture of the insecure unknown—the why do I matter questions. So, trying to get at what this all means, I have more contempt for life itself and less for the poor beings who are held by its strings, dancing as part of a ridiculous show. But maybe people agree to play a part in the show, and perhaps the consent lives in all the little practices and decisions that bury our heroism.

Life, your hero has come to think, is best thought of as unreal and unknowable on the surface. You know what, *the Matrix* is correct in terms of ideology. I do not take that film literally, but everything we see daily is not the pure expression of that particular thing or person. I can say that having lived for too many years as someone who only received information as it was conveyed, rather than as it was intended, has been a significant limitation. I never came close to gaining insights into people, past their costumes, to those places where they might reveal themselves.

In the past, I was unable to measure any situation accurately. Well, maybe that is an overstatement, but it is correct in spirit. If that darn time machine ever came my way, then I would tell the young hero not to be disappointed in the reality that is easily seen. Reality is not real. As for more guidelines, spend your time only on those people and situations worth working on, to see past the facade. As for all others, try to let all those hassles drop to the ground. Imagine you are shedding your skin, or if you had rather, taking off an ill-fitting piece of clothing.

The younger self could have benefited from training in all the subtle ways humans manipulate one another. In the not-so-distant past, I recall being perplexed by ordinary interactions, such as holiday gatherings, that should not have been so challenging. My hated enemies were gossip, rumors, and small talk that led to both. I think I wanted to share that, "hey, I have good things to offer! I am not terrible!" It was apparent that no one cared about important stuff and that average folks were schemers and connivers. Meanwhile, I was like a CIA operative who was not able to divulge any information about his secret mission. Feeling judged at all times is perhaps akin to being in the bright lights on some stage, sweating, with the heat felt sharply on my skin. I can still feel this way now. If I had to clarify my mission, it was to get away from the torture room and back to the haven of Home.

It is the teacher's job to enrich people, entreat and inspire them to consider the big questions, and help them embark on a more meaningful life. So, this would also include striving to be less Shakespearean. Yes, I am suggesting that education can influence people to do good rather than the alternative. So, my love for the Humanities is more than academic, as I had theorized. Furthermore, I am now more confident that my chief purpose in life is to be a teacher. Whatever or whomever planted Hannah in my life may also have stressed this as a basic truth. However, my convictions had been heading toward that conclusion for a handful of years.

It took something outside myself, and the introduction of appropriate medications, for my brain to be able to arrive at a definitive determination on teaching. Hannah was probably encouraging me to view the CRC and all the drama preceding it as a new education. For now, I am obliged to consider that this additional instruction puts me in a unique position to teach more than history. All we are is mental health, and that is inseparably entangled with history: both personal and the textbook kind. So, do

I not have a useful pedigree to share with this old world? It is like I am sitting in life's waiting room, anxiously, of course, to provide teaching of the most authentic sort. In disastrous scenarios, he fears that he may not be permitted to be a teacher again. He cannot forget and should include here his progress toward his purpose over the last several months, teaching without being paid for it.

The friends of Socrates once upon a time counseled us to believe in teaching, as I do now more than in the past. The ancient Greeks made it clear the value of what were called philosophers, but they were more than that. They meant "philosopher" to refer to someone who would probably be termed an intellectual or professor today. Or, as I see it, ancient philosophers such as Plato and Aristotle were teachers of every facet of life that they considered important. Plato argued that society should look to someone like himself as the most worthy of leadership. So, teachers should be in charge, I guess. Please take to heart, dear reader, that I am not comparing myself to Plato nor running for office.

Kirk enthusiastically claims, however, that teachers are as vital to this world as any occupational group. He thinks teachers are special, exceptional even, and he declares himself as one now and forever. I must use the word 'we,' and so we are essential and needed for defeating the Nothings of the world. The zero-sum game mindset must be countered by a spirit of cooperation, which is much more challenging to achieve than merely discussing it. He hopes to enlighten as many people as possible, as that is what people need more than Othering. Yes, there is that voice now belittling these optimistic forecasts while putting him down for impudent dreams of grandeur. I reject that voice. There is a risk of arrogance, but I am willing to accept it to maintain my mental health and security as I advance my life's purpose. I think this is far preferable to letting pent-up frustrations lead to my downfall.

Over the past year, I have learned about the concept of purpose and how it aligns with my new approach to life. I came across an interesting book title in my research on the big questions, titled *Man's Search for Meaning* by Viktor Frankl. I am hesitant to refer to any book in the way people too casually speak of "a book that changed my life." Although Frankl's classic work comes as close as any to turning Kirk's head toward a new course, mission, or what have you. The author proposed that the meaning of life is to discover one's purpose and then live it out daily. As I am sure you gather, each individual has a separate purpose and his or her own path to walk. It is essential to note that Frankl maintained that purpose is not the same as searching for happiness. By making happiness the ultimate goal and striving to attain it, we miss the point and sabotage our well-being. I think we cannot snatch happiness and put it in our pocket, because human beings are too complicated and restless. Happiness is too relative and thus not concrete; therefore, I believe it is dependent on too many variables to be firmly established. It is too slippery to hold in our hands with supreme confidence. Plus, the grass is always greener, you know, and uncertainty about happiness appears to be very close to unhappiness.

Frankl stated that happiness falls upon us only as a byproduct of living with a defined purpose. So, only by not looking for it will contentment begin to flavor all the little scenes and struggles that compose our lives. All of this commentary, then, turns finding a dedicated cause into the most important part of being human. There is more heavy-lifting to be done; more to this game than pointing a finger in some direction and calling that my intention in life. I appreciate Frankl's advice that we should not focus on what we deserve in life, as the real aim is to understand what life expects of us. I am not positive Frankl's message works without this key piece of information.

In my humble interpretation, this means that bizarre entity called life casts us in a particular role we are suited to play. By that word life, I reckon you can substitute a higher power if you choose to. Evolution can fit into this schema if that appeals to you. So, we are selected to become what we are in the most fundamental sense and perform a purpose that may or may not be obvious. Likewise, one's purpose can change over the course of a lifetime. As for me, I glean from these considerations that I have a purpose based on my talents and circumstances revealed during/after a gauntlet of tribulations. I am afraid to say it, but it is likely that purpose was bound to enter my conscious brain, regardless. While I am throwing out maybes, Hannah played her part by reassuring me during a life-threatening crisis. This sounds alright so that I will proceed with a little faith.

I must declare, dear reader, that my calling was not entirely unknown before Vegas threatened to end my life. It has been a few months since a voice within informed me that I was meant to be a teacher. Then, the Vegas ordeal and other situations of late intervened to make me again reinterpret my identity. I become disheartened by thoughts of a wearying job that holds no appeal for me. What could be more soul-destroying and less authentic than performing unfulfilling tasks to survive? Serving a purpose is a higher calling and feels much different. Not easy, but affirming.

In contrast to research, teaching offers immediate results without the long wait for any impact whatsoever. Yes, that uncertainty of publishing without anyone noticing is real. Teaching means receiving instant feedback on what is being heard and what is not being heard. As a teacher, one can be assured of receiving some form of results, whether favorable or unfavorable. Your work, when all the stars align, reverberates within and around a student as they traverse life. Therefore, what a teacher does is passed on and on with that romantic dream of becoming immortal.

So, I carried with me many notions of what it meant to be a teacher before the CRC reinvented my mission. Was he meant to be a teacher of life lessons? He has a divided inside, with his country boy and fancy professor voices not always singing the same tune. Well, what if life picked him to bridge a gap between both worlds? Is it part of my responsibility to speak as a mentally ill man and as an educator of the humanities, and maybe more? Perhaps I have been given a mandate. I would like to reiterate my earlier statement that I arrived at the CRC feeling defeated and dejected. There was nothing for me anywhere, just like during those awful teenage years. As you now understand, a turnaround began around this time, which led me to where I sit now: a shabby couch. I started to come out of my shell a little through conversations with the good folks who worked there, and somewhere the big questions reemerged. As it happened, I was given some latitude to think of topics, and those speculations eventually led to my newfound teaching. The treatment team likely planned a curriculum to help me feel better about myself. I imagine there was some conversation, and some person spoke up and said, "Sure, let him do it, it might be good for him."

It turned out that my ideas worked as topics, and classes were regarded as something that could be done under very stressful conditions. His classes increased, and the reviews remained largely positive. I attempted to integrate relevant academic lessons applicable to my setting with real-world insights into mental health. This last part was born out of all those classes and my lifelong struggles to find a better sense of well-being. With so many hours spent in classrooms, such as at Bynes, one should be expected to gain insights, information, and at least one or two epiphanies. Somewhere along the way, I found a method to begin the rewrites necessary to turn my story into something heroic. This work continues.

Now I see a story unfolding where the protagonist overcomes the Nothing aided by the hand of providence. By the way, all I am saying is not dependent on that lady of mystery. This hero is not immune to the instinct to find patterns in life's twists and turns. I am betting it was a combination of closely supervised medication and the teaching experience that reignited my curiosity. There are at least two key points I would like to emphasize about these past few months of my life. The first is that my interest in the intellectual side of life died. It had been gone for about ten years before 2022, and it came back as the under appreciated virtue we term curiosity. Without curiosity, societies cannot advance. It is the basic element of a wise soul whatever their age, and curiosity is the antidote for the modern blahs and the big bad Nothing. I also need to mention how the rekindling of that analytical, inquisitive spirit not coincidentally led to a more authentic self. At least, it was a step in the correct direction. The culprit was depression, unchecked, with a few more allies as well.

I'm not sure, but it may be hard for you to imagine how a teacher lost his mojo for at least ten years. That loss was complete. So much so that I had not realized it was gone until my reawakening. Indeed, I am twice-born like William James wrote about. Like him, I lived through an existential crisis and lived to tell the tale. Most of humanity's best nature begins with a childish, naive desire to explore the dreams we dream. That did not exist at all, and it would be inaccurate to say The Darkness alone perpetrated the crime. Life's pressures and endless petty matters drained him until the addiction disease delivered the killing blow. From the d-word event until roughly 2021, no need-to-know questions stirred in his head. His in-class time was a welcome respite from the anxiety, and always too brief. It was like filling my tank enough to teach, and doing that very well, and then going dry until the next appointed time. Drinking worked along the same lines, as I reached record levels of drunkenness and then diligently sobered up, and then repeated. Mental illness buried my good parts and let loose the Shadow self.

The guitar just vanished from my worldview for those many years. It simply did not come up in any regard, including playing guitar and hearing others do so. Sure, there was music here and there, but not like it was when his boyish fascination with the guitar held a voodoo-like spell over him. As I am positive you know, depression cancels those activities that enable enjoyment/excitement. For me, it was a little more diabolical, as depression caused any relationship to my passions to be especially and doubly odious compared to all else. The realization that your life-loves are depressing begets dire hopelessness. So, you put that guitar, or violin, piano, canvas, brush, pen, pencil—you get the picture—away, far away. You shut it up in a closet and shut it out of your mind. The same story applies to all that brought the young man peace previously to The Darkness. The man almost smiles, thinking about his days of drawing and creating stories. There was innocence to all of that.

At the heart of the matter, the young man loved the Blues generally and the Blues guitar, especially. The discovery occurred around the age of fifteen, and it changed his outlook on the possibilities of music. Previously, I listened to "Top 40" radio, which featured songs that were manufactured and popular at any given time. He did not know any better. These were the days of stereos, tape cassettes, then CDs, and stores where one would go in person to purchase music. The Blues and other music molded from it or related to it were more authentic and soulful than that other stuff.

Blues burned a path through the barriers of his stale world, straight to something inside, rousing in him the type of soulfulness that moves people. Sadness is essential, but we are talking about emotions that are life-affirming and unlike the despondency of depression. Real music makes a human feel more like a human. The Blues are a primal, dance-around-a-fire kind of music. My second favorite word for Blues is urgent, in that how I feel matters, and I am going to howl, scream, or moan it so you really understand. There can be a droning, repeating, trance-like rhythm, that gave its fire to the early Rock and Roll beat. Country blues is more sparse, with a touch of evil contained in it. My favorite became electric blues, such as performed by B.B. King, Albert King, Stevie Ray Vaughan, and many more. It is those guitars that cry that better represent the insides of a teenage youth than anything else found.

The uninitiated do not grasp that the Blues do not give someone the sadness that people also call "the blues." It is unimaginable to think I would respond positively to music that made me more depressed. No way. Now it is time for my favorite word to describe this musical style: catharsis. In my mind, the word represents a process of cleansing, akin to a ritual that is truthful in acknowledging the bad stuff and then letting it go. That is the Blues to me. Before I put this in words, I felt it as a young person. The Blues indeed has lots of references to hard times and especially a "mean woman" who did somebody wrong. In this regard, the music deals with real life, not happy jingles, which do genuinely make me sad. Blues are diverse, so my remarks are intended to be a general summation. With that being said, the Blues admit the low-down nature of life and then urge us to say: "Oh well, we might as well have a good time." Additionally, the term 'mean women' sometimes refers to something else in life, such as a work boss. There is a lot of coded language.

Well, that last word prompted this: my immersion in the Blues was like learning a new language. I went to work to learn more about the music. My brother was aware of it but did not speak it fluently. So, there was no human source around to further my education, but thankfully, the early days of the Internet did help. I recall hours sitting before the computer and listening to samples on one or two websites. Yes, the Internet was much smaller and slower then. They did not teach anything about real music in high school. After about three years, at the age of 18, my parents bought me a guitar for Christmas. It was a solid guitar for a beginner. From this day forward, I practiced intensely almost every single day.

I did not indulge in my favorite things for what felt like forever. His guitar playing, enthusiasm for all music, and part of the young man's soul all died around 2011. This could have been and looked like a permanent passing away. It was around the time of the d-word, when many harmful trends got behind the wheel and started driving his life. I remember thinking how much I failed at the guitar, unable to bend the strings to make those sounds that altered my musical paradigm. It was all or nothing-ism, because falling short of the greatness of B.B. King sent the message that I had no business playing the instrument. Perhaps mental illness tricked me, as I was not conscious of any compromise with myself to stay with my Blues pursuit. In other words, I did not have the mental capacity to think the kind of thoughts that allowed for compromise. No reassuring voices complained that my comparisons were unfair or that it is possible to settle for being good and not great. I desired never to look at or think about guitars and the Blues again.

My recovery coincided with breaking that pact to forget about playing guitar. The turnaround began in 2021 and continues to this day. It is not hyperbole to say that I had ceased all artistic endeavors for at least ten years. Perhaps worse, I had no clue that it happened. Now that I reflect on this subject, I realize my state of mind guarded against all creative projects so the man would not be reminded of what he had lost. Or, there was more at work. I had internally confirmed the suspicion that I was not good at any of the creative arts, and yes, had sky-high, unrealistic, pressured expectations for myself. Perfectionism is such that it can finally make a person submit and say, "Uncle, I am not trying anymore."

I started drawing and playing the guitar again while at Bynes. This became an everyday habit wherever I ended up, functioning as a saving grace while enduring torturous boredom and war stories. There was a cool fellow at rehab who played quite well. Furthermore, my sister brought an old guitar to me—that first one I received at the age of 18. So, all that created reasons to play again. To be honest, some of the enthusiasm for playing music initially stemmed from a desire to pass the time. While in lockdown facilities, there are always long, empty hours to fill. I had those notebooks, even the one with Leaving Las Vegas scribbled on it, and I filled them with strange little drawings that were probably not as good as my perceptions. It is uncanny how one's viewpoint can change with time and healing. Most likely, various mental health personnel said words I needed to hear.

With the guitar, I found that my playing was better than it had been years before when I put it down, and this time my self-assessment was right. Before long, I reached a level of playing that is "not bad" in guitar speak. Medications and counseling have played a huge part in my improvement. When I think of art, the word possibilities comes to mind, which is like staring into the unknown in a good way. All things live, rules mean little, x can equal anything or nothing, and on a good day, I dig deeper, combine, extract, disassemble, and reassemble according to my own will. That approach only comes with a view of the horizon and the confidence that wonderful stuff exists just beyond it. In short, all that is only doable for me when depression is in the background instead of front and center. So, for the first time in my life, I have uttered the words "I am a guitar player" more than a few times. Yes, saying that is a real accomplishment. There was something about greater wisdom that aided my playing, methinks. Additionally, life struggles tend to clarify what is important and eliminate wasted effort. One thing I know, or at least hope for, is that I can maintain a healthy attitude toward the interests that give me an identity.

What about belonging and being a whole, or real, person? The golden-haired boy turned out to have most of the answers about where the hero should go with his life. The more specific answer is that the boy had some vague impression of who the man was. He wanted to be an artist like those pros who illustrated comic books, and the man has finally circled back to his truest self. In short, creativity, self-expression, and sharing spellbinding emotional intensity with another, which is only found when receiving the signal and not thinking, magically materializes when art strikes some core aspect of the individual's condition. All this must be raw and partly instinctual. I get those chills all on my own, but it is even better if another human being can vibe on the same wavelength. It must be that I am an artist first and foremost, and an analytical thinker, intellectual, and explorer of the big questions, or however you want to put it, second.

Only by becoming yourself, like through the process of Individuation, can one rest easily in the belief of embodying a whole person. Like Dorothy, the tools to better my life and achieve personhood were always there within our hero, waiting for activation. I know doubts linger, and I still have apprehension, but we must wear our identity daily to supplement our mental health. It has also come to my attention that not belonging was likely to happen. It was true that I did not fit in much of the time, but why would I want to act out the tired old roles, as others expected, in a world with upside-down priorities? Finally, I realized that other people were often the issue, and the youth and then the young man should not be shamed for every failure to connect with others. Besides, other people tend not to be comfortable around uniqueness and often choose to be sheep rather than a shepherd. So, the hero was not always wrong; he was just talented and creative.

Some serious incident traumatized that golden-haired child, though it is unknown. Finding that dividing line in my young life, between the boy artist, showman, and impressionist, and the youth left out of life, is comparable to the old search for the evolutionary missing link. It must be there, as other evidence indicates the probability of its existence. I am not sure, but it is a reasonable proposition that there was not one event but several that combined somehow to repress and disturb him. Perhaps it was an ongoing issue unsettling to the boy, but the man could only guess. So,

I admit feeling cheated out of happiness as a boy and all the other things associated with childhood. He can say the same about his adolescent and teenage years. I need to reveal this rather than hiding it away, as that serves no healthy purpose. There are no candidates to blame even if he felt like playing that game. It is also factual that regrets are not helping him right now, or at any time, because no time machine is available to him. If one yet existed, the chances of the hero pushing to the front of the line are very low.

Mourning my youth brought disaster but then a clarification of my identity and mission. I think being sidelined in childhood and then in college created a bitter creature within my soul. Let's call him Jim. He was and is sorrowful for failing to appreciate the good times when they were sitting there waiting for him. Jim is not all bad, but he is very impatient and seeks out relief from pain in worldly things instead of within Kirk. Jim prefers to instantly alter his mood when bad feelings arise and threaten to overwhelm his body and mind. He has been rejected, and Jim holds onto the hurt of his unrequited love for the rest of his life. You see, Jim proposed to life once long ago, and life simply said, 'No, I'd rather not.' So his frustrations drove Jim to build up hostility toward life, leading him to believe that he was right in thinking it was meaningless and a waste of time. His voice can be heard loudly on those occasions when Kirk is vulnerable and ready to say goodbye to all things real, for as long as possible, and escape. Jim will say something like, "There is no use in trying in this pitiful, cursed place." Yet, Jim is not very truthful and deep down knows his hatred for life is just a cloak of self-preservation. Kirk and Jim must find a way to get along and reroute the pain of mourning into projects worthy of a hero.

I believe Western Civilization is built on mourning. Well, okay, not completely, but Christianity is a rock-solid pillar of Western Civilization, and most religious cultures are steeped in the laments for eras and people long gone. The conventional origin story most influential to us casts Adam and Eve in the primordial Garden of Eden. We all have heard it before. Life was almost perfect, and humanity was largely ignorant of the big questions. They were unashamed and content to live simply, unencumbered by labor or the struggle to find food. Then, we all know how that perfect lifestyle crashed. And every day from that date we mourn the pure, authentic beginnings of humanity. The communion rite is a remembrance of Christ and all that he did for and meant to this earth. So, many of us mourn as individuals and collectively for our origins, but those desires are mostly unconscious. I will say once again that such a powerful thing as that surely is part of us, and that part of us is surely mental health.

As I related previously, our modern, secular prophets firmly established the decline of religious faith. I cannot think of any way to disagree with this assessment, dear reader. I singled out Frederick Nietzsche and Henry Adams as two, and they had nothing in common except for this. Religious or not, I do not think most people sit around and consider whether going back to earthly Eden is a real option. So, I want you to know that I am not in fairy-tale land. Moreover, people seek to recover values, ideologies, and locations that are more accessible. In our time, half of the political discourse has been that whatever is wrong with America can be made right by a return to the beliefs and practices of those men on our money. More pleasant to discuss, though, is how we mourn the loss of nature and "old-fashioned" means of living, believing, and producing. As a romantic, I feel the pull of these things as clearly as hunger makes me think of food. I do not remember if *Dead Poets Society* ever addressed this topic, but the Romantic poets certainly loved the wonders of nature. We moderns standing on the cliffs of the world sometimes need romance to assuage our fears.

Mourning has much to do with me as an individual and my mental health. At every stage of adult life, I have remembered a previous time and wished I had learned of its greatness sooner. With hindsight, every part of the journey appears more favorable in retrospect than it did during the time. That may be the most often-used but not so great definition of a romantic: someone who reflects on the past and celebrates only what they prefer to see. Every class one teaches will never be repeated. It does not matter how many times U.S. History is taught. There is a set time of day and a specific group of people, and these factors can never be reconstituted. There is some mourning associated with finishing a class, and I'm unclear whether this is normal or unusual.

But most salient to my mental health, I have mourned the security and safety of an early childhood that I can barely recollect. I do not know how much it matters whether this has been a yearning for something real or some fantasy. It is there and has shaped each chapter of the hero's story and will likely continue to do so. There is little better than belonging, along with the warm glow of being secure, lacking all worry and doubt, with no prying eyes of disapproval. How do I know? I'm not sure; maybe it is just something I imagined.

Of course, drinking provides a reliable sense of warmth for a short time. So, I am an addict and romantic by nature, but it is not the substance itself that I have been chasing. Now I am only humbly suggesting that this might be true of others too, that we do not put everything worthwhile to us, including our lives, in jeopardy for a mere liquid. There must be more prizes available in our wager where death stands guard in the shadows. It entered my mind recently that I am addicted to a state of being that, admittedly, I cannot promise to have ever experienced sober. I cannot say with absolute certainty that it exists. Is this what Eastern religions refer to? A kind of oneness with all matter? I think not, as of right now. However, the warmth of belonging and simply being a real person, like imaginary arms wrapped around you, is quite priceless and merits the dedication of a significant portion of our precious time.

Childhood is the most probable place to look for such things. William Wordsworth and the other Romantic poets tend to agree. Certainly, it is tragic when any person has that magic snatched away by any type of abuse. Millions go to a bottle or other drug of choice to find something we have a difficult time putting into words. So, all of us are in mourning, but we each have our own points of view and methods, including the choice of words, that we use to articulate our stories. I, for one, do not think Jim ever considered himself in mourning.

Jim, though, is not the only occupant of this person who goes by Kirk. We all have different voices within our souls. When I started this project, I heard voices that insisted that it was folly. More specifically, the inner voices barked at me, claiming I had no business trying such a thing. As mental health education instructs us all, I listened to the content of the voices but forged ahead anyway. Our cast of characters within, like actual people, have various points of view to respect but disagree with.

Teaching gave Kirk the performer a voice for the very first time. Little by little, he moved forward cautiously, grooming that part of himself. And it slowly leaked out here and there. To the best of my knowledge, no one has been hurt thus far as a result. A sage professor once told me something close to this: "Every teacher is a performer and every class is a performance." The young me greeted his words with enthusiastic approval. Oh, and I should add that this unnamed person who occupies some space in Kirk is quite needy. Yes, he requires that someone highlight him and what he is capable of doing with pats on the back if not applause. And I may have to invent another person; I'm not sure yet, but they also want to make art and be respected for it. Yes, I am aware that the artist-as-rebel does not seek the attention of the masses who will not understand his art. I mean, that is part of an archetype. This seems silly to me, and I honestly believe that most, if not all, artists have an inner burning desire to be noticed and rewarded.

I sense that the tone has shifted too far toward the optimistic, so let us return to a more somber tone. Beginning with The Darkness, I have learned that Kirk lost many of the characteristics that once defined him. These were traits to be proud of, and he was. I venture to say that witnesses would support my statements. Somewhere, I incorporated timeliness and being true to one's word as part of my overall outlook. My dad for sure had more to do with my veneration of time than any other influence. Now I am speaking of time in the sense of not being late. This was another way in which I was and still am obsessed with time. More often than not, in my younger days, I would be early so as not to risk the unthinkable gaffe of failing to appear somewhere at the agreed-upon hour. I was also mortified by the chance of wasting someone else's time by being inefficient and/or slow. Keeping promises is also part of the equation. We sometimes call that honor. So, yes, my word on any matter was something to take to the bank.

The Darkness began the stripping away of some of my cherished qualities. And I say cherished because I held these listed above, and more, in very high regard. When things went wrong, I could at least tell myself that I had done what I was supposed to, in a commitment to worthwhile principles, and I could then hold my head a little higher. Using substances erodes such noble things as these. One finds oneself in situations where lying appears to be the best option. No question about it, the addicted person will often be late and miss appointments entirely. The suffering user will then need to lie about a bad thing, as in not showing up somewhere, so frequently that dishonesty itself functions almost as an addiction. Bad qualities are acquired due to the nature of the addiction beast. Little dramas like this will add up and then neutralize most of the attention to any code of conduct. No, addiction manufactures a perilous desperation to endure where most standards are thrown away. This is what happened to me. It was not intentional, nor was it even visible until the train had left the station, so to speak.

Addicts develop instincts and talents that are essential for survival. As far as I can tell, these replace those admirable characteristics either partially or entirely. And that survival depends on one's position in life and what they are trying to hold onto. So, it could be a wife, husband, and/or family that is slipping away from the poor addicted soul. One could be scared of losing that middle-class existence, with riches, possessions, and respectability. On the other end of the spectrum, an addict is barely alive at all and holding on to life itself. You will get to a spot somewhere along this road of losing something, dear reader, if addiction comes your way.

The concept of respectability is important and warrants further commentary here. Alcoholics are Othered in our society, as are all addicts. But with alcohol, a sufferer can maintain credibility as a whole person as long as he or she is a functioning addict. Crossing the line to non-functioning brings a kind of shame down on the shoulders of the afflicted. Again, what I am trying to say applies only to alcohol. Within the manly arts, not handling your booze is akin to running from a fight. As a society, we judge alcoholics with less sympathy and are eager to throw disgust in their direction. I find this logic reckless and foolish. But as we know, a functioning addict is just a non-functioning one waiting to happen (but this is not why it's ridiculous).

None of these inferences would have come without a lengthy period of treatment and uninterrupted reflection. Again, I am reminded of the teachings of Eastern religions. As an adult, I had never quieted my mind long enough to do some of this necessary work. In addition, my thoughts can become extremely rambunctious, like an unruly child, and refuse to conform to my commands. More than once, all that stuff reached a boiling point in my life, and I could no longer handle everything all the time. Beginning at Bynes, but especially at the CRC, I had the opportunity to engage in some meditative thinking. That peace was inseparable from the efforts of reestablishing some link to the golden-haired boy.

The culmination of some soul-searching and the knitting together of a few strands of ideas has its roots in the quiet time. This is when I began a comeback and formed some of the beliefs necessary to try writing this mental health memoir. Some people reason that the biggest question of all is: What is the meaning of life? Nothing gets me worked up quite as much as existential musings, but I do not know why. In my opinion, no answer to the meaning of life questions found in books is finite enough. The great books I have read tried and failed to arrive at an explanation any more plausible than one you or I can deduce. It may be this way because the meaning of life is not a fair question. No simple statement can adequately represent all that it means to be alive. Still, just the challenge of it is the kind of exercise that can serve humanity and force us to look at ourselves in the mirror, and look at each other. I like the question, too, as it can tear away all that is trivial until only the soul of life remains. As far as I can gather, the most reasonable answer thus far to the meaning of life (by the great intellects) is that there is not one, and that every individual has to decide the issue for themselves.

All human beings should take some kind of long timeout for self-discovery. In the 1980s, I recall people on television occasionally saying they were taking a year or so "to find myself." However, I cannot discern whether this was merely a television culture phenomenon or if real people did it. When this hiatus from life's chaos arrived, and I could look back with insight instead of only sadness, parts of my life made more sense. By quiet, I do not mean inactive. So, I developed some theories, for lack of a better word, and yes, formulated preliminary ideas about the meaning of life. I mean, the way I look at it, if geniuses cannot succeed, then I am justified in giving it a try.

So, let us get down to the meaning of life already. For me, the most important question is this: how do we feel that rarefied warmth of belonging while also establishing a unique identity for ourselves, both at the same time, in synchronicity? The pursuit of these almost opposites, singing in unison, is what we call life. The will to belong and the need to form an identity are not equally balanced in all people. So, singing together does not mean everyone partakes in the song equally. By this, I am saying that some of us esteem one or the other of this contradictory pair in a greater proportion of life's song. Many insist that being part of the group is a little, or far more important than standing out, while many would vote in favor of singular identity over belonging. In my manner of thinking, two things do not have to be perfectly balanced by weight to be harmonious. The journey itself—the search to secure duality—might be of greater relevance to a good life than any assumption that we have achieved a result. In summary, all the words in this paragraph lead me toward a familiar refrain: every human being chooses a meaning of life that is not the same as the next. All my life experiences and recent reappraisals of the past prove that distinction from the crowd means much more than belonging.

My inclination at present is to prioritize this balance of group and individual identities as essential to my inner contentment. Please take note, I said nothing about happiness. This elusive thing is not the meaning of life, and this I say with confidence. In the Grail stories, what is gained is not the original prize but an unexpected thing picked up along the way.

So, for you and me, our real holy grail is not what is originally chosen to be the sacred thing of our dreams. Happiness cannot be sought and won like a first-place ribbon in some contest. What we can reach out and take into our possession can always be snatched away from us. In addition, humans have this unlimited, incorrigible tendency to notice that the grass is greener somewhere else, with someone else, doing something else. So, I feel no need to have that word happiness bouncing around my head. I am making progress on my task understanding the meaning of life with the hope of finding comfort and satisfaction.

For most of my days so far, there was an empty chamber in my soul where evidence of belonging was meant to be stored. Or, that was the assumption. This is the space where the proof of being a whole person should be. I did not read the instructions, such as the chapters on the manly arts, to gain what I needed to satisfy the requirements. Also, Kirk could spot the phonies out there. More accurately, it was less about people and more about situations, trends, art, causes, and ideas that should not be but were (and still are) repeated all the time and promoted as real. Therefore, I was unable to resolve this issue in my mind and heart. There was nothing I could do. At least, there was little chance of bettering how I felt without some aid, information, medication, and personal time. One should not pursue a mismatched relationship, and I had no genuine interest in being part of one that revolved around interests that held no appeal. So much of how I thought was indeed very backward, but I guess nothing can be done about that now. Yes, I still don't have a time machine.

I have come to believe that we are not different people at various stages of life, but rather different versions of ourselves. So, Kirk has heard a particular notion put forward frequently that goes something like: "I am a new person" due to some life-altering or therapeutic situation. I have never said that, and more importantly, at no point has my mind turned in that direction. I remain skeptical about overnight conversions and complete metamorphoses of any kind. I think we costume the outside to look like whatever inside "person" is winning the debate at a given moment.

It may be that a healthy person forms their outside self to resemble their favorite inner voice. Yeah, I think this idea is reasonable and possibly true.

Although this is a minor consideration given the mysteries of the past that I have vowed to confront and resolve, and maybe that is too much to hope for. In the early stage of writing, I knew I wanted to come to terms with a hard-to-remember childhood, addiction, and all the mental health hardships. I sincerely wished that through writing, the puzzle pieces would begin to assemble and some whole picture would emerge. Maybe this is my holy grail? I have at least one more something that it could be, however. Anyway, perhaps I have done exactly what I set out to do. At the least, an image has been formed from the puzzle, but I am not confident that it is enough of an answer. You know, I have to weigh the probability that Jim has a hand in all of this, because what I allude to may be a quick-fix answer that does not come for anyone on this earth. I sometimes feel impatient and prefer resolutions that are simple yet have enormous explanatory power. I like to wrap everything up as neatly as possible, and summaries of very complex variables can be unreasonable.

For my well-being, it seems critical that I discover how nighttime holds some special intrigue to the hero, and it has been this way all his life. First, you might rightly shout that this is too simple and ordinary a statement to warrant any emphasis at all. If you are especially sarcastic, it may be that I have only now realized that I am a vampire. However, my affinity for the dark hours has something to do with long-held insecurities and habits. I think there is more to it. I have not been fond of sleeping too much or going to bed early. For all time, there has been an inner craving, perhaps even a need, to stay awake until midnight and then a little bit after that. I recall that when my cousin or someone else came to stay overnight, it was not unusual for the young hero to be the last to succumb to sleep. Late at night, the television shows became more interesting, scarier, or racier. I relate staying up longer than one should to something approaching stealing. It feels like something is being done that perhaps shouldn't be, and that brings a thrill or two. I am stealing time itself. As you know, late-night comedy was simply the best thing televised in my younger days. SNL and David Letterman were almost revolutionary to a sheltered person with a large imagination but a small world.

Nighttime equaled freedom. Daytime was callous, cold, and chaotic. There was no order or meaning to be found among the hundreds of unintelligible scenes of everyday life. There were no reassuring faces. More likely, I detected disapproval in almost every look and life situation. All of this died sometime after the sun went down. It was a reprieve. Yet, I tried to make the nighttime last for the rest of my life, and I really cannot find how to untangle and refine this to make more sense. To try, it must be that avoidance of the day was the last refuge available to defend against untreated anxiety. Suddenly, everyone was on my side. My television comedy choices skewered the events and people of the day—the real people. Things made sense now, guards could be lowered, and self-loathing subsided. Being the last person still up was the preferred outcome, but I had no idea why.

During later years, the nighttime habit continued while new elements were acquired. Before I knew my way around a liquor store, I looked forward to that moment when my head hit the pillow. There were almost no other considerations past the day's intellectually stimulating work. That meant reading, writing, and school-related stuff. For the most part, I went to bed and woke up at roughly the same times every day. Later, the Darkness came and modified the nightly routine. For a long while, it was necessary to have some soda on hand to mix with liquor during the warm-up stage. It took several minutes to establish the intoxicant in my body and achieve enough pleasure to dispense with mixing the drinks. Then, I could listen to music and watch entertainment that might make me too emotional when not under the influence. Feeling something that I cannot describe almost every night replaced the feeling of finding no authentic connections during the day. If sober, the intensity of letting loose my heart to feel was lovely, painful, and hard to take. So the routine was altered, but the night remained that thing to look forward to.

I must look back on my youth and be able to pinpoint the creation of my nighttime rituals. They have been there since the start. I do not want to define ritual and separate it from routines, because it is challenging, and I am not presently convinced it matters to us now. Both are intended to salvage order and meaning out of a nonsensical, belabored existence. For anyone paying attention, it is easy to feel out of control as if one is not the prime mover of the forces that govern one's life. Therefore, a ritual must be repeated and infused with meaning that transcends the words and actions carried out to perform it. This is my understanding, regardless. My rituals have been used to lighten the load of life, such as that longing for belonging, authenticity, wholeness, and identity. They indirectly fight back against enemies I could not even name. Nighttime rituals were performed to seize some control over my discordant universe. Most of all, my rituals have been unknowingly related to this desire to reengage with and mourn the enraptured state of mind of some lost thing, actual or imagined. This is what ritual participants seek.

I have some ideas about what I have looked for in rituals, but I am confident that some pages from the book are missing. I am aware of my limitations in fully understanding. With addiction, the sufferer wants to find a way to get that original high from the substance, and that project gets more difficult the further one sinks into the grip of the disease. So, part of my ritual was to surround myself with greater amounts than were ever needed to achieve drunkenness. And, the over-supply must be maintained at all times. There is more at work than just the bodily reactions to the drug, as far as the reasons for continued use. With intoxication, there is an association of love and belonging that goes away from flesh and blood life but does not entirely disappear from the addict's consciousness. So, somewhere inside, I scavenged my memories to try to recapture those sensations of intimate bonding and camaraderie with other human beings. This remained even as addiction pulled him into increasing isolation. So, I was in mourning, and I believe addicts to be especially susceptible to this state of mind.

Our modern lives have become alienated from what makes us human. The magic has been lost, and nothing is mesmerizing. As a result, something of the greatest magnitude will always be looked for again and again, and ritual forms a huge part of that longing. Most romantics are not accurate about the past and are not looking to be. We all have some form of long-gone "splendor in the grass" that tugs at the nostalgic part of us now and then. Youth usually provides the context for those "firsts" of life that are not yet besmirched by the cynicism that unfailingly buys real estate in our hearts and minds. When I ask myself why addiction, one part of the answer is all about a misspent childhood. I am sorrowful to have been sidelined to the maximum degree, having foregone and wasted those occasions to have fun and be young. In a way, a "lost" childhood has plagued the hero and is a major source of the not-great aspects of his adult life.

Among all the days of my existence on earth, a common thread has been facing most challenges in solitude. My default setting assumed that no one would truly appreciate the issues that plagued me. I also lacked the words to express myself and feared being less of a person by exposing my weaknesses. I have conducted nighttime activities as the sole participant, as others would complicate things. When drinking, the last thing desired was for any other person to be watching. I did not share this with anyone before, during, or after. Now what I do at night is different and preferable, but others are still unwelcome. I eat too much, and in a way that makes sense to me, but not to anyone else. It is obvious to me that there is shame in performing my ritual, and I would rather maintain it as a secret. I should repeat, however, that my normal point of view is chaotic, and the day never satisfies the need to replace a disjointed mind with order and peace. Rituals help toward this end.

While deliberating on rituals and my relationship to them, I came upon an interesting revelation: most of the rituals of my life have disappeared. The church is often the first place one considers when seeking human rituals. Religious ceremony and activities are not far removed from the practices of addiction, in that all rituals seek to impart an original intention or state of mind. In the Church of Christ, I was not immersed in as many time-honored observances as customary with other Protestant sects. There was the Lord's Supper every Sunday morning and the occasional baptisms. Yet, there was a time for class, for preaching, for singing, and for the beginning and end of services. So, acts performed in church had some level of significance and were repeated again and again for each assembly. From my perspective, rituals occur all the time. However, all that changed as I drifted away from church attendance and eventually stopped going altogether. It has been several years since I entered a church door for reasons not related to A.A., but this is not me confessing that going to church would have stymied and crushed the sins of addiction. Not exactly.

Also, other rituals that once impacted the hero's life have been extinguished over the years. First and foremost, I am thinking about holidays and family gatherings. There was Thanksgiving with one side of the family, Christmas morning with the immediate family, and Christmas afternoon and night with the other side of the family. In addition, one could expect well-attended events around July 4th followed by other spontaneous meetings throughout the year. Not surprisingly, the constant was food and lots of it. All my family likes to eat and can cook in that old-fashioned, southern-grandmother style. It was great. There was an initial time set aside for eating and conversing with all involved, with people grouped by age and other factors. Within holiday celebrations, there exist a hundred mini-rituals that are done without thinking but with consistency. Watching football, time spent outside, who parks where, topics appropriate for discussion, things you don't say, and information that you imply openly so everyone hears, and more, constitute what I am calling rituals or at least steps in a ritual.

Without a doubt, the repetitive behaviors and formalized events of the past had some great influence on the golden-haired child, the youth, and the young man. Apart from family matters, I would like to add that school has its rhythms in life and things that might be considered rituals. I have been taking classes as a student, teaching, or both simultaneously, for the majority of my life. As someone who requires routines, basic logic dictates that having rituals benefits the hero and having few to none is less than ideal. As you can guess, family engagements are not like they used to be. Only shadows and remnants of what was remain intact. This is natural, no? This is part of life. I recognized how rituals are essential, for the first time, during my quiet meditations. I do not have children, and I also lack the predictability and constancy of all rituals except those that are solitary and not so healthy. I believe these facts matter and will continue to do so for this author.

The value of rituals to all human beings, regardless of age, is not in question. We require them to feel complete. Humans create rituals just as they do language, government, and religion. Rituals must do more than just mark and commemorate a special set of circumstances. There is something that people must recognize for a renewal of spirit to take place. Since mourning has become a central aspect of modern sensibility, rituals should be at the forefront of our consciousness. But, is that true? It does not seem to be the case, but maybe I am not looking in the right places.

As a society, our collective mental health is in peril and has been for a long time. I believe what smart people say, for the most part, and they indicate something approaching a mental health crisis. I have noticed that everyone has OCD these days. Well, I speak of this trend where any person suddenly declares, "I am so OCD," or something of that nature. Usually, the comment is made with the indication that someone feels very comfortable, if not gleeful, about their self-diagnosis. I hope we can agree that this trend is not the greatest thing in the world. I do feel there is a correlation between the decline of rituals and a greater preponderance of mental illness symptoms. Please note that some relation between the two is not the same as stating that one causes the other.

Social, weekend drinking once served as a ritualized behavior for Kirk. It was not all bad for his health and peace of mind, either. This once seemed like a sustainable and suitable lifestyle for him, but that did not last for very long. I had two real friends at the time while finishing my degrees. Gwen was there, and life chugged along reasonably well. Every weekend night, the hero would make his way toward the hangouts, and all present indicated a good time was had. The nightlife made him wonder if this was finally an entryway to a life similar to that of real people. Unlike later on, Saturday night drinking did not bleed into Sunday morning, then afternoon, then Sunday night. I was able to attend to matters that needed attention on Monday almost every time. There was the same regret of it all ending, and trying to stay up all night, like always. It was a social thing, and then it was not. How and when that difference came to be, I cannot say.

I bring this up in part to make a sad admission about my days thus far on Earth, learned, once again, only recently. All the things that I enjoy doing or thinking about, now or in the past, have made me incredibly lonely. Now, it is not that these recreations are inherently lonely-making. Instead, for whatever reason, the few interests that grab my attention and vitalize the best version of Kirk have been things not shareable with others in my life. My passions are not the same as those who play a role in this hero's journey, and the same is true in reverse: I cannot pretend to care about those things they find important or interesting. Now, of course, this is not entirely true, but it is generally accurate. I refer to comedy, the Blues, the big questions of humanity, and drinking. It is probably correct to conclude that drinking is the one not-like-the-others here, but I cannot deny my love for it even if it is inconvenient. Each brought me to a place of seclusion. The hero reckoned that whatever is enjoyed must be done alone. He learned this lesson and dealt with the consequences through whatever means were available to him. Since no one cared about what he did, the world became that much colder.

On the other hand, recovery usually includes building relationships with peers who are in some stage of fighting mental illness. A.A. preaches the socializing element of coping with addiction, certainly. A community of those aligned with your own recovery goals, happy to offer helping hands, and nearby, is a great and maybe necessary thing. Before the Las Vegas stage of awfulness in my life, I came very close to having such a state of affairs. I was attending meetings and trying to fit in somewhat among my comrades from Bynes. But I have an ambiguous opinion on all this.

Never did I find contentment or belonging among others I have met during recovery. Just as a last reminder, I use the term mental health to include those with depression and other diseases of the mind, as well as brothers and sisters in the substance abuse camp. The overlap between the two is immense. Or, the more professional terminology is that many, many folks have a dual diagnosis of a mental health issue and addiction affliction. Per usual, I rigorously evaluate if I am understanding and relating to them on any real level, or if I am just useful for rides to and from meetings. Also, part of me recoils at the potential of helping others with their stuff, and having to walk with them down the path of fears, insecurities, resentments, traumas, and the like. I do not enjoy this aspect of Kirk, and perhaps it makes him a worse person for feeling such a way. This may be another instance of avoidance of things I would rather leave behind. Part of the hero, I think, desires to turn back the clock and not be an addict or a frequent guest at mental health facilities.

Another thing must be divulged. Part of my reasoning for sometimes describing my life as if I were someone else is because I needed that to be true. Yes, but more directly, it was necessary to refer to this hero of a story without implicating myself in that person's misdeeds and shortcomings. This was especially the case at the start of writing this project about my mental health journey, amid the existential fog, the not-belonging, and the lack of a unique identity. I want the hero to be the one who is tasked with slaying these beasts that have stalked his life from the beginning, instead of me. Indeed, dear reader, I still shudder in fright when faced with everything that has happened and what I must do to continue with an enlightened, sober, and purpose-driven life. I have grave doubts that I will be able to be victorious over my notorious enemies, who have drowned countless people in shame, hopelessness, and despair. The hero at least has a chance against the Nothing, I believe.

Thankfully, a coordinated support system is in place for me, but it is likely to come to an end eventually. There are people and outlets for help that surround me, and those I have come to know have good hearts. Much of my days are already mapped out in accordance with the mental health system. Daily, I make an effort to teach. Sometimes I do so in a classroom setting. I cannot say how long it will continue. The recalcitrant voices often inform me that it is easier to have a positive attitude and purpose now, but it is possible that I will return to hopelessness once confronted by the full power of the real world. So, I have fear and trepidation concerning the future. Truthfully, I have never led a balanced and successful life. That is to say, the hero has not been able to maintain a professional and personal lifestyle that is enriching and complete, in every way I wish it to be, without self-sabotaging tendencies. I have not fed every part of my soul that needs nourishment to be healthy and whole. That might be my holy grail, or it might be the completion and publication of this book. Upon doing so and sharing my story with the world, I hope to achieve closure on past regrets. As I have mentioned a few times, I must do something creatively that is rewarding and publicly respected.

I never intended to write a story where the hero rode off into the sunset and all loose ends were tied. I did not plan to offer a great narrative of overcoming, and I have not done so. Too often, people revel in victory over things where doing so is unlikely. At least, I think it plausible to have prevailed to some degree, but smashing my nothing into pieces in some final and absolute manner is unrealistic. There are a few things I can say with clarity. My mission moving forward is to speak and teach on both the Humanities and mental health, utilizing the extensive knowledge I have acquired. I am an artist who must satisfy that weird and sometimes rebellious nature. And being weird is fine, but may put me at odds with the world, and that must be accepted as okay. This hero must identify and maintain a social equilibrium that does not leave him in isolation, but also will not totally exhaust him. Either pitfall leads to addiction. I have made significant progress toward aligning my outward personhood with my inner self. Above all, I must make the most of my time. This person, should he accomplish all of this, would find it easier to exist, love, and be loved.

I wish I had recognized that I was a hero on a journey many years before. Standing on stage to receive my doctorate should have closed the era of not belonging and opened one where greater stability enshrouded my life. Thus, I am saying that a great chapter of the story should have been over, right then. I had achieved a rare and important thing, even in this age of watered-down education. I said at first that writing this thing would maybe provide answers to some mysteries. It has, but not totally. I will likely always find it illogical how little I esteemed myself and valued everything and everyone else so much more. Also, there is no use pretending that I enjoy the flavor of the month in popular culture. I do not. Once again, I will state with conviction that I will not build birdhouses. Every day must be taken on its merit without need to hold on tightly to an unknowable future, anyway. So I have a plan, and the results must turn out in a way that honors my heroic purpose. I shall not let any person or thing dissuade me from advancing in the journey. Perhaps I should name that voice that offers hope, and mourns correctly and not destructively, but what should I call him? Or her?

So, with all that said, I decided to make an effort to translate my story into the hero's journey. It will be quite brief and vague. Also, the story is not over, so I prefer to analyze all that has occurred as one installment of a multi-volume epic. Kirk refused the call to adventure many times over the years by maintaining that all was well. He put off self-exploration and healing in favor of the attainment of things like marriage. He tried to pretend to be alright. The Darkness is an example of him rejecting all the work and reflection necessary. His monsters were so many, including abject loneliness, jail, and being forced to sit in his thoughts and regrets alone behind locked doors. His identity as a teacher has been imperiled and still is. The CRC enabled the hero to initiate the long journey home, which is still ongoing. I did bring back something to the community in the form of knowledge and wisdom unique in this world, based on a strange life, advanced learning, and firsthand battles with my mental health devils. Being a teacher, I can impart it all back to the people in whatever format is called for. Who was my wizard, or the Jedi of this story? The professors, of course, who first provided access to the world of ideas. They were the heralds of all he could become and do, along with inspiration for attaining powers completely foreign to his closed-off youth. That is not bad. The next story should describe how I proceed to share my education with others. This is a giant task. I must do this while resisting temptations to fall to the dark side.

One lesson from my history has become crystal clear: we are mental health. Sometimes people working in separate areas of life, such as mental health vs. substance abuse, use different words to mean similar things. And this is a pertinent example, but it is not the only one. I have employed my favorite terms throughout this project, including transcendence, authenticity, and identity. Occasionally, I felt that a section was moving toward something we can classify as spiritual, and so I chose that word. Carl Jung said more than once that mind studies provide modern people with a new frontier of mystery that was once found in religion. Psychology is a world of wonder, in other words. The collective unconscious is both scientific and mystical, known and unknown. The spiritual and all else here in the previous pages must at some time belong to everything that our brain is and does. The heart and soul of a person is actually what one thinks, has done, wants to do, and all the other stored information. And that data is not a nebulous nothing somewhere, invisible to our eyes. Our spirit and everything we are is mental health. This is no small thing and needs to be emphasized at an early school age. I must not hold much hope that a time machine will become a reality and allow me to be at the front of the line to use it. Dear reader, I must have faith in my life that I can do and feel great things, even though the beginning of the story did not go as it should have. Tomorrow, I do not have to be concerned with, as that contented affirmation just has to be good enough for today.

The conclusion of all conclusions is this: I must learn to excise people and things no longer consistent with the hero I have become. With that, my confidence must not waver. Here I sit, with my finger on the delete button, all is ready, and only the future matters. Well, I misspoke a little. Kirk will always be a romantic laden with memories and nostalgia. However, now is the time to write the obituary for that person whom I have described in most of this book. For those who do not understand, I have no time to sit around and wait. Most people I have ever known demonstrated zero interest in who I am and what I wanted to do. But, it is not the doing I must concentrate on the most. I must be and let what follows from this supreme faith in myself play out without too much interference and impatience. This is like a beginning, back to the beginning. I look forward to my story with the belief that the best is yet to come. The most real thing I can offer right now is—my story continues.

ENDNOTES

1   Dylan, Bob. "My Back Pages," From album *Another Side of Bob Dylan*, 1964.

2   Simon, Paul. "Rewrite." From album *So Beautiful or So What*. 2010.

3   Buck, Pearl. "The Chinese Novel" A lecture delivered before the Swedish Academy. (Stockholm, 1938.)

4   Nietzsche, Friedrich. *Thus Spoke Zarathustra: A Book for All and None,* (Lepizig: 1885).

5   Wordsworth, William. "Ode: Intimations of Immortality; Recollections From Early Childhood," in *Poems, in Two Volumes*. (London: Originally published 1807).

6   Becker, Ernest. *The Denial of Death*. (New York: Simon & Schuster, 1973).

7   James, William. *The Variety of Religious Experience: A Study of Human Nature*. (London: Longman, Green, and Co. 1902).

8   Jung, Carl. *Modern Man in Search of a Soul*. (New York: Harcourt, Brace & World, 1933).

9   Lewis, C.S. *The Weight of Glory*. (London: Society for Promoting Christian Knowledge, 1942).

10 Carlyle, Thomas. *On Heroes, Hero-Worship & the Heroic in History*. (London: James Fraser, 1841.)

11 Jung, Carl. *Modern Man in Search of a Soul*. (New York: Harcourt, Brace & World, 1933).

12 Ibid.

13 Adams, Henry. "The Dynamo and the Virgin" in *The Education of Henry Adams.* (Boston: Houghton Mifflin, 1918).

14 Braun, Bruce. *The Intemperate Rainforest: Nature, Culture, and Power on Canada's West Coast.* (London: University of Minnesota Press, 2002).

15 Jung, C.G. *Collected Works of C.G. Jung, vol. 10.* "Civilization in Transition." (Princeton Press, 1970).

16 Wallace, D.F. "This Is Water: Some Thoughts, Delivered on a Significant Occasion, about Living a Compassionate Life."(New York: Little Brown & Company, 2009).

17 Nietzsche, Friedrich. *The Gay Science.* (Leipzig: E.W. Fritsch, 1887).

18 Becker, Ernest. *The Denial of Death.* (New York: Simon & Schuster, 1973).

19 Firmage, George. ed. *E.E. Cummings A Miscellany Revised.* (October House, 1965).

20 Becker, Ernest. *The Denial of Death.* (New York: Simon & Schuster, 1973).

21 Nietzsche, Friedrich. *Thus Spoke Zarathustra: a Book for All and None.* (Cambridge: Cambridge Press, 2006).